THE GOSPEL IMAGE OF CHRIST

THE GOSPEL IMAGE OF CHRIST

by

VESELIN KESICH

ST. VLADIMIR'S SEMINARY PRESS
CRESTWOOD, NY 10707–1699
1992

Library of Congress Cataloging-in-Publication Data

Kesich, Veselin, 1921–
    The Gospel image of Christ / by Veselin Kesich.
        p.   cm.
    Includes bibliographical references and index.
    ISBN 0–88141–102–7
    1. Jesus Christ—Historicity. 2. Jesus Christ—Person and offices—Biblical
teaching. 3. Bible. N.T. Gospels—Criticism, interpretation, etc. I. Title.
BS2650.2.K47   1991
226'.06—dc20   91–42120
                                                                                    CIP

© 1991

ST. VLADIMIR'S SEMINARY PRESS
ALL RIGHTS RESERVED

ISBN 0–88141–102–7

PRINTED IN THE UNITED STATES OF AMERICA

Contents

To Carol and Gregory,
who to my surprise still maintain their interest in
biblical interpretation.

Preface

Twenty years have passed since I wrote *The Gospel Image of Christ: The Church and Modern Criticism*. For a long time out of print, this book has now been completely rewritten and enlarged. New material, topics and approaches in gospel research are discussed and evaluated. For all practical purposes, this is a new book with the old title, which best conveys its main purpose. It retains some of the previous material and the basic perspective of the first edition.

In preparing this edition, I am grateful to my students in the course on the Synoptic Gospels, with whom I discussed and clarified many aspects of gospel interpretation over the years. I am particularly grateful to those who have read the manuscript this year, eagerly looking for misprints or unclear expressions. I wish to express my thanks to William Congdon for his editorial work and his many helpful suggestions. He also compiled the selected bibliography, biblical references and general index. To Eleana Silk, librarian at St. Vladimir's Seminary, I owe my heartfelt gratitude for putting the text on disk and supplying me with some of the bibliographical references. My friend and colleague, Fr. John Breck, contributed valuable comments. Special thanks to my wife Lydia for reading the material in its various drafts and for her comments and editorial skills.

Veselin Kesich
Crestwood, N.Y.
1991

Introduction

Each Christian generation has had to respond to Jesus' questions addressed to his disciples: "Who do men say that I am?" and "But who do you say that I am?" (Mk 8:27-29 and parals.) The question "who is Jesus?" has been repeatedly asked throughout the centuries both by those "outside" and by those "inside" the Church. This book is written to give an answer to these questions with the help of modern historical gospel research.

The early Church practiced its own version of "biblical criticism." Some early Christian theologians and biblical scholars discussed, among other topics, the question of the authorship of the canonical books and examined the nature of the language used in them. The early church, therefore, did not practice literalism. On the day of Pentecost, the historical beginning, the Holy Spirit descended upon Jesus' followers, enabling them to exercise "criticism," to separate truth from falsehood. To keep the image of Christ pure, the church had to "judge" and "separate," to respond to attacks from outside as well as to "criticize" the dangers of superstition and magic from inside.

The Orthodox Church, therefore, cannot oppose modern biblical investigation as such. For Orthodox Christians biblical criticism is based theologically on the Church's teaching of the Incarnation and understanding of the charisma of inspiration. God became man, and his words received "the fleshly garment" of Jesus' time and country. We cannot repudiate all historical examination of the Church's record of revelation. To do so would undermine the importance of the historic incarnation and revive docetic tendencies. The evangelists wrote their gospels under the inspiration of the Holy Spirit, yet one Gospel of Christ was attributed to four different writers. "The Gospel according to" implies that the evangelists were not passive but active in composing their works. Their natural qualities were illuminated but not replaced or superseded by the gift of inspiration they received. "The word became flesh and dwelt among us" (Jn 1:14) and the diversity of the inspired books invite and encourage biblical research.

Why then do biblical scientific studies occupy a rather insignificant place in the Orthodox Church? Until recently there has been little interest among its members in the field of biblical criticism. Primarily this is due not to their reliance upon Tradition, but to historical circumstances—to the state of isolation in which Orthodox churches lived for so long. This isolation fed suspicion and shaped the mistaken notion that the so-called "critical" historical method used in biblical research is not for Orthodox Christians but for "Protestants," who had broken away from the universal Church.

This book is written with the conviction that the proper function of biblical criticism is to build, not to destroy; to illumine, not to obscure; to bring members of the Church to a better understanding of the gospels, not to lead them away from Jesus, whose recorded sayings and deeds mirror his image. It is written to contribute to the ongoing discussion among Orthodox Christians as to the place, value and use of biblical criticism in the Church.

1

Jesus in History

The question of whether or not Jesus existed has often been raised throughout European history. On British television in 1984, for example, G. A. Wells, a professor of German at Birbeck College, London, expressed doubts about Jesus' existence. In a series of three programs entitled *Jesus: The Evidence,* he argued on the basis of the writings of Paul that the Jesus of the gospels is a fiction. While Wells admitted Paul's existence and the authenticity of several of his letters, he claimed that Paul revealed no details of Jesus' earthly life. Paul appears to be ignorant of the place where Jesus was born and lived, as well as of his movements and his public ministry. Nor did he record any of Jesus' parables or miracles. Wells pointed out Paul's own admission that he never knew the human Jesus. He was silent regarding the historical Jesus, for the Jesus of the gospels never existed.[1]

I

To judge the validity of these charges, which is based on the so-called "silence of Paul," described above, we too must turn to the sources on which the charge is based. Paul's letters belong to the earliest writings in the New Testament. Did Paul imagine Jesus? Let us see what Paul himself reveals to us about his knowledge of Jesus of Nazareth.

Paul, or Saul, was born in Tarsus, Cilicia, but was "brought up in Jerusalem at the feet of Gamaliel" to be trained as a Pharisee (Acts 22:3). It is usually assumed that his father or grandfather was from Judea. As one who lived and studied in Jerusalem, Paul was well acquainted with the religious and political life of Judaism in his time and surely must have heard about Jesus. The Pharisees were critical of Jesus for associating with "sinners" and for holding a "relaxed" attitude toward the law and the

1 Ian Wilson, *Jesus: The Evidence,* (London: Pan Books, 1984), p. 46ff., and James D. G. Dunn, *The Evidence for Jesus,* (Philadelphia: Westminster, 1985), p. 29.

rules of purity. When the Christian Church came into existence, immediately after the death and resurrection of Christ, Paul persecuted this Jewish-Christian group. He knew some of its leaders, with whom he entered into many heated disputes regarding the role and the claims of the "prophet" from Nazareth. Thus in the period before his conversion, Paul knew Christ "in a fleshly way." It was during this period that he understood Jesus "from a human point of view," as a false Messiah who undermined traditional beliefs which Paul regarded as approved by God (2 Cor 5:16).

Paul was called and converted to Christianity about three years after the death of Jesus. After he had met the Risen Christ on the road to Damascus, Paul joined the Christian community there and learned more about Jesus. He spent fifteen days with Peter (Cephas in Aramaic) and the other apostles in Jerusalem. These men must have told Paul even more about what they had seen and heard while they accompanied Jesus during his ministry in Galilee and Judea. Undoubtedly they told him all they knew about Jesus: how he had lived, taught, died and was raised up. This was the historical record of the early Church, a memory based on vivid accounts of eyewitnesses. This exposure to the living oral tradition must have confirmed in Paul the conviction he acquired on the road to Damascus: namely, that his previous understanding of Jesus of Nazareth was utterly incorrect. Jesus was not one among many false pretenders to the title of messiah, but the true Messiah of God. Far from denying the human existence of Jesus, Paul now affirmed it.[2]

---

2 This is the meaning of 2 Cor 5:16: "From now on, therefore, we regard no one from a human point of view; even though we once regarded Christ from a human point of view, we regard him thus no longer."

The biblical scholar marshals a number of facts and techniques when he considers this verse. First, he turns to the Greek text from which all modern translations have come, to see what was originally said. Then, he uses grammatical knowledge to clarify precisely the meanings of difficult expressions. In the passage we have just quoted, for example, we must understand the grammatical form of the expression κατὰ σάρκα, "from a human point of view," as well as its literal meaning. Is Paul saying that we no longer regard Christ as "human," "in the flesh," or "humanly," "from the human point of view"? Grammatical analysis reveals that the expression in our text is adverbial, modifying the verb "to regard," and not an adjective referring to the noun, Christ. Therefore, it is the way we look at Christ, not his existence in the flesh, which is described here. If κατὰ σάρκα is taken as an adjective, then the first part of the verse, "we regard or know no one according to flesh" or "in the flesh" would make no sense (see Jerome Murphy-O'Connor, *Becoming Human Together*, (The Pastoral Anthropology of St. Paul), Wilmington, DE, Michael Glazier, 1982, p.34). Even the preceding short passage, which directly concerns those who question Paul's knowledge of the

When we ask why Paul did not speak more fully about the concrete details of Jesus' life, we confront first of all the question of his purpose. His epistles were written primarily for pastoral reasons. In them, he never had to recount the facts that he had learned about the Jesus of history. But we learn a great deal about Jesus from these occasional letters, written to answer the questions raised by the Christian communities of the Hellenistic world. We learn about the Jewish origins of Jesus (Rom 9:4-5), that he came from the line of David (Rom 1:3), and that he was "born of woman, born under the law" (Gal 4:4). We learn of the Last Supper which Christ celebrated with the Twelve on the eve of his death and his betrayal (1 Cor 11:23ff). His death, burial, resurrection and post-resurrection appearances are presented as well attested facts (1 Cor 15). Paul calls the Christian message the "word of the cross" (ὁ λόγος τοῦ σταυροῦ), and the core of his preaching was "Christ crucified" (1 Cor 1:18, 23). This shows that Paul preached the historical Jesus, not only the resurrected Lord (2 Cor 11:4). He was familiar with the teachings and instructions of Jesus (1 Cor 7:10), and, when the issue at hand demanded it, he readily referred to them (1 Cor 10:27; see Lk 10:8). There are echoes of the Sermon on the Mount in Rom 2:14 (Mt 5:44); 12:17 (Mt 5:39f); and 14:10 (Mt 7:1). The apostle to the Gentiles was acquainted with Jesus' life of humiliation and perfect obedience (Phil 2:7-8). Some suggest on the basis of 2 Cor 8:9 ("For you know the grace of our Lord Jesus Christ, that though he was rich, yet for your sake he became poor, so that by his poverty you might become rich") that the story of the life of Jesus was given, "at least its general outline," in the Church's instruction to new members.[3]

Paul was acquainted with and used images from Jesus' parables as well. Although the apostle could have known the metaphors of sowing and harvesting from the Hebrew Scripture or from rabbinic literature, he still depended upon Jesus' use of these metaphors. Harold Reisenfeld argues that there is a strong link between Jn 12:24 ("Truly, truly, I say to

historical Jesus, is an example of the approach that the reader of the Bible must use in order to understand the meaning of the text. He must search for what was actually said, the original context, and the relationship between the passage and the author's experience and his writing as a whole.

3 See for example John J. O'Rourke, "The Second Letter to the Corinthians," *Jerome Biblical Commentary,* 52:28.

you, unless a grain of wheat falls into the earth and dies, it remains alone; but if it dies, it bears much fruit") and 1 Cor 15:36 ("What you sow does not come to life unless it dies"). The expression "unless it dies" is essential to both texts, since both bind death and the new life inextricably together. In John the phrase points to Christ, whereas in Paul it refers to the destiny of Christians. "If Christ has not been raised, your faith is futile" (1 Cor 15:17). Christ's resurrection was of primary importance for Paul. To establish this in the minds of his audience, he adapted the saying of Jesus and applied it to the death and resurrection of Christians. Riesenfeld, who offers a detailed analysis of Paul's "grain of wheat" imagery in the context of his interpretation of 1 Cor 15, concludes that Jesus' saying in Jn 12:24f was faithfully transmitted and was already known to Paul "in basically the same form" which was later recorded in John.[4]

Paul would never have been able to write some of the most inspiring passages in his letters "unless the historical portrait of Jesus, as it appears in his words, his deeds, and his suffering were the living background and primary foundation" of his theological insights.[5] The historical image of Christ, as well as his glory revealed on the road to Damascus, were constantly present to Paul. He knew no division between the historical Jesus and the glorified Lord. From the eyewitnesses of the life and suffering of Jesus, and from the witnesses of his resurrection, Paul received knowledge about the historical Jesus. Only through them and from them could Paul know Jesus. The testimony they rendered to Christ is incorporated in the gospels, which are the only source for our knowledge of Jesus of Nazareth. There is no other way to communicate historical facts except by bearing witness to them. Out of this witness the gospels emerged.

Efforts to separate Paul from the "historical" Jesus and from the authors of the gospels contradict the record as it has been transmitted to us. We know from Acts and from his own writings that he was constantly in touch with the disciples and with those to whom the gospels are attributed. Mark and Luke were in his company (Acts 13, 15-16; Col 4:10ff). Mark knew Peter and Paul (Acts 12, 1 Pet 5:13), and Luke was with Paul and James in Jerusalem (Acts 16:10ff, 20:5-21:17). The so-called

4 See his *Gospel Tradition*, (Philadelphia: Fortress Press, 1970), pp. 171-186.
5 See the essay "Jesus, St John, and St Paul," in Anton Fridrichsen and others, *The Root of the Vine: Essays in Biblical Theology*, (New York: Philosophical Library, 1953), pp. 50-52.

"we" sections in Acts, where the narrative is written in the first person plural instead of the third person, indicate that Luke was with Paul at the time of his last visit to Jerusalem, where Paul again met James. The earliest Christian documents confirm that the apostles, including Paul and the future evangelists, shared the knowledge of common traditions relating to Jesus. All these contacts and personal relationships are mentioned "in a matter-of-fact and incidental fashion without apologetic purpose and have a high degree of historical probability," observes E. Earle Ellis.[6]

II

Non-Christian sources, both Jewish and Roman, attest as well to the reality of the historical Jesus. The Jewish historian Josephus (37–ca. 100), who was born in Jerusalem, refers to Jesus, Pilate, John the Baptist, James, "the Lord's Brother," (Gal 1:19) and other disciples. It is true that *The Jewish War*, the history of the bloody conflicts between Judea and Rome from 66 to 73, mentions Pilate but not Jesus. We may surmise that this omission reflects Josephus' caution. Taken prisoner in 67, Josephus was given his freedom when Vespasian became emperor in 69. He knew the Roman sensitivity to messianic stirrings in Palestine, and most probably for this reason he kept silence about events which would antagonize the Romans. But the earliest Jewish testimony to Jesus appears in another work of Josephus, *Jewish Antiquities*, written about twenty years later. Here Josephus mentions Christ. Most scholars agree that statements in the passage that have reached us have been supplemented by later Christian interpolations, such as that the man Jesus appeared, "if indeed one ought to call him a man." Other additions include: "He was the Messiah...he appeared alive again on the third day." In 1972, however, Schlomo Pines of the Hebrew University in Jerusalem announced the discovery of perhaps the earliest version of *Antiquities* 18:63f, in an early Christian Arabic manuscript, where the text runs as follows: "His disciples reported that he had appeared to them three days after his crucifixion and that he was alive; accordingly he was, perhaps, the Messiah."[7] Josephus appar-

---

6 E. Earle Ellis, "Gospel Criticism—A Perspective on the State of the Art," *Das Evangelium und die Evangelien. Vorträge vom Tübingen Symposium 1982*, Peter Stuhlmacher, ed. (WUNT 28, Tübingen, 1983), p. 46.
7 Gaalyah Cornfield, *The Historical Jesus*, (New York: Macmillan, 1982), p. 184.

ently revealed some of his knowledge of Christian origins at the end of his life. Another passage, also in chapter 18, describes Jesus as a "wise man" and as "a doer of wonderful deeds," whom Pilate condemned to the cross "on the indictment of the leading men among us." Josephus also reveals intimate knowledge of political intrigues in first-century Palestine.[8] He reports that after the death of the Roman procurator Festus in 62, who was mentioned in the Book of Acts (25-26), and before the arrival of his successor Albinus, "Ananias called the Sanhedrin together, brought before it James, the brother of Jesus who was called Christ, and certain others...and he caused them to be stoned." However fragmentary the evidence, there is no doubt that Josephus knew of Jesus' existence.

The Talmud, a collection (c. 200 A.D.) of various rabbinical traditions, also attests to Jesus' historical life, although in a polemical manner intended to contradict the claims of the first-century written Christian tradition. According to this body of writings, Jesus of Nazareth used magic to perform his miracles. He beguiled the people of Israel and led them astray. He was tried as a deceiver and was crucified on the evening of Pesah (Passover), which happened to fall on the Sabbath. At the time of his death he was thirty-three years old. He had a group of disciples, five of whom are mentioned.

The most important text comes from the Talmudic tractate Sanhedrin (43):

> On the eve of Passover they hanged Yeshu [of Nazareth] and the herald went before him for forty days, saying, "[Yeshu of Nazareth] is going forth to be stoned in that he hath practiced sorcery and beguiled and led astray Israel. Let everyone knowing aught in his defense come and plead for him." But they found naught in his defence and hanged him on the eve of Passover.[9]

In the opinion of J. Klausner, the statement about the herald "has an obvious 'tendency,' and it is difficult to think it is historical."[10]

The importance of these rabbinic references is threefold. First, they

8 See C. K. Barrett, *The New Testament Background: Selected Documents*, revised edition (San Francisco: Harper & Row, 1989), pp. 162ff.
9 Translated by Joseph Klausner in his *Jesus of Nazareth, His Life and Teaching*, (Boston: Beacon Press, 1925), (PB, 1964), p. 27. This book was composed in Hebrew, and the translator informs us that this is probably the first time that a modern Hebrew book of any considerable size was translated into English. Klausner was born in Russia, studied in Germany, and came to Palestine in 1920. His book contains the most complete account of Jesus in the Rabbinic tradition.
10 *Ibid.*, p. 28. He also adds that the Talmud speaks of hanging in place of crucifixion, "since this horrible Roman form of death was only known to Jewish scholars from Roman trials, and not from the Jewish legal system."

attest to the existence of Jesus, even while casting doubt on his message. Their arguments against the miracles of Jesus are essentially the same as those used by the scribes in the gospels: "And the scribes who came down from Jerusalem said, 'He is possessed by Beelzebub, and by the prince of demons he casts out the demons'" (Mk 3:22 and parallel passages). Second, they attest that the Temple authorities tried him before Pilate, who condemned him to death. Third, the rabbinical account supports the chronology of the Gospel of John, which assumes that in the year of Jesus' crucifixion the Passover fell on the Sabbath (Jn 19:31). Thus, among earliest accounts, both the Jewish historian Josephus and the Talmud confirm Jesus' historical existence.[11]

III

The earliest extant Roman reference to Jesus' existence comes from Pliny the Younger, who was governor of the province of Pontus and Bithynia. He wrote the emperor Trajan in 112 to report that on certain days the Christians came together and "sang hymns to Christ as to a god." The Roman historian Suetonius, who composed *The Lives of the Twelve Caesars* around 120, when discussing the reign of Claudius (41-54) reported that "the Jews constantly made disturbances at the instigation of Chrestus," and for this reason the emperor "expelled them from Rome" (Claudius 25.4). Suetonius used the Latinized form "Chrestus" instead of the Greek "Christos." Tertullian (160-220) wrote that the Roman rulers pronounced Christianus as Chrestianus (Apologeticus 3). Suetonius implies that the controversies between Jews and Christians had caused a turmoil in Rome, and that a certain "Chrestus" was responsible. He also confirms what Luke wrote about Claudius' order that all Jews leave Rome (Acts 18:1-2).

11 The evidence from Jewish sources is well arranged and discussed in R. T. Herford, *Christianity in Talmud and Midrash* (Clifton, NJ: Reference Book Publishers, 1966. Reprinted from the London edition of 1903). A convenient summary and evaluation of the references to Jesus in Rabbinic literature is given in Howard Clark Kee, *Jesus in History: An Approach to the Study of the Gospels* (New York: Harcourt, Brace & World, 1970), pp. 37-43.

There are several other references in the Talmud to Jesus, but they are of no value as testimony to his historicity. They are polemical in spirit and are the product of the bitter struggle between Judaism and Christianity in the early centuries.

Our third Roman source is the historian Tacitus (c. 55-117), who wrote in the *Annals* (c. 116) that the Emperor Nero accused Christians of setting Rome on fire in the year 66. Tacitus explained that the name Christiani came from Christ, who "was executed during the reign of Tiberius on the orders of the procurator Pontius Pilate" (*Annals* XV, 44). Of the Roman sources, this is the most precise and direct. Some scholars have suggested that Tacitus drew not only on hearsay but also on official Roman archives dealing with the trial and death of Jesus. The rulers of the provinces kept careful records of what was happening in their dominions and regularly informed the emperor of their activities. Pilate, who tried and condemned Jesus as a dangerous rebel, presumably sent Tiberius records mentioning the case of Jesus. Justin Martyr claimed that this occurred. These records have not come down to us, and we can only guess at what sources Tacitus used.

Thus, in discussing a modern challenge to the existence of Jesus, we must conclude that the historical sources and the evidence of Paul's epistles confirm the historical presence of Jesus. In the words of Peter on the day of Pentecost, Jesus was "attested to you by God with mighty works and wonders and signs which God did through him in your midst, as you yourself know" (Acts 2:22). Since the gospels are the principal sources for the life and teaching of Jesus, we now turn to the evidence that they supply.

IV

From the gospels we learn that Jesus "was born at Bethlehem of Judea in the days of Herod the King" (Mt 2:1), during the reign of Herod the Great, who died in 4 B.C. We learn as well that he was "the son of Mary" (Mk 6:3), that he was a Jew from Galilee, that he was baptized by John in the Jordan around 27 A.D., and that after his baptism he experienced trials or temptations in the wilderness. Capernaum was the center of his missionary activity in Galilee, and according to the Gospel of John, Jesus was active both in Galilee and in Jerusalem. At the beginning of his ministry he proclaimed the coming of the kingdom of God and gathered a group of twelve disciples, the nucleus of the new Israel. During his public ministry, which lasted about three years, Jesus associated with sinners and outcasts. He was seen in the company of the despised, the poor, and women.

The gospels tell us that Jesus performed many "mighty works," or miracles, and that he taught in parables. He came into conflict with the Pharisees and the religious authorities in Jerusalem, for he challenged the oral traditions and on some occasions even the law of Moses. Above all, his "cleansing" of the Temple led directly to his arrest and his trials before the Jewish and Gentile authorities. The Jewish leaders accused him of the blasphemy of attributing divine authority to himself and of profaning the Holy Temple, both crimes punishable with death by stoning. Having lost the right to inflict capital punishment, the Temple authorities handed Jesus over to the Romans, and around 30 Pilate delivered him as "King of the Jews" to be crucified. The gospel narrative ends with an account of his resurrection following his death on the cross. His tomb was found empty and he appeared to his disciples.

As the gospels show, Jesus lived a human life and shared human experiences. Yet his demands upon those who would follow him far exceeded any that had been made by any other leader or prophet in the history of salvation as it is recorded in the Bible. He realized in his short historical existence the highest possible perfection of human life, and claimed unity with the Father. The intimate word *Abba* (Father), which he used as a form of address to God, expressed the heart of their relationship. It demonstrated that Jesus is God's son, who made God known and present. He practiced unlimited, non-judgmental love and goodness of God in his own life and ministry. He overcame evil by doing good. Jesus called concrete human beings to the new life which he so visibly exemplified and lived, not to a theory or an ideology.

The gospels give us a portrait of Jesus in which his history is reflected and interpreted. Each of our four canonical gospels has distinct characteristics. There are differences among them in reporting about what Jesus said and did and on what occasion. Yet the basic external data of his life and the most outstanding characteristics of his person are present in all of them.

2

The Gospels and the Critics

When so much depends upon the gospels, it is no wonder that they have been subjected to the most thorough historical and literary investigation, particularly in the last two hundred years. No other ancient document has been read so closely and analyzed so meticulously. Biblical criticism was not unknown in the early Church, but critical questions that are now at the center of interest were, then, marginal. The growth of modern criticism is a relatively recent phenomenon. In this chapter we shall discuss modern methods of interpretation, utilizing some of the findings of modern criticism and reflecting upon the views of some leading critics. Our purpose, first of all, is to focus upon the exegetical method and the various kinds of biblical criticism. We shall pay particular attention to the questions that the critics raise in connection with the historicity of the gospel material and the Church's role in the formation of our documents.

I

The exegetical method described below is recognized, accepted, and used by all scholars. The first task of a critic is to understand what the author of a particular passage or book conveys. The precise text of the passage must be established before the meaning can be derived from it, and the passage is studied within the context of the passages which precede and follow it. This may mean studying the whole chapter in which it is found, or even the entire book. Secondly, the critic tries to determine the source or sources of the narrative that he deals with. Does it come from a source used by two or three evangelists together, or from a special source drawn on by only one evangelist? Once the sources have been identified, the third step is to investigate the pre-literary form of oral tradition, that is, to go behind the literary sources in an attempt to find the place of the passage in the ongoing life of the early Church. Finally, the origin of the tradition is investigated, to determine whether the saying, miracle, parable, or any particular event reported in the gospels has its origin in the life of the community or instead goes back to Jesus himself.

This exegetical method presupposes several kinds of "criticism." The first kind is textual or "lower" criticism. If we possessed the original copies of the books of the New Testament in their final and complete form, we would have no need for textual criticism. The books, originally written in Greek, were copied and mistakes crept in. Consequently, the goal of the textual critic is to provide us with the best possible text. The task is not easy, for there are approximately three thousand ancient manuscripts of the gospels alone. Often, variant readings of a particular verse are found in them, and a choice must be made between them. In making this choice, the textual critic must be well acquainted not only with the style and grammar, but also with the theology of an author before he takes the decisive step of accepting one reading and rejecting another. The theology of the textual critic himself may affect the process of selection, especially when it is opposed to the biblical author's theology and when the critic tries to impose his own theology upon the text.

In some ancient authorities, for instance, Jn 1:18 is recorded as "No one has ever seen God; the only God, who is in the bosom of the Father, he has made him known." In others, instead of "the only God" we have "the only Son." Which of these two readings will the critic decide for? Scholars have concluded that both readings would fit the theology of John, but the more difficult reading, "the only God," best fits the prologue of this gospel. Another example from John is the account of the woman taken in adultery (Jn 7:53-8:11). We may surmise that it is an insertion, as it does not follow naturally from the preceding dialogue at the end of chapter 7, nor does it lead into Jesus' monologue in chapter 8. The authenticity of the story is not in question, since it clearly relates to the life of Jesus, but there is a question as to whether it belongs in this place in the text of this particular gospel. The best Greek manuscripts do not include it in John's gospel. Origen and St John Chrysostom both wrote extensive commentaries on the fourth gospel, and neither one dealt with this particular narrative. On the basis of these facts and other evidence, the textual critic concludes that the passage did not originally belong in this gospel. Some manuscripts placed the story after Luke

21:37-38, which reads: "[Jesus] lodged on the mount called Olivet. And early in the morning all the people came to him in the temple to hear him." It is quite possible that a scribe transposed the story from one manuscript to another because of the similarity of the introductions; Jn 8:1-2 reads: "Jesus went to the Mount of Olives. Early in the morning he came again to the temple; all the people came to him, and he sat down and taught them." Another reason for preferring Luke's gospel to John's as the proper context for this passage is Luke's interest in collecting narratives about women. On the other hand, its placement in the Gospel of John could have served as a concrete application of Jesus' words: "You [Pharisees] judge according to the flesh, I judge no one" (8:15). This dilemma is an example of the problems with which the textual critics must cope.

In spite of both the enormous amount of textual evidence and its fragmentary nature, textual criticism has made a fundamental contribution. It has established an authoritative text which can be the foundation for critical discussion. "It cannot be too strongly asserted that in substance the text of the Bible is certain. Especially is this the case with the New Testament," writes Frederic Kenyon.[1] Many who have no love for modern criticism of any sort are nevertheless quite ready to accept the necessity (and the fruits) of textual criticism.

II

It is the "higher" historical criticism which fills some observers with misgivings. "The higher critic seeks to penetrate higher up the stream, nearer the source (which is the actual writing of the book)," explains H. A. Guy; "the textual critic deals with matters lower down the stream, after the book has been written and copies made and circulated."[2] Observers note that those critics who are working "higher up the stream" use procedures they regard as arbitrary. A critic may be led by his work to discover and define sources which are merely hypothetical and to use them as the basis of his reconstruction of how the gospels were written. While recognizing the difficulties these hypotheses may lead to, we must also recognize the valuable results that these "higher" critics have achieved.

1 See his *Our Bible and the Ancient Manuscripts* (London: Eyre and Spottiswoode, 1958), p. 55.
2 *The Gospel of Mark* (New York: St Martin Press, 1968), pp. 5-6.

A reader approaching the gospels wonders first of all about the relationship between them. The Church's interest in this problem began as early as the second century, when the Christian writer Papias, Bishop of Phrygia, wrote his *Expositions of the Word of the Lord* (c. 140). A certain elder had told Papias: that "Mark, having become the interpreter of Peter, wrote accurately everything he remembered," and that Mark "did not hear the Lord, nor did he follow him." He was a follower of Peter and was with him in Rome.[3] About forty years later, Irenaeus, Bishop of Gaul, summed up the tradition concerning the origins of the gospel: Matthew wrote his gospel in Hebrew "while Peter and Paul were preaching and founding the church in Rome." After the death of these two leading apostles, "Mark, the disciple and interpreter of Peter," wrote in his gospel "those things which Peter had preached," and Luke, a member of Paul's company, recorded what "Paul has declared" (*Adv. Haer.* 3,1,1). According to Eusebius, Clement of Alexandria knew of a tradition that Matthew and Luke were written before Mark and John, that the gospels with genealogies came before the gospels without them. Clement reportedly believed that John, the author of the fourth gospel, "perceived that the external facts had been made plain" in the gospels already written, and was prompted by his close associates to write his own gospel, and "composed a spiritual gospel" (Heb 6:14-17). Augustine of Hippo believed, as did the Western Church after him, that Matthew was the first, then Mark, who abridged Matthew; Luke followed Mark and John was the last. Augustine also believed that the first gospel was written in Hebrew and the three others in Greek. Although modern criticism relegates all these statements to a "pre-critical period," certain aspects of the relationship among the gospels, noted by these early commentators, are also themes of their modern counterparts. The preoccupation of modern critics with discovering written sources on which the gospels may have been based is what particularly distinguishes them from the Fathers. The early Church displayed no interest in discovering the gospel sources.[4] Contemporary source critics, on the other hand, have made it their primary task to define these sources.

The first three gospels are known as the Synoptic Gospels, since the material from Matthew, Mark and Luke can be arranged in parallel columns to be "seen together" (synopsis). When this is done, we notice

---

3 Eusebius, H. E. 3,39,15.
4 Ellis, *Gospel Criticism*, p. 34.

that the material is arranged in a similar manner, and that very often they use the same words to describe events or to record the sayings of Jesus. The degree of agreement or difference defines what is called the "Synoptic problem." Most modern scholars agree that the Gospel of Mark is the earliest of the gospel accounts about Jesus. Both Matthew and Luke knew Mark's gospel and used it as one of the sources for their gospels. Since Matthew and Luke share other material, which is not found in Mark, scholars concluded that these two evangelists also drew on a source called Q (from *Quelle*, the German word for source), which was lost soon after they used it. There are still disagreements about its contents. In addition, Matthew's gospel contains some material found in no other gospel. Presumably it came from another hypothetical source, designated by the letter M ("Matthew's special source"). Luke's special source is similarly designated by the letter L. The fundamental assumption of this hypothesis, the historical priority of the second canonical gospel, is accepted by most New Testament critics of all critical persuasions.

The results of source criticism are questionable, however, because they are tentative and subjective. Some respected modern scholars do not subscribe to the priority of Mark's gospel. They employ modern methods and skills to argue for the traditional view of the priority of Matthew. Some object to the hypothetical Q, since the critics are incapable of showing that it was one document with a clear structure and content. Yet we must recognize that the majority of modern exegetes adhere to the theory that there were two or more written sources, finding this to be the best working hypothesis.

III

Form criticism builds upon source criticism and goes beyond it. While not displacing source criticism, the results of which have been generally accepted, it seeks to overcome its excessive tendency to "discover" new sources by going behind the written documents to investigate the oral traditions which preceded them. This allows form critics to try to classify the literary forms of the small units out of which the gospels were composed. Form critics study the period when the stories and sayings of Jesus were circulating within the oral tradition (without chronological order, as some form critics insist). They attempt to trace the steps in the growth of the traditions about Jesus and to describe the role of the apostolic church in this development.

Our understanding or misunderstanding of the gospels depends to a considerable degree upon the answer we give to the question of their literary form. Are they biographies, chronicles, or the testimony of witnesses to Jesus? The answer to this question has a definite bearing upon our interpretation of them. Unless we determine the literary form of any biblical book, we have difficulty determining its message. What message does the book of Jonah convey, for instance? Before we answer this question, we must ask what its literary form is. Is Jonah an account of an actual happening, or is it a parable? "If the reader knows that Jonah is a fictional parable," writes Raymond Brown, "he knows that the author is not giving a history of relations of Israel and Assyria and is not presenting the story of Jonah in the whale's belly as a serious account of a true happening."[5] The Book of Jonah, therefore, conveys the truth that God is concerned with the Ninevites as well as with the elect people of Israel. This understanding of the story of Jonah's preaching and his sojourn in the belly of the whale for three days and nights is used by Christ, who applies it to his mission (Mt 12:40-41, Lk 11:32). "Something greater than Jonah is here."

It is important to define not only the literary form of each gospel as a whole, but also the forms of the small units that each incorporates. Within the gospels we find several literary types, including the short sayings of Jesus, stories, miracles, accounts of personal experiences, the records of eyewitnesses, infancy narratives and genealogies. Some critics prefer to speak about "mixed" rather than "pure" forms. Others express doubts about the historical value of these small units on the basis of the very classification to which they assign a particular passage. For example, the story in Mark 3:1-6, about the healing of a man with a withered hand, is classified by the form critic Rudolf Bultmann not as a miracle story but as a pronouncement story, which expresses the attitude of Jesus toward the Sabbath. The climax of the account, therefore, would come when Jesus says: "Is it lawful on the Sabbath to do good or to do harm, to save life or to kill?" This type of story Bultmann calls an apophthegm,

5 "Hermeneutics," *Jerome Biblical Commentary*, 71:27.

because it is similar to such sayings in Greek literature. Martin Dibelius, however, calls them "paradigms," for he thinks they were used as modes or illustrations in preaching. This shows how divergent the approaches to the Synoptic Gospel tradition of two of the best known and most creative form critics can be. Whereas Dibelius uses the so-called "constructive method" (that is, attempting to analyze the formation of the tradition "from a study of the community and its needs"), Bultmann proceeds "from the analysis of the particular elements of the tradition" and tries to identify the needs that produced and handed it on. These two approaches are not in opposition to each other. In Bultmann's words, they are "mutually complementary." However, they differ in assigning historicity to a particular saying of Jesus or to an event in the gospels.[6]

We should stress once more the importance of the knowledge of literary forms. What does the listener expect from a particular story? On Halloween in 1938 American radio listeners panicked when they heard that the world had been invaded by men from Mars, since they thought they were listening to a news bulletin. They did not know that they were listening instead to a radio play by Orson Welles. Their reaction resulted from misjudging the broadcast's "literary form."[7]

If form critics had limited their work to the identification and classification of literary forms, they would have disturbed very few people and would have performed an indisputably important task. But by passing judgment on the historical value of the material embodied in a particular form, the form critics aroused controversy. According to Dibelius, such judgment was not originally the business of the form critics. Bultmann, on the contrary, was convinced that it was. The form critics who follow Bultmann note that the healing miracles of Jesus, for instance, have the same form as the miracle stories of the Hellenistic age. Healing miracles in both the gospel and the Hellenistic traditions were described in stories containing three elements: the setting, with a description of the sickness; the healing, with a description of the healer's actions; and a depiction of the cure. On the basis of this similarity, the radical form critics conclude

6 See Rudolf Bultmann, *The History of the Synoptic Tradition* (New York: Harper & Row, 1963), p. 5.
7 Celestin Charlier, *The Christian Approach to the Bible* (Westminster, MD: Newman Press, 1961), p. 130.

that the miracle stories in the gospels were not descriptions of the works of Jesus but creations of the primitive church. Accordingly, they reject them as actual events. But is the similarity of the gospel miracles to the Hellenistic miracles a sufficient reason for their elimination from the life of Jesus? Could we tell the story of a cure in any other way? "A sufferer from hay fever who describes how Dr. Brown has cured him uses precisely the same 'form,' as that of the miracle stories of the gospels," comments Alan Richardson.[8] Regarding the same problem, Lucien Cerfaux writes: "The local correspondents, when they report a fire, resort to clichés. Does it follow there was never any fire? We crave pardon for such a simplistic argument, but it is neither more nor less so than the fundamental fallacy of the school which calls itself 'the method of history of literary forms' and denies in principle the objective truth of every story whose 'form' already existed."[9] The miracles of Jesus are an integral part of the most primitive gospel tradition. There is no single gospel source that does not contain miracle narratives. Jesus explicitly claimed that he performed miracles:

> Woe to you, Chorazin! woe to you, Bethsaida! for if the mighty works done in you had been done in Tyre and Sidon, they would have repented long ago...And you, Capernaum, will you be exalted to heaven? You shall be brought down to Hades (Lk 10:13-15; Mt 11:20-24).

Not even the opponents of Jesus rejected his miracles. Thus it becomes apparent that the subjective views, presuppositions, or concealed assumptions that the critics impose upon the text have played a significant role in the rejection of the miracle stories.

According to classical form criticism, the needs of the Church played a determinating role in the preservation, selection, and incorporation of the gospel stories and sayings. These needs also influenced their elaboration. The great achievement of this type of criticism, therefore, is its demonstration that the gospel tradition did not exist in a vacuum but had its setting in the life of the Church. It put stress on the New Testament as the book of the Church, since the Church relived the words and deeds of the Lord in its life and worship. The early Christians "devoted themselves to the apostles' teaching and fellowship, to the breaking of bread and the prayers" (Acts 2:42). Within the contexts of

8 *The Miracle Stories of the Gospels* (London: SCM Press, 1952), pp. 27-28.
9 *The Four Gospels* (Westminster, MD: Newman Press, 1960), pp. 122-123.

baptism and the eucharist, the words and acts of Jesus were remembered and interpreted. It was the eucharistic celebration that served as the context for the narration of Christ's passion, as well as the context for preserving accounts of the mighty works of Jesus and particularly those which modern scholars characterize as epiphanic—the ones which focus on Jesus' appearance as a divine person. One such miracle, for instance, is the stilling of the storm in Mark 4:35-41. The form critic asks how the Church used and relived this story of the miracle. According to Paul Achtemeier, who has closely analyzed Jesus' miracles in Mark, the original setting was the eucharistic celebration. By telling how Jesus rebuked the wind and calmed the sea, the participants in the worship expressed the epiphanic character of the Eucharist. The miracle focuses upon Jesus, who has divine power; the Eucharist underscores that he is still active and that his power is at work.[10]

In its preaching and teaching, the Church used the gospels to answer questions about the teachings of Jesus, to give examples which explained his attitude toward the Law and the various groups and institutions within Judaism, and to explain his teaching about the Kingdom of God and about himself. As Christianity spread and the number of converts grew, the Church, as should be expected, prepared collections of the sayings and deeds of Jesus for those who were involved in the work of catechetical instruction. These written catechetical manuals allowed the Church to control the transmission of the gospel tradition and to guarantee that the new members of the Church were acquainted and entrusted with the authentic sayings and stories of Jesus. As was shown above, the needs of the Church determined which traditions concerning Jesus were selected for the written accounts.

10 For Achtemeier's analysis of Mk 4:35-41 as the epiphanic miracle story, see Raymond F. Collins, *Introduction to the New Testament* (New York: Image Books, Doubleday, 1987), pp. 192-195, "Select Bibliography."

The Christians focused their baptism and eucharist on Jesus, who was the Messiah and who himself underwent baptism and instituted the Eucharist. Thus, any one baptized in the Church was informed about Jesus' baptism and about all the events that led up to and followed the Last Supper. "The Christian sacraments formed motives for the development of the relevant traditions and in addition offered guarantees for the remarkable continuity of these traditions when spread to various circles of believers" (Bo Reicke, *The Roots of the Synoptic Gospels* [Philadelphia: Fortress Press, 1986], p. 66). In a worship setting, the participant does not invent the words and deeds of Christ. He remembers, understands, and applies them to the ongoing life of the Church.

The Church did not create the words and deeds of Christ, but it did apply them to the new situations in which it found itself. For example, when the Council of Jerusalem (c. 50) debated the need for circumcision of the Gentiles, the Church could not find any word of Jesus that was directly related to this problem. If the radical form critics are right in their view that a considerable part of the gospel narrative was created by the primitive community to satisfy its needs, then the conditions in the late forties of the first century were ripe for inventing a saying or story that would indicate Jesus' attitude toward the circumcision of the Gentiles. Since at the time no single gospel had yet appeared in its final written form, the temptation to produce a suitable "saying of the Lord" must have been great. But the Church and those who were actively involved in the dispute yielded to no such temptation. They could not ascribe to Jesus any saying to which they could not bear witness.[11] The question of the circumcision of the Gentiles was solved at the Council at Jerusalem, not by creating a new saying of Jesus, but by relying on the authority of the apostles and elders to decide against imposing circumcision.

Form criticism had shed a much-needed light on the gospel tradition before it received its definite written form. On the other hand, those who have been skeptical regarding our ability to "know the Jesus of history" have tended to ascribe to the community more traditional material than the evidence supports. This minimizes the important role of the original witnesses in the transmission of the words and works of Jesus, as well as the activity of the evangelists in the composition of their gospels. If the pioneers of the form-critical school were right, according to Vincent Taylor, then we have to assume that "the disciples must have been translated to heaven immediately after the Resurrection." And according to Bultmann, "the primitive community exists *in vacuo*, cut off from its founders by the wall of an inexplicable ignorance."[12] The New Testament itself tells us, however, that after the Resurrection and the descent of the Spirit some of the disciples were active in laying the foundation for the spread of the Church and were in charge of the proclamation and transmis-

11 This problem in connection with Acts 15 is treated in Birger Gerhardsson, *Memory and Manuscript: Oral Tradition and Written Transmission in Rabbinic Judaism and Early Christianity* (Uppsala: 1961), pp. 257f.
12 *The Formation of the Gospel Tradition* (London: Macmillan, 1949), p. 41.

sion of the gospels. In sum, while no one can deny the valuable information brought to light by the form critics, not all of their conclusions contribute constructively to the study of the formation of the gospels.

IV

An offshoot of form criticism known as redaction criticism tries to compensate for the weaknesses of form criticism, described above. The two criticisms are closely related. Form criticism, however, is community-oriented, while redaction criticism concentrates upon the evangelists and their contributions. Redaction critics investigate the ways in which the evangelists used their sources, and what particular theological views they constructed by editing them. After determining the literary form of a book, a redaction critic studies the composition and the process of editing through which the book passed. To the redaction critic, the evangelists were not simply compilers of traditional material, but authors who had their own point of view and who arranged their material with the particular aim of expressing their own theological interests.

For example, Matthew 8:23-27 and Mark 4:35-41 record the story of Jesus stilling the storm. When we compare these two accounts of the same miracle, we realize that there are some "editorial" differences between Matthew and Mark. In the Marcan record of the event Jesus' boat is not alone, since "other boats were with him" (Mk 4:36). When the great storm arises, the disciples wake the sleeping Jesus and ask him: "Teacher, do you not care if we perish?" (Mk 4:38). After Jesus stills the storm, in awe they say to one another, "Who then is this, that even the wind and sea obey him?" (Mk 4:41). By contrast, in Matthew's account there is only one boat. The disciples address Jesus not as "teacher" (διδάσκαλε) but as "Lord" (κύριε): "Save us Lord; we are perishing" (Mt 8:25). At the end Matthew reports that the disciples "marvelled, saying, 'What sort of man is this that even the winds and sea obey him?'" (Mt 8:27). Essentially we have the same miracle, but Matthew emphasizes the disciples' recognition of Jesus' divine power.[13]

Radical redaction critics, like radical form critics, may overemphasize the uniqueness of each gospel account. Willi Marxsen, one of the best

13 Raymond F. Collins, *Introduction.* See the literature he cites, pp. 224-229.

known redaction critics, came to the conclusion that the written gospels do not belong to a single literary form. The evangelists expressed or created so much of their own form, he asserts, that the common gospel pattern was broken. Thus each gospel stands completely by itself. From the viewpoint of literary forms, according to Marxsen, "there are no 'Synoptic' gospels."[14] But this, of course, is not the only viewpoint available to biblical scholars.

V

Other critical approaches to the books of the Bible and to the gospels include the new literary approach ("new" because literary critics devote more care and attention to the very text, the story itself). They ask questions about the story's structure and its unifying principle or theme. Form critics rightly insist that the literary form of a book or of a unit within the book must be defined before a text can be properly interpreted, but style is not their primary concern. Redaction critics are concerned with the creative editing performed by the author, but are less interested in the literary structure used by the editor. A critic who uses the new literary approach concentrates on what the form critic only touches upon. He asks: How is the story structured? How is it developed or ordered? What is said and how is it said? What is the meaning of the images and symbols and the other language forms used in the story? The answers to all these questions help to elucidate the meaning of the text.[15]

One rhetorical form which has attracted considerable attention is *chiasmus.* This form involves "placing crosswise" the words or themes in a literary unit, arranging them so that the sequence of terms from the beginning to the middle is mirrored from the middle to the end of the same sequence in reverse. A simple example of *chiasmus* would be a passage with terms arranged in the pattern ABBA. Such a passage occurs in the introduction of the Gospel of Mark. A literary critic approaches this passage by exploring its structure in order to discover its meaning.[16]

14 *Mark the Evangelist: Studies of the Redaction History of the Gospel* (New York: Abingdon Press, 1969), p. 217.
15 See the discussion on historical criticism and the new literary approach to New Testament interpretation in Donald K. McKim (ed.), *A Guide to Contemporary Hermeneutics: Major Trends in Biblical Interpretation* (Grand Rapids: W. B. Eerdmans, 1986).
16 Robert Alter and Frank Kermode, eds., *The Literary Guide to the Bible* (Cambridge: Harvard

Mark roots his work in the "sacred present": "The beginning of the Gospel of Jesus Christ, the Son of God" (1:1,A). This introduces Jesus not just as a figure from the past, but as alive and active. By quoting the prophets Isaiah and Malachi: "Behold I send my messenger before thy face, who shall prepare thy way; the voice of one crying in the wilderness: Prepare the way of the Lord, make his paths straight" (1:2-3,B), Mark roots it in the "sacred past" of ancient Israel as well. The Gospel of Jesus is thus firmly "fastened" to the present and the past. The messenger sent to prepare for the coming of the Lord appears in the person of John the Baptizer, who "appeared in the wilderness preaching a baptism of repentance for the forgiveness of sins" (1:4, B). Finally, he who was introduced first, "Jesus Christ, the Son of God," reappears: "Jesus came from Nazareth of Galilee and was baptized by John in the Jordan" (1:9). At the time of his baptism, Jesus is identified as "my beloved son" (1:11, A). Thus, the structure of the passage is chiastic: ABBA. "Its subliminal effect is to rouse us to the possibility that something momentous is happening in 1:1-15—something to do with John that brings Jesus into the lead," Frank Kermode observes. The baptism of Jesus by John is the central event; its centrality is underscored by its placement in the center of the chiastic structure of the unit. The structure and the meaning of Mark's introduction are organically linked, as are the structure and meaning of any other chiastically ordered text. The structures of such passages focus upon a particular "pivotal theme," in this case Jesus' baptism.[17]

Source criticism is sometimes called literary criticism, because it deals with literary sources that were used in the composition of the gospel or other biblical books. However, the main preoccupation of a source critic is to show how the author employed his sources. The new literary criticism goes beyond source criticism and builds upon it, by showing how the author used literary structure to convey his thought more effectively.

Amos Wilder has been particularly successful in combining the results of form criticism with insights from literary criticism and from his own exploration of the language of the New Testament. He recognizes the unique power of New Testament forms and language, power which

University Press, 1987), pp. 407-408.
17 For additional insights into *chiasmus* and a clear distinction between "parallelism" and "*chiasmus*" see John Breck, "Biblical Chiasmus: Exploring Structure for Meaning," *Biblical Theology Bulletin*, v. XVII (1987), n. 2, pp. 70-74.

throughout the centuries has never failed to take effect whenever the gospel is read. In his study of the literary form of the gospels, Wilder points to "the faith they carry and the sources of that faith." He reminds us that Jesus' words and parables were remembered and retold "often with great accuracy," and that this is due not to formal memorization but to the clarity with which Jesus told the story or pronounced new ideas. The words of Christ reached the hearts of his disciples, and these words recorded in the gospels still tend "to evoke or restore the face-to-face encounter."[18]

The language of the gospels, as Wilder notes, is the language of freedom and revelation. The gospel accounts are direct and short because the evangelists are recording revelation, not trying to persuade the reader. Whereas "persuasion may take a great deal of talk and argument, revelation does not." Thus the forms of early Christian literature are "deeply determined by the faith or life orientation that produced them."[19]

This approach reveals a new dimension of the language of the gospels and makes us appreciate even more the meaning of the Word of God. The human language in which revelation is recorded is full of power; in every generation it effects profound changes and performs deeds of its own. Jesus' words have a life of their own.

VI

Finally, we must take note of canonical criticism. The canonical critic is concerned with the final form of the canonical text and its place within the Bible. Whatever literal or historical meaning the author conveyed in his book before it was included in the canon must now be seen in a much larger context. From this new perspective of the wholeness of the biblical revelation, the original meaning can acquire a new interpretative dimension. Raymond Brown points out an example from the book of Job, in which Job apparently rejects the idea of an afterlife. However, in many other sections of the Bible, and especially in the New Testament, life after death is taken for granted. How then can we understand Job's rejection in the context of the Bible as a whole? Certainly the view of an

18 *Early Christian Rhetoric: The Language of the Gospel* (Cambridge: Harvard University Press, 1971), pp. xxx, 13.
19 *Ibid.*, pp. 16-25.

afterlife in Job cannot be taken as complete or final but "could be seen as a step in the gradual perception of a larger truth."[20] From the canonical perspective we can determine the meaning of Job's rejection of an afterlife within the Bible as a whole, as well as within the book itself, without minimizing the literal impact of the statement. Canonical criticism assumes the results of other approaches and simultaneously insists that no canonical book can be interpreted in isolation, but only in connection with the other parts of the canon. This approach avoids the arbitrary use of isolated texts to prove a theological point which may have no relation to the text as a whole ("prooftexting"). Those who practice canonical criticism take seriously what the inclusion of a book into the canonical list may mean. The canonical perspective allows us to interpret differences between biblical authors, not in terms of the contradictions among them, but as expressions of various levels of development and experience at different stages in the history of salvation. The canonical approach does not overlook the human condition of the biblical writers. Rather, it acknowledges the inspiration of their books and sees them as free of deception, but not as free of limited human views. This type of criticism encourages a holistic approach to the biblical texts. Only in the light of wholeness, in the context of the life of the Church, can we determine the full meaning which the books convey to us. The Church exercised "criticism" or "judgment" to produce the canon. The result has been a principal criterion for the Church's life and growth throughout its historical existence.

"Christianity has nothing to fear from scholarship," writes James D. G. Dunn. "Scholars may be a different matter! For individual scholars have their biases and prejudices, like every human being. Individual scholars may see a particular truth only partially or in a fragmentary way or in a distorted light. They may even bend what they see of the truth to serve their own or narrowly party ends...Thankfully, scholarship is larger than the opinions of any particular scholar, however eminent," Dunn concludes in his admirably balanced evaluation of the present state of New Testament scholarship.[21]

20 *The Critical Meaning of the Bible* (New York: Paulist Press, 1981), p. 20.
21 J. D. G. Dunn, p. 103. To reject the historical knowledge acquired over the last two hundred years and the method used to obtain it is theologically untenable and historically impossible, argues Brevard S. Childs (*Interpretation,* April, 1980). But he also warns that it is equally naive

In itself, the critical method is neutral. In the hands of some scholars, it reveals their shortcomings. In the hands of others, it has opened many doors that were closed, thereby enormously helping us to enter into the meaning of the words and deeds of Christ.

to welcome the new knowledge with uncritical enthusiasm. The accumulation of historical and literary data in itself does not necessarily guarantee that one is in a better position to understand the biblical text. As Childs continues, "One can end up with a distorted picture much like a malfunctioning television." For an interpretation of the biblical text in the light of our newly acquired knowledge, he suggests a few guidelines. One is a holistic approach to the Bible: every part must be understood in the context of the whole canon, as one constituent element in the whole and in the light of the whole history of God's activity. Old and new critical knowledge should be used. The integrity of the biblical narrative must be maintained. Finally, the interpreter should come to the text with a sense of anticipation and openness.

3

The Drive To Objectivity

The field of Biblical studies has incorporated not only genuine research, but also "the prejudices of an epoch," as Sergius Bulgakov stated more than fifty years ago.[1] More recently, E. Earle Ellis observed that "the presuppositions of the investigator govern the historical study of the gospels more than one might suppose, [since] they include both confessional attitudes and methodological assumptions."[2] The vision of the critic or theologian of what Christianity is, of how it began and developed, influences his study of the gospels more than anything else.

I

At the beginning of this century, Adolf von Harnack presented (in his influential book *What is Christianity?*) an archetypal statement of the nineteenth-century liberal position on the gospels. He claimed that the message of Jesus "has to do with the Father only and not with the Son." He recognized that the Synoptic Gospels are the sources for the Church's teaching of Jesus and that they are historically reliable. To arrive at the "historical" core of Jesus' message, the Fatherhood of God, Harnack had to classify many other elements of the gospels as peripheral or non-essential. He divided the eschatological sayings and discourses of Jesus from what he considered as the core of the gospel. By considering Jesus' proclamation as something that would be consummated within history, Harnack reflected a nineteenth-century optimistic view. But the Jesus of *What is Christianity?* is not the Jesus whom we encounter in the gospels or in the life of the Church. He has very little to do either with the first-century Jewish-Hellenistic world or with the sacred history of the Old Testament. Harnack's views recall those of Marcion, who in the second century fought for the exclusion of the Hebrew scriptures, the Old Testament, from the canon of the early Church, on the grounds that they obscured the revelation of the "true" God.

1 *The Orthodox Church* (Crestwood: St Vladimir's Seminary Press, 1988), p. 17.
2 Ellis, *Gospel Criticism*, p. 27.

Soon after the appearance of Harnack's book, Albert Schweitzer published his monumental work *The Quest of the Historical Jesus* (1906). His examination of the "lives of Jesus," written during the eighteenth and nineteenth centuries, led him to the telling conclusion that each was completely influenced by its author's cultural and religious environment. Each interpretation of Jesus, according to Schweitzer, reflected above all the historical period in which it was written. "Each individual created Him in accordance with his own character." Schweitzer believed that in order truly to understand Jesus' actions and teachings, he had to be viewed within the context of apocalyptic Judaism. Accordingly, in contrast to his liberal predecessors, Schweitzer depicted "the true historical Jesus" as "an imperious ruler" who "could think of Himself as the Son of Man."[3]

Matthew 10 was central to Schweitzer's image of Christ. He claimed that when Jesus called his twelve disciples and sent them on a mission out into Galilee, charging them: "Go nowhere among the Gentiles, and enter no town of the Samaritans, but go rather to the lost sheep of the House of Israel," he expected that the end would occur before they had gone "through all the towns of Israel" (Mt 10:5-6, 22-23). When this expectation failed, Jesus decided to go to Jerusalem to set in motion and to accelerate the coming of the Kingdom of God by undergoing the experience of death and thereby bringing about the apocalyptic end. Schweitzer thus replaced Harnack's "harmless preacher of the fatherhood of God" with "a stranger and an enigma," with "an apocalyptic fanatist."[4] This lent impetus to even more radical challenges to traditional interpretations. Gustaf Aulen observed that, paradoxically, Schweitzer's devout and powerful work encouraged a skeptical attitude toward the possibility of knowing the historical Jesus.[5]

Rudolf Bultmann (1884-1976), a leader in the field of form criticism and one of the most influential scholars in gospel research before and after World War II, espoused an extreme skepticism. He separated the Christ of the apostolic preaching ("*kerygma*") from the historical Jesus, thereby denying the possibility of knowing Jesus as he really lived and worked and taught. He regarded the gospels as the product of the

3 *The Quest of the Historical Jesus* (New York: Macmillan, 1968), pp. 4, 403.
4 *Ibid.*, pp. 389ff.
5 See Aulen's *Jesus in Contemporary Historical Research* (Philadelphia: Fortress Press, 1976), p. 8.

Christian Church, the creative work of the community, claiming that the Jesus of history was obscured by the layers of dogmatic interpretation present in the gospels. Thus, Christianity as we know it cannot depend on the historic Jesus, but only on the Christ of faith. Bultmann's well-known method of "demythologization" consisted not simply in removing so-called "mythical" features from the gospels but also in interpreting them according to a new existentialist understanding of human existence derived from the philosophy of Martin Heidegger (1889-1976). This is why Bultmann's Jesus has been called the "Heideggerian Jesus."[6] Bultmann's skepticism led him to divorce the faith of the New Testament from the person, works and teachings of Jesus and to call the message of Jesus "not part of the theology" of the New Testament, but one of its "presuppositions."[7]

The foregoing paragraphs show how the world-view of an interpreter inevitably affects his study of the gospels. The historical method, as understood and used by some modern critics, includes the presupposition that history is a "closed continuum," in which events "are connected by a succession of cause and effect." This closed universe cannot be disrupted by powers from above.[8] When a critic with such a perspective comes to the miracles of Jesus, the result of his work differs radically from that of a scholar who considers history to be open to powers beyond it. Joseph Cardinal Ratzinger, in his 1988 New York address concerning modern methods of studying the Bible, remarked that early and influential scholars "had mistakenly tried to imitate natural sciences," and that their methods reflected a modern philosophical assumption that "there is no way of knowing about 'God's intervention in history'." For theologians, this belief "is a contradiction." He urged biblical scholars to reexamine such philosophical premises, which have sometimes become

---

6 J. Daniélou and others have indicated a certain similarity between Origen's use of allegory and Bultmann's "demythologization." Even though Origen used excessive allegorism, he preserved the unity of the Bible, and through non-biblical categories he secured the Hebrew historical outlook for the early Church. On a deeper level, Bultmann is closer to the second-century Gnostics than to any other group in this early period. Neither the early Gnostics nor the modern demythologizers accept the witness of the New Testament to the Word become flesh. For both of them, history is an "external shell."

See our article, "Criticism, the Gospel, and the Church," *St Vladimir's Theological Quarterly*, v. 10, n. 3, 1966, pp. 160ff.

7 Rudolf Bultmann, *Theology of New Testament* (New York: 1951), p. 3.

8 Bultmann, *Existence and Faith* (Cleveland: 1960), pp. 291-2.

"academic dogmas." In other words, he asked critics to be as critical of their own methods and presuppositions as they are of the texts they approach to analyze.[9]

Bultmann was fundamentally influenced by philosophical trends prevalent in his own time, but he was hardly the first interpreter of the gospels to be affected in such a way. For example, Hegel's dialectical pattern of thesis-antithesis-synthesis was applied to the gospels by the Tübingen School during the nineteenth century. Interpreting John's gospel as a synthesis of the faith of the primitive Church (thesis) and Pauline theology (antithesis), they effectively dismissed its historical value. The effect of the Hegelian method in this instance was to separate Jesus from the records of his work and teaching and even to remove the fourth gospel from its Palestinian setting and deny its apostolic origin.[10]

Concern for the historical Jesus is a positive result of these debates. Historical scholarship has produced new solutions to basic problems in biblical history. It is "an ongoing conversation about the past in which no one has the last word."[11] This "conversation" has led the various Christian groups to realize that they must participate in intense intellectual and spiritual efforts to know as much as is humanly possible about Jesus in the context of first-century life and history. Christian scholars and theologians are more aware than ever before of the perils of modern-

9 As reported in the *New York Times*, January 29, 1988. There is no serious disagreement among New Testament scholars regarding the task of the historical critical method. There is, however, a dispute among them over some of the philosophical and theological presuppositions of criticism. It has been recognized that "more than a few of them are raising questions about the adequacy of the classic historical-critical method to deal with transcendence" (see D. K. McKim, *A Guide to Contemporary Hermeneutics*, p. 16). For some, the method is closed to the idea of transcendence and properly should remain so, while for others the method should take transcendence into consideration.

10 See J. N. Sanders, *A Commentary on the Gospel According to St John* (New York: 1968), pp. 56-66. Even today Hegel plays "a subtle but influential role" in the work of some of the scholars who are particularly involved in reconstructing the life and history of the early Church. Here, Hegelian dialectic is used in connection with the expectation of *parousia* (the Second Coming of Christ), its delay, and solutions to the problem. "The apocalyptic expectation of Jesus and the earliest Church (*thesis*) encounters the problem of the delay of the *parousia* (*antithesis*) and is resolved by a salvation-history theology (*synthesis*) of Luke-Acts...or of all the gospels." E. Earle Ellis notes that in this interpretation "an inference or implicit assumption" is made that "the gospels are a response to conflict. It also creates *a priori a caesura* between Jesus and the gospels and thereby imposes a substantive and not only a chronological distance between them" (*Gospel Criticism*, p. 34).

11 Gerd Theissen, *The Shadow of the Galilean* (*The Quest of the Historical Jesus in Narrative Form*), (Philadelphia: Fortress Press, 1987), p. 55.

izing Jesus, for as they come closer to the Jesus of history through their research, they realize that he transcends the boundaries both of his world and of the categories and patterns of their own culture and theology. We should therefore be particularly wary of shaping our view of Jesus in accordance with the experiences and ideas of our own time. Such subjective interpretation diminishes his significance and his message. The Christian Churches would obscure their own historical origins if they cut off the story of Jesus from its contemporary religious context and interpreted it according to their own modern experiences. On the other hand, we should also reject the "otherworldly Jesus" who has nothing in common with our experience. If Jesus were beyond the common experience of human beings, he could not be known by us today. The Schweitzerian Jesus comes close to being such an alien figure. While the Jesus of the gospels transcended the culture and religion of his time, he interacted fully with the people he met and was understood by them.

Bultmann's students have broken through the boundaries imposed by their teacher in a search for historical facts in the gospels which went unrecognized by their master. Overall, Bultmann's school contributed substantially to an interest in critical study of the gospels. By raising radical questions and producing its own images of Jesus, it also inspired profitable discussion of the formation and historical character of the gospel narrative. Its members offer a compelling challenge to all of us to go back to our primary sources and to search for new and more adequate answers to the questions they raise. While their own perspectives and prejudices may have led them to false conclusions, they have been instrumental in formulating new approaches and forcing fresh readings of the gospel texts.

III

If we criticize certain tendencies in gospel scholarship, it is not to reject the exegetical method itself, but to point out certain assumptions which the scholars bring to their work. Some critics want to believe that the life and ministry of Jesus must be different from the way they are presented in the gospels. They accept and understand his message according to their own subjective presuppositions. We have already suggested that even in the field of textual or "lower" criticism these presuppositions can play a significant role in the selection or rejection of a particular variant.

If all interpreters shared the same presuppositions and were absolutely objective, they would eventually arrive at the same acceptable interpretation, since, according to John L. McKenzie, "the meaning of the Bible has been determined by its authors, not by its interpreters." However, McKenzie recognizes the practical difficulty of attaining such objectivity, adding that it is "doubtful if we ever shall be [entirely objective] before the Second Coming."[12]

Complete objectivity is not only unattainable, but also undesirable. "One has to check, severely and strictly, one's prejudices and presuppositions, but one should never try to empty one's mind of all presuppositions," as Georges Florovsky put it. "Such an attempt would be a suicide of mind and can only issue in total mental sterility."[13] The most dangerous kind of presupposition is to believe that one does not have any. "The important thing is to admit and examine one's presuppositions, realize their potential strength and dangers, and allow them to be addressed and challenged by the text."[14] The Christian interpreter is free in his research, but free within a perspective. He should be guided by the whole tradition of the Church—biblical, liturgical and dogmatic. Scripture is not a field by itself; its meaning is revealed within the life of the Church.

We now recognize that the New Testament exegete should cultivate the incarnational approach to the sacred writings and should be guided by the principles that come from this biblically grounded view. The Bible owes its existence, in the words of St John Chrysostom, to the condescension (συγκατάβασις) of God . A more accurate translation of this Greek term might be "the divine act of considerateness by which God (particularly—but not pre-eminently—in the Scriptures) makes allowance for human limitations by the language he (through the sacred author) employs."[15] The words of God took form in the languages of different cultures and civilizations. God's care and love for all of his creation were manifested in his desire to be personally present among his

12 See his article, "Problems of Hermeneutics in Roman Catholic Exegesis," *Journal of Biblical Literature*, 77:20, (1958), p. 199.
13 "The Predicament of the Christian Historian," in W. Leibrecht, ed., *Religion and Culture: Essays in Honor of Paul Tillich* (New York: Harper & Brothers, 1959), pp. 148-49.
14 John P. Meier, in "Introduction" to R. F. Collins, *Introduction to the New Testament* (Garden City, NY: Doubleday, 1987), p. xvii.
15 R. C. Hill, "St John Chrysostom and the Incarnation of the Word in Scripture," *Compass Theology Review*, 14 (1980), p. 34.

people: "Let them make me a sanctuary (a tabernacle) that I may dwell in their midst" (Ex 40:35). Finally, "the Word became flesh and dwelt among us, full of grace and truth; we have beheld his glory, glory as of the only Son from the Father" (Jn 1:14). Thus God's faithfulness to his promises in the Bible was fulfilled in Jesus. The glory of God dwelt fully in Jesus of Nazareth.

In the incarnation the Word of God became flesh, and in the Bible the words of God became human language. The words of Scripture are simultaneously the record of God's revelation and an expression of human response to God's actions. These words inevitably consist of both divine and human elements. The truth of God becomes incarnate in the reception and contemplation of it by human beings. The fact that the books of the Bible, and particularly of the New Testament, are ascribed to individual authors indicates that it contains a human factor. It is by nature subject to historical research. We are fully justified in taking into account the historical, social and literary contexts of a passage from the gospels, its "human factor," to grasp its full meaning. Origen (d.c. 254), the great biblical scholar of the early Church, was among the first to insist upon intellectual and spiritual efforts in understanding a biblical text. "Readers need an open mind and considerable study, and if I may say so need to enter into the mind of the writers to find out with what spiritual meaning each event was recorded" (*Contra Celsum* 1:42).

Among those of our time who have emphasized the importance of the incarnational approach to Scripture is Urs von Balthazar. A biblical book or text, according to Balthazar, has two meanings: the literal (or historical) and the spiritual. The relationship between these two senses corresponds to the relationship between the human and divine nature in Christ. Like Christ's two natures, these two senses, while distinct from one another, are ultimately indivisible. Just as the human nature of Christ simultaneously reveals and conceals his divine nature, so that the literal historical meaning of the Scripture both reveals and conceals its spiritual meaning. Just as the divine nature of Christ is not "beyond" or "behind" the literal meaning, but "within" it, so the spiritual manifests itself "through" the letter.[16]

Our knowledge, however extensive, of historical or literal elements in the Bible cannot be sufficient to grasp adequately all the implications of

16 *Word and Revelation* (New York:Herder and Herder, 1964), pp. 22ff.

a biblical text. While we may know history, biblical archaeology, the social environment and customs, the "spiritual" meaning may still elude us. In the setting of faith, in the Body of Christ, the Bible reveals other meanings that are not opposed to the historical.

At first the incarnational approach appears to oppose the historical-critical method described in the preceding pages. This is not the case. We cannot dismiss the contributions of modern approaches to our understanding of the Bible. To reject the historical-critical method would be to reduce or even to neglect the importance of the human response to the Word of God. The incarnational approach presupposes historical inquiry and justifies historical research and historical questions. It is necessary to realize that the questions and interests of ancient and modern exegetes are different. While the patristic writers tended to interpret historical data spiritually, modern commentators tend to understand spiritual matters historically. Each period has its own questions, the best answers to which always remain with us. The insights upon which the patristic approach to Scripture was built and the insights of modern historical exegesis need not be contradictory.

4

Tradition and Interpretation

The task of New Testament criticism is to lead us to see Jesus as he was seen by his contemporaries. Modern criticism, however, cannot exhaust the meaning of the gospel. It may bring us to a clearer understanding of Jesus, but "no one can say, 'Jesus is Lord' except by the Holy Spirit" (1 Cor 12:3). The proper function of criticism is not to destroy the tradition of the Church, but to illumine it; it is not to reject old insights, but to open new avenues of understanding of God's ways and purposes in history.

I

The gospels themselves invite criticism. Many events in the life of Jesus are recorded in more than one gospel. One does not need to be a biblical critic to notice both similarities and differences between parallel reports of the same episodes. We find varying wordings and emphases even in the accounts of the authentic words of Jesus. Jesus' works are not reported as neutral facts, nor are his words recorded without their meaning. The gospels combine the facts with interpretation and the words with their meaning. The task of the critic is not only to explain variations between parallel passages, but also to bring out explanations built into the gospels, if their sense is not immediately evident.

No layer of the gospel tradition records an event without interpreting it. An example is the report of the death of Christ in Mark 15:37-38. "And Jesus uttered a loud cry, and breathed his last. And the curtain of the temple was torn in two, from top to bottom." Jesus' death and the tearing of the curtain go together. But while we see the death of Jesus as death in the real sense, we do not need to take literally the statement that the veil of the Temple was split in two. It is quite possible that the curtain which the evangelist had in mind was the one in the Temple in Jerusalem, which separated the Holy Place from the Holy of Holies. In the

Holy Place, daily sacrifices were offered. The Holy of Holies was the place of God's invisible presence. Only once a year could the high priest enter it. The sense of Mark's account, therefore, is that the barrier which separated man from God, symbolically represented by the curtain, has been removed through the death of Jesus.

Let us turn to Matthew's account of the same event:

And Jesus cried again with a loud voice and yielded up his spirit. And behold, the curtain of the temple was torn in two, from top to bottom; and the earth shook, and the rocks were split; the tombs also were opened, and many bodies of the saints who had fallen asleep were raised, and coming out of the tombs after his resurrection they went into the holy city and appeared to many (27:50-53).

The images which here follow the tearing of the curtain in the temple are unique to Matthew. Their literal interpretation obscures their deeper meaning. The description functions, not as an eyewitness account, but as a symbolic interpretation of the death of Jesus. Matthew adds new elements not found in Mark. The images of the shaking of the earth and the splitting of rocks were traditionally used in the description of the Day of Yahweh.[1] Both Matthew and the gospel tradition on which he drew tell us that the Day of the Lord is here: the day of judgment and salvation which the prophets had announced is inaugurated with Jesus' death on the Cross. What, then, about the opening of the tombs and the resurrection of the Old Testament saints? Is the resurrection of Lazarus multiplied here? Can we take this account from Matthew's gospel in its literal sense? Not only modern exegetes, but also many Church Fathers interpreted this passage theologically rather than historically. If this passage is taken only literally, its meaning is missed. "It is difficult to imagine Abraham coming out of the tomb, wandering round Jerusalem for two or three days and then dying again later," as Pierre Bénoit puts it.[2] According to both ancient and modern interpreters, notes Bénoit, with Jesus' resurrection the way to heaven is opened, and the holy city where the saints appear is probably meant to be the heavenly Jerusalem (Heb 11:10; 12:22-23; 13:14, and Rev 3:12; 21:2-10; 22:19).

The death of Jesus is a revelatory event. Any other interpretation of the death of Christ must be judged by its faithfulness to the interpretation already given here. Both the facts and their interpretations used by

1   See Is 13:9f; Zeph 1:14-18; Am 8:9; Jl 1:15, 2:1f.
2   *The Passion and Resurrection of Christ* (New York: Herder and Herder, 1969), pp. 203-4.

the evangelists come from the pre-literary gospel tradition, which began with Jesus himself and with the interpretation that he himself gave his disciples concerning his death.

If the gospels do not simply give us the "bare facts" about the life of Jesus, do they give us his "pure words?" The fundamentalist critic and the radical critic both have clear and easy, if diametrically opposed, answers to these questions. An extreme form critic would maintain that the words of Jesus are lost to us, and that only the words of the community as expressions of its faith are recorded in the gospels. We have to agree that the sayings of Jesus are not recorded verbatim in the gospels. For example, the four different accounts of the institution of the Eucharist are not contradictory, but their wording does differ at some points. The Church meditated upon the words of Jesus, lived them at the eucharistic gathering, and was led by the Spirit to their meaning. Therefore, the gospels present both the eucharistic words of Jesus and their meaning. The disciples remembered the words of Jesus in the sense that they not only repeated, but also understood them. It was equally vital to transmit the message that the sayings conveyed and the truth that they revealed about Jesus. The words of Jesus and the words of the Church that expressed their meaning were united in the gospels.

In *Memory and Manuscript*, Birger Gerhardsson compared the transmission of the words of Jesus by the early Church to the transmission of the oral teaching of the great rabbinic teachers. He related three elements of the New Testament (the Old Testament, the words and works of Jesus, and the Church's interpretation of them) to three elements of Judaism (Scripture, Mishnah, and Gemara). Mishnah ("repetition") is the early third-century collection of the rabbinic law. Gemara ("completion") is the commentary on the Mishnah. Gerhardsson's thesis inspired an illuminating critical response from W. D. Davies,[3] in which he argued that whereas it is comparatively easy to distinguish three strands in Judaism, this is not the case with the Christian tradition. Here "the three corresponding items are merged. We suggest that they are so merged because the point of reference in the Church is Jesus Christ, who has

3 For criticism by W. D. Davies, see "Reflection on a Scandinavian Approach to 'gospel Tradition'," Appendix XV of his *Setting of the Sermon on the Mount* (Cambridge: Cambridge University Press, 1964), pp. 464-80.

become in himself Scripture, Mishnah, Gemara." The tradition in Judaism leads to Mishnah, but the tradition in Christianity leads to the gospel. Jesus and the Church are inseparable; he identifies himself with the Church. The words of Jesus and the "Gemara" of the Church are one and the same, as far as the evangelists are concerned.

The Spirit-inspired words of the Bible have a life of their own and imply new meanings beyond those governed by their original context. The Bible has its own design, which naturally resists any interpretation that would distort it. Athanasius, in his fight with the Arians, contended that by "playing" with arbitrarily selected proof-texts they ignored "the scope [pattern] of the Divine Scripture." According to Georges Florovsky, "*skopos*" in Athanasius' response to the Arian mishandling of the biblical text was closely equivalent to the term *hypothesis* ("underlying idea, or design") used by Irenaeus in the second century in his fight with the Gnostics. Irenaeus contended that the Gnostic use of biblical texts to support their own teachings was too free and too selective. In order to illustrate the Gnostic attitude toward Scripture, Irenaeus offered his readers the story of an artist who used many precious jewels to make an image of a king. After someone destroyed the image, the artist began to make an image of an animal with the same jewels. Although the material was the same, the image was no longer the same (*Adv. Haeres.* I, 8:1). "Now the point which St Irenaeus endeavored to make is obvious," argues Florovsky. "Scripture has its own pattern or design, its internal structure and harmony. The heretics ignore this pattern, or rather substitute their own instead. In other words, they rearrange the Scriptural evidence on a pattern which is quite alien to the Scripture itself."[4] The interpretation of Scripture, according to Irenaeus, must be guided by "the rule of truth," which is the apostolic preaching, the *kerygma*, handed over and faithfully witnessed to in the Church. In other words, the living tradition, the continuous life in the truth guided by the Holy Spirit, became for Irenaeus the indispensable context and hermeneutical principle for interpreting Scripture.

The fulness of the faith is given in the Scriptures. The Fathers of the Church spoke of the "sufficiency of Scripture." For Anthanasius the Scriptures "are sufficient for the proclamation of the truth."[5] None of the

4 "The Function of Tradition in the Ancient Church," *Greek Orthodox Theological Review*, 9:2 (1963), pp. 184-85.
5 The term "self-sufficiency" is not to be understood in a negative, exclusive sense. Chrysostom

Fathers regarded the Bible as a *self-interpreting* book, however. Their view of its sufficiency organically linked Scripture to the living past of the Church. Without the Church there would be no New Testament, and without the gospel revealed and proclaimed there would be no Church. Tradition is the application of Scripture to the life of the Church. What distinguishes the testimony of Scripture from all subsequent testimony is that as the record of and response to revelation, it is the criterion by which the Church judges any other subsequent expressions and formulations of the truth of God. Without the record and contemplation of revelation, the Church would be without an "appointed road."

Scripture lives and reveals its meaning within a tradition that is scripturally inspired. Therefore Scripture and Tradition, "the life of the Holy Spirit in the Church,"[6] can be neither opposed nor subordinated to each other. Neither is it justifiable to isolate Scripture from the life of the Church. There has been a temptation throughout history to view the Bible as "intelligible in itself," and to view subsequent dogmatic and liturgical growth as signs of a break with the "purity and simplicity" of the gospel. Some have tried to understand the Christian movement in terms of its "pure origins;" others, in terms of its growth and development. Now we know that what is "pure" and "authentic" in the formation of the Church is also manifested in its growth as a hierarchical and charismatic body. The growth comes from the seed, and the seed is the gospel itself. This is the framework within which our principles of interpretation must be set forth clearly and without concealment. Tradition is a help, not a hindrance, to the work of biblical research. Gustav Weigel expressed it well when he said that "the presence of tradition does not hinder" the exegete "any more than gravity hampers the racer. It only keeps him on the ground."[7]

describes Scripture as "the appointed road" on which we must start. Self-sufficiency for the Fathers does not exclude, but actually includes the Church and its tradition. The Church finds her identity in the Scriptures. For the views of the Fathers and other Orthodox theologians, see my articles, "Research and Prejudice," *St Vladimir's Theological Quarterly*, 14:1-2 (1970), pp. 16f, and "Criticism, the Gospel, and the Church," 10:3 (1966), pp. 155-157.

6 See Georges Florovsky, "Scripture and Tradition: An Orthodox Point of View," *Dialog: A Journal of Theology*, 2 (Autumn 1963), pp. 298ff. For Vladimir Lossky, tradition in its "pure form" is "the life of the Holy Spirit in the Church." It is the truth of Christ revealed by the Spirit (V. Lossky, "Tradition and Traditions," in L. Ouspensky and V. Lossky, *The Meaning of Icons* (Crestwood: St. Vladimir's Seminary Press, 1982).

7 *Catholic Theology in Dialogue:* (New York: Harper & Row, 1961), p. 48.

II

As we have seen, Scripture must be understood within the context of the Church and Tradition. Moreover, the same God unites the Old Testament and the New with his promises and with their realization. The unity between the Old and New Testaments is apparent in the gospel texts themselves, and the early Church fought against the Gnostics to retain it. One of the permanent results of early Christian exegesis is precisely this unity. The early exegetes demonstrated that Jesus did not abolish the Old Testament, but fulfilled it. The early Christians saw the New Testament as the climax of the Old Testament, the realization of its messianic promise. This is attested by what may be a very early Christian hymn: "In many and various ways God spoke of old to our fathers by the prophets, but in these last days he has spoken to us by a Son, whom he appointed the heir of all things" (Heb 1:1-2). In writing the New Testament, the evangelists often described or interpreted events by referring to Old Testament texts. But only the authority of their experience of Jesus could determine which passages from the Old Testament were to be used. Their reading of the Old Testament in light of this experience was the only perspective they could have accepted.

The gospels present Jesus as the one who brought the Church into existence. Jesus' choice of the Twelve, in the words of Schnackenburg, was "a kind of prophetic parable," the beginning of the messianic community.[8] The activity of the Messiah began with the selection of those who would follow him. The Incarnate One called ordinary men to share his life and destiny. He was not an isolated individual, but the head of a community. His intention was not to bring into existence one more group to add to those already existing in first-century Israel, but to incorporate everyone into his community, which would then follow after him and proclaim the coming of the reign of God. The "little flock" (Lk 12:32) was intended to be inclusive. The Twelve were sent on a mission to announce Jesus' own message, that "the Kingdom of God has come upon you" (Mt 12:28), that it was already present and already at work. They were asked to go and to preach that "the kingdom of heaven is at hand. Heal the sick, raise the dead, cleanse lepers, cast out demons" (Mt 10:7). Their preaching and activity were no different from those of Jesus.

8 Rudolf Schnackenburg, *God's Rule and Kingdom* (New York: Herder and Herder, 1963), p. 215.

The messianic community was not yet the Church in its present sense. Its transformation into the Body of Christ occurred only after the resurrection. After the glorification, death, resurrection, and ascension of Jesus, and the giving of the Spirit, the newly-created Church continued the work and relived the life of Christ in the world. The resurrected Christ promised that he would remain with his own "to the close of the age" (Mt 28:20). Thus the Church is his body, in which those who are incorporated by baptism "have tasted of the goodness of the word of God and the powers of the age to come" (Heb 6:5). While the effects of God's reign are active in the Church, this community brought to life by Jesus looks forward to the future consummation of this reign. It was to this eschatological society that Jesus left his words and works: to the Church and not to an anonymous community that fabricates myths and legends about him. In the Church, the risen Christ lives and rules. He is the head and the savior of his Church (Col 1:18; Eph 4:15; 5:27). According to Emile Mersh, the Church as his body "is in the same relation to him as a building to its foundation, as the stem to its root, as the organism to the life that animates it. The Church continues Christ; she expresses him."[9]

III

As the head is always united with the body, so Jesus is always united with his Church, "which he obtained with his own blood" (Acts 20:28). Scholars who apply to Jesus' teachings the principle of "double dissimilarity," however, imply that he can be separated from it. Some followers of Bultmann claim that to determine the earliest form of a saying of Jesus does not necessarily determine its authenticity. As one spokesman has defined it, "the earliest form of a saying we can reach may be regarded as authentic if it can be shown to be dissimilar to characteristic emphases both of ancient Judaism and of the early Church."[10] By using the criterion of double dissimilarity, these critics try to discover material that can be ascribed without doubt to Jesus alone, making this uniqueness the only grounds for true authenticity. Paradoxically, the method tries to use skepticism to overcome skepticism.

9   *The Whole Christ: The Historical Development of the Doctrine of the Mystical Body in Scripture and Tradition* (Milwaukee: Bruce Publishing House, 1936), p. 121.
10 Norman Perrin, *Rediscovering the Teaching of Jesus,* (London: SCM Press, 1967), p. 39.

This method assumes that Jesus was an isolated individual who had nothing in common with Judaism or with his Church. In effect, it "disincarnates" him by separating him from his time and his followers. If we accept as historical and authentic only those sayings which are "out of character with the beliefs of the Church," we risk eliminating as secondary what may be primary, for no other reason than that Jesus and the Church had a particular saying in common.[11] The principle of double dissimilarity reflects a limited view of the originality of Jesus. Those who vigorously apply it presuppose not only that Jesus should be isolated from the Church, but also that the name "Jesus" and the title "Christ" are not related. However, astute critics, Edwyn Hoskyns and Francis Noel Davey (*The Riddle of the New Testament*, 1947), question the validity of any reconstruction of first-century events which assumes a breach between the faith of the primitive Church and the Jesus of history. This gap, they emphasize, would not explain the origin or the growth of the Church or give due attention to the New Testament evidence that the life of Christ is the source of the Church.

IV

Our approach to Jesus is guided by the principle that the historical Jesus and the resurrected Christ are the same person. To Jews and Gentiles alike, the apostles preached both the risen Lord and the Jesus of history. When they proclaimed the resurrection of Jesus on the day of Pentecost, they spoke of "Jesus of Nazareth, a man attested to you by God with mighty works and wonders and signs which God did through him in your midst, as you yourself know—this Jesus delivered up according to the definite plan and foreknowledge of God, you crucified and killed by the hands of lawless men ... This Jesus God raised up, and of that we are

11 In "Christology and Methodology" (*New Testament Studies* 17, pp. 480-87), M. D. Hooker writes: "No one can seriously doubt that in some things Jesus' view must have overlapped those of the Jewish leaders and those of his followers, yet these must be set aside from our reconstruction. But to exclude details from our picture of Jesus may lead to distortion as serious as (or worse than) that which comes if we include too much" (p. 481). "The application of the method is bound to be subjective. How do we decide what is 'dissimilar'?... To be acceptable as genuine, a saying of Jesus must at one and the same time be 'dissimilar' from contemporary Judaism, and yet use its categories and reflect the language and style of Aramaic. In other words, authentic sayings must not be reflected in Judaism (as far as it is known to us) but must sound as if they could have been spoken at that time" (p. 482f.).

all witnesses" (Acts 2:22-23; 32). "This Jesus" is again emphasized in the apostolic proclamation to the Gentiles in Acts 10:38-40: "We are witnesses to all that he did both in the country of the Jews and in Jerusalem. They put him to death by hanging him on a tree, but God raised him on the third day and made him manifest." To these first witnesses of the resurrection, there was no separation between the Jesus who called them while passing by the Sea of Galilee and the Lord whom they met and worshipped after the resurrection. They bore witness not only to the historical continuity between "Jesus" and the "Christ," but also to the personal continuity.[12]

If the Christ preached by the apostles was not the same person as Jesus of Nazareth, then he is merely a mythological figure. This would root the proclamation of the gospel not in an historical event, but in subjective visions and human imagination.

We have seen that New Testament scholars continue to debate vigorously the historicity of the gospels and that they are by no means of one mind. These controversies have been particularly fruitful in their definition of the gospels as historical documents and of Jesus as a historical figure. They draw us out of mythology and into history. They have contributed much to our attempts to define the image of Christ in the gospels; more simply, they help us discover who Jesus really was. In pursuit of this goal, we turn now to consider the gospels and their authors.

---

12 Jesus was called "Lord" (κύριος) after his resurrection, and yet the evangelist Luke, for example, used the same title for Jesus in his account of the public ministry (Lk 7:13; 10:39, 41). In doing so, he did not falsify history. Rather, he made the same "mistake" that all historians make when they try to describe past events in the light of present knowledge and experienice. By ascribing the title κύριος to Jesus before his death and resurrection, the evangelist simply expressed the faith of the Church, which he shared, that the risen Christ and Jesus of Nazareth were one and the same person.

5

The Gospel and the Gospels

When we use the word "gospel," we usually have in mind a book ascribed to one of the evangelists; the reading from the gospel in church during a service is a reading from one of the four books called the gospels. This term has another meaning as well: the passage that is read contains the "gospel," the "good news" or message of salvation for those who hear it. Thus the word "gospel" means both the good news brought by Jesus and the written proclamation of this good news.

I

From the second century on, the two meanings of "gospel" have always been used in the Church. But in the first-century, when the gospels were written, the word "gospel" (Greek εὐαγγέλιον) never denoted a book. There is not a single example of this usage in the New Testament. The epistles of Paul, at least some of which are probably our earliest Christian documents, used the word εὐαγγέλιον about sixty times, either alone (τὸ εὐαγγέλιον) or with epithets: "the Gospel of God" (τὸ εὐαγγέλιον τοῦ θεοῦ), and "the Gospel of Christ" (τοῦ Χριστοῦ). In each case he meant the message, not a book.

Paul admitted the existence of only one message of salvation. He wrote to the new members of the churches in Galatia not to turn from the gospel which he had proclaimed to them to another "gospel." For there is not "another gospel," he insisted, and "if any one is preaching to you a gospel contrary to that which you received, let him be accursed." He emphatically stressed that it was not "man's gospel" (τὸ εὐαγγέλιον κατὰ ἄνθρωπον) that he preached, but the gospel that "came through a revelation of Jesus Christ" (Gal 1:6ff).

In Romans he defined the gospel as "the power of God (δύναμις θεοῦ) for salvation to every one who has faith, to the Jew first and also to the Greek" (Rom 1:16). For him, the gospel was not merely "a series of propositions about Christ, e.g., 'Jesus is Lord,' which human beings are expected to apprehend and give assent to," but rather the dynamic power of God acting "in human history through the person, ministry, passion, death, and resurrection of Jesus" for human salvation.[1] The gospel came to the members of his communities not only in words, "but also in power (ἐν δυνάμει) and in the Holy Spirit" (1 Th 1:5).

Paul's gospel was the gospel of the primitive Christian community. It was the message of salvation, the apostolic proclamation or κήρυγμα, in which the gospel, revealed and experienced as the power of God, received the formulation that served as the early Christian credo. Paul received this *kerygma* from the Church and delivered it to the members of his communities. He cites it in 1 Cor 15:3-8:

> For I delivered to you as of first importance what I also received, that Christ died for our sins, in accordance with the scripture, that he was buried, that he was raised on the third day in accordance with the scriptures, and that he appeared to Cephas, then to the twelve. Then he appeared to more than five hundred brethren at one time, most of whom are still alive, though some have fallen asleep. Then he appeared to James, then to all the apostles. Last of all, as to one untimely born, he appeared also to me.

Kerygma expressed the faith of the apostolic Church. Yet not all that the Church believed and lived by was necessarily included in this formalized apostolic preaching. The infancy narratives, for instance, were not included in the primitive creed in 1 Cor 15:3-8. This does not mean, however, that the material in the first two chapters of Matthew and Luke was considered less important by the early Church. The gospel of the birth of the Messiah belonged to the faith from the start. The troparion of the Feast of the Annunciation in the Orthodox Church expresses this in its first verse: "Today is the beginning of our salvation." Why then was such "good news of great joy" not included in the *kerygma*, which was above all the *kerygma* of salvation? With reference to Lk 2:19: "Mary kept all these things, pondering them in her heart." Vladimir Lossky suggested that this was due to the "personification of tradition."[2] The good news of Jesus' birth affected only a few persons, especially Mary. The *kerygma*, on the other hand, was the public proclamation of the events in the life of Jesus which did not belong to a

1 See Joseph A. Fitzmyer, "The Gospel in the Theology of Paul," *Interpretation*, vol. XXXIII (1979), no. 4, p. 343.
2 In his article on "Panagia," in E. L. Mascall (ed.), *The Mother of God* (London: Dacre Press, n.d.), p. 28.

"private tradition," but which was observed by many. Many other details in the infancy narratives, such as the virginal conception of Jesus, are beyond the reach of historical investigation. W. F. Albright rightly ascribes this to "their highly intimate, personal and transcendent character," adding that "the historian cannot control the details of Jesus' birth and resurrection and thus has no right to pass judgment on their historicity," and that "the historian, *qua* historian, must stop at the threshold, unable to enter the shrine of the Christian *mysteria* without removing his shoes, conscious that there are realms where history and nature are inadequate, and where God reigns over them in eternal majesty."[3] The gospel of the birth of the Messiah remains within the Holy of Holies of Christian revelation.

II

Of the four evangelists, only Mark used the word "gospel" in Paul's absolute sense. Matthew always qualifies it with the words "of the kingdom," while Luke uses the term "gospel" only in Acts (see 15:7 and 20:24), preferring in his gospel "to proclaim the good news" (εὐαγγελίζομαι). In John the term for "testimony" or "witness" (ἡ μαρτυρία) takes the place of "gospel." The opening verse of Mark begins with "gospel": "The beginning of the gospel of Jesus, Christ, the Son of God." Matthew begins with "the book (βίβλος) of the genealogy of Jesus Christ, the son of David, the son of Abraham." Luke in his preface uses the word "narrative" (διήγησιν), and John after the prologue opens his historical account with a reference to "the testimony (ἡ μαρτυρία) of John" the Baptist (Jn 1:19). For the meaning of "gospel," then, we turn to Mark.

Mark's use of "gospel" in the "title" of his book implies not that the word stands for the book, but that it refers to "the good news of salvation." The saving work of God is what he means by "gospel." The gospel in Mark includes what Jesus did and said, and this "gospel (τὸ

---

3 *From the Stone Age to Christianity*, rev. ed. (New York: Anchor, 1957), p. 399.
The birth stories of Matthew and Luke, writes Bo Reicke, "do not indicate any complicated mythology but just contain artless reports on the experiences of a man and woman graced by God." The events narrated in their sequence in these two infancy gospels are essentially the same. Matthew has consistently described the experience of Joseph (Mt 1-2), whereas Luke has suggested recollections of Mary (Lk 1) and directly emphasized this in two cases (2:19, 51) (p. 72).

εὐαγγέλιον) must be preached to all nations" (Mk 13:10). The gospel may therefore be characterized as a reality in which we must believe and to which we must be utterly committed: "Repent and believe in the gospel (πιστεύετε ἐν τῷ εὐαγγελίῳ)" (Mk 1:15). This goes beyond believing that something exists, that something is true, to include forming a relationship with the one we believe in. Jesus and the gospel are one and the same, "for whoever would save his life will lose it; and whoever loses his life for my sake and the gospel's (τοῦ εὐαγγελίου) will save it" (Mk 8:35). The complete commitment to Jesus and the detachment from everything else is equated with the gospel (Mk 10:29). Where Jesus is, there also is the gospel. When Jesus reveals his power to teach and heal, he reveals the gospel as well.

Εὐαγγέλιον in Matthew is the good news of the Kingdom of God (Mt 4:23; 9:35; 24:14; 26:13). Matthew emphasizes Jesus' role as the teacher of the gospel of the Kingdom. Luke, on the other hand, emphasizes the act of bringing and proclaiming the good news. Despite such differences in emphasis, all three Synoptics proclaim a Messiah in whose life, death and resurrection the Kingdom of God is manifested. While the term "gospel" has different connotations in the Synoptics, these are not contradictory but complementary.[4]

Like many other key words in the New Testament, the εὐαγγέλιον was not a completely new Christian creation. It had already been used centuries before in Homer's Odyssey to indicate a "reward given to a herald of good news" (14; 152, 166).[5] More significantly for the New Testament, εὐαγγέλιον was used to announce the birthday of the Roman emperor. An inscription in Priene, Asia Minor, from around 9 B.C. states: "And the birthday of the God [Augustus, the *divi filius*] was for the world the tidings of joy (εὐάγγελ) due to him."[6]

Therefore Paul and Mark used an already extant term, giving it a new content and a new context. The question of their motive for using

---

4 In Mark, Jesus proclaims the coming of the Kingdom and thereby becomes the object of the gospel. In Matthew "Jesus is the communicator of the gospel," and in Luke the "act of preaching" is emphasized (see Raymond F. Collins, "Gospel," *Encyclopedia of Religion* [New York: Macmillan, 1987], v. 6, p. 81).

5 J. A. Fitzmyer, "Gospel," p. 349.

6 For this inscription and other details see Wilhelm Schneemelcher, "Gospel," in Hennecke and Schneemelcher, eds., *New Testament Apocrypha*, trans. R. M. Wilson (London: Lutterworth Press, 1963-65), v. I, pp. 71-75; J. Fitzmyer, p. 350.

εὐαγγέλιον as they did remains: did it come from Greek literature, from the Roman imperial cult, or from the Old Testament? New Testament commentators generally recognize the Old Testament as the background for this usage. The Hebrew noun *besora* ("good news or tidings announced by a herald") meant in the pre-exilic period a "victory proclamation" (2 Sam 18:19-22), but took on a more religious connotation in the post-exilic period, particularly in the writings of the so-called "second Isaiah." One Isaianic text in particular relates closely to the use of εὐαγγέλιον in the New Testament: "How beautiful upon the mountains are the feet of him who brings good tidings (*bissar*), who publishes peace, who brings good tidings of good, who publishes salvation, who says to Zion, 'Your God reigns'" (Is 52:7). Bissar in this verse is translated in the Greek Old Testament, the Septuagint, with εὐαγγελίζεσθαι (to announce good news or good tidings). In a religious sense, this is much closer to the usage of Paul and the evangelists than that of Greek classical literature or of the Roman world of the time. Paul quoted this verse in Romans when referring to the preaching of the gospel: "And how can men preach unless they are sent? As it is written, 'How beautiful are the feet of those who preach good news'" (Rom 10:15). This use of Isaiah 52:7 by Paul proves "that his notion of εὐαγγέλιον is heavily dependent on the Old Testament idea of God's herald and his message."[7] Mark presented Jesus and his ministry as the fulfillments of God's promises and of the people's hope, and employed the term "gospel" to announce this theme.

The non-Christian term thus became distinctly Christian and was embodied in a unique literary genre. In time, this genre also was designated by the word εὐαγγέλιον. This usage does not occur in the New Testament, nor does it occur in the plural in first-century documents. The writings of the second-century Christian apologist Justin Martyr contain the first use of the term in the plural (*First Apology*, 66-67). The word "gospels" has been applied ever since to the four written accounts of the words and works of Christ.

---

7 J. A. Fitzmyer, p. 350.
   In Second Isaiah LXX uses εὐαγγελίζειν also in 40:9, 60;6, 61:1. The messenger announces that the time of salvation is at hand, YHWH will reign as king, and a new age is about to come (R. F. Collins, p. 80). For the Old Testament background of Mark's usage of the term "gospel" see E. Hoskyns and F. N. Davey, *The Riddle of the New Testament* (London: Faber & Faber, 1952), pp. 74ff.

The written gospels were composed as a response to the needs of the Church. The message of salvation, εὐαγγέλιον, was at first proclaimed orally. But soon it became necessary for the Christian movement to preach the gospel both orally and in writing. Church growth demanded written records for missionary work, for instruction of new believers and for worship. Thus the gospels were written for a diverse audience, for both Jewish and Gentile Christians who lived in different areas of the Roman world.

III

Jesus left no written record, but he entrusted his message to those whom he called and appointed (or "made," ἐποίησεν, Mk 3:14) his disciples. The word "disciple" (μαθητής) appears only in the gospels and in Acts. Paul never used it in his letters. A disciple is one who follows, who is attached to and dependent upon the person from whom he received the call. In the New Testament, "the technical word 'follow' is never used of 'following' anyone but Jesus, e.g. the disciples themselves do not have followers or disciples."[8] Nor did Paul have "followers" in the sense in which Jesus had them. Jesus constantly called disciples to him, not to imitate him but to commit themselves to him and to obey him. To be a disciple of Jesus was to know him, to believe in him. "The sheep follow him, for they know his voice," and he knows them: "My sheep hear my voice, and I know them, and they follow me (ἀκολουθοῦσίν μοι)" (Jn 10:4, 27). To follow Jesus was to follow him wherever he went (Mt 8:19), to take up his cross and to share in his glory. He who did not do so was "not worthy of me" (Mt 10:38). After Christ's resurrection, discipleship received a new dimension and a new expression of "being in Christ," and the circle of Christ's disciples was enlarged (see Acts 6:1; 9:18-19).

To follow is to listen. This is made clear by the constant recurrence of the verb "listen" in the present imperative in the Synoptic Gospels, demanding "continuous attention and obedience" and that the hearer "listen to me always."[9] To listen to Christ was to bind oneself to him.

8   J. Massyngberde Ford, *Bonded with the Immortal, A Pastoral Introduction to the New Testament* (Wilmington, DE: Michael Glazier, 1987), p. 189.
9   Ceslaus Spicq, *Agape in the New Testament* (St. Louis: B. Herder Book Co., 1963), v. 1, p. 44.

The twelve were the disciples of Jesus in this sense of "listening," and to them the message of salvation was entrusted. During his public ministry, Jesus sent them to preach the gospel and manifest its power to the people. After his death and resurrection, the twelve proclaimed Jesus as Christ, Lord and Savior. They were, therefore, the link between Christ and succeeding generations, the guarantee of the authenticity of Christ's words and works for all future followers and disciples of Christ. The evangelists depended upon the witness of the disciples. What Jesus taught and accomplished we know from those who were closest to him, those who after his death and resurrection, endured trials and suffering for following—for still listening—to him.

The written gospels, while they reflect the gospel and the response of the disciples to it, did not suddenly drop from the sky. There was definite development of the written gospel tradition. Luke's preface to his gospel (1:1-4) strongly suggests three stages in this development. First came the events of Christ's life, "the things which have been accomplished among us." The second stage was the transmission of these happenings by "eyewitnesses and ministers of the word," the followers of Jesus. Finally, the third stage was the composition of the gospels by the evangelists.

Christ was central to all three stages of the development of the gospel tradition. He was its beginning, its origin. He was the one who is proclaimed and preached after his resurrection. Finally, the gospels bear his imprint, his portrait. Consideration of the period of Jesus' public ministry, of the apostolic *kerygma* and the mission of the first Christian community, and of the period of the writing of the gospels all lead to an encounter with the same Jesus of Nazareth. These three stages of the gospel tradition were linked into one organic whole, not only by the memory of past events, but also by the living presence of Christ himself. For those who were with him, those who preached him, and those who wove his image in human words, Christ was more than the founder of a new movement. They experienced his promise, "I am with you always" (Mt 28:20), as a new reality. According to C. F. D. Moule, the expression "through Jesus Christ" in the New Testament alludes to the importance and influence, not of "a founding-figure of the past" for which the expression "because of whom" would have been adequate, but of Christ as a "formula of mediation through a contemporary presence." The expression "through whom" expresses the disciples' experience of Christ's living presence. Christ is the full revelation of God, and the New Testament books reflect his presence in the life of individuals and of Christian communities in a variety of ways. "It is not only through Jesus Christ, but in him that Paul finds access to God."[10]

While the gospels contain biographical elements, they are not and could not have been biographies of Jesus. They portray one who belonged to the past, belongs to the present, and will come in the future "to save those who are eagerly waiting for him" (Heb 9:28). The Church never tried to produce a biography of Jesus. Any such attempt would be doomed to failure. This is due to the very nature of the person of Jesus. To write a biography of Jesus would imply that whoever undertook the task would be obliged to divide the human from the divine presence of Jesus. This would be impossible and self-defeating, since in him the human and the divine are inseparable.[11] To presuppose a separation or division between the human and the divine in Jesus leads to both theological and biographical distortions. In theology it has produced Nestorianism, the separation of the human nature of Jesus from his divine nature; in gospel research, it has produced the so-called "lives" of Jesus which appeared in the nineteenth and twentieth centuries. For the Church, both Nestorianism and the lives of Jesus are alien to the image of Jesus in the gospels.

Jesus never asked his disciples to write a biography of him. He gave them power to cast out demons (Mk 3:14-15), to heal the sick (6:12-13), to preach the Kingdom of God (Mt 10:7, Lk 9:1-2), and (after the resurrection) to "make disciples of all nations, baptizing them in the name of the Father and of the Son and of the Holy Spirit, teaching them to observe all that I have commanded you" (Mt 28:19-20). When John the Baptist's disciples asked Jesus, "Are you he who is to come, or shall we look for another?" (Mt 11:3), he did not give them autobiographical data, but turned their attention to his works: "Go and tell John what you hear and see: the blind receive their sight and the lame walk, lepers cleansed and the deaf hear, and the dead are raised up, and the poor have

10 See Moule's article, "The Christ of Experience and Christ of History," *Theology*, v. 81 (May 1978), p. 166.
11 Bishop Kassian, *Christ and the First Christian Generation* (in Russian) (Paris: YMCA Press, 1950), p. 3.

good news preached to them" (Mt 11:4-5). In the same way, the gospels turn our attention from biographical curiosity to Jesus' works and to his message.

It has been argued that the New Testament is not biographical, because biography was not a form of writing cultivated by the Jews. All the disciples of Jesus were Jews and all the evangelists, except St Luke, were of Jewish origin. "Neither prophet nor wise man, scribe nor later rabbi was the subject of an extended continuous biographical account."[12] The gospels are not meant to provide a literal description but an image of Jesus; not a photograph, but a portrait. They offer little personal description. By contrast, "literal portraiture" appears in the apocryphal books of the New Testament.[13] Since a photograph portrays one person at one point in time and space, its representational value is limited to one particular instance. A photograph "can be used to confirm or contradict, but not to replace the stories told by human witnesses."[14] The gospels have been called the verbal icon of Christ, an image produced not by the extraordinary creative talents of the evangelists, but by the tradition with which they were acquainted, within which they experienced the living presence of Christ, and from which they drew their material.

No biography of Christ could adequately convey his living presence. A new literary form was needed. In the gospels, historical facts are understood, lived and interpreted. A "tape-recording" of Jesus' sayings, and a "cinematographic production of his deeds" would not instill a better or more "accurate" understanding of Christ than that presented by the evangelists. In the gospels this understanding is augmented by its incorporation of four different points of view. From these we learn how Jesus was perceived in his own time, how his words and works were understood and applied in the life of the first Christian communities. Of the evangelists, two, according to early tradition, belonged to the Twelve, and two others to Jesus' post-resurrection following. The gospel image of Christ, therefore, was conveyed by four distinctly different persons,

12 Frederick C. Grant, *The Gospels: Their Origin and Their Growth* (New York: Harper & Brothers, 1957) p. 27.
13 In the apocryphal Acts of Paul, for instance, there is this description of Paul: "A man little of stature, with bald head and bent legs, strong...full of charm, sometimes he appeared like a man, and at others he had the face of an angel."
14 H. Palmer, *The Logic of Gospel Criticism* (New York: St Martin's Press, 1968), p. 38.

united in their commitment to him and moved by the same Spirit in their writings.

IV

The Holy Spirit acted in all three stages of the gospel's growth: in the life of Jesus, in the development and transmission of the apostolic preaching, and in the work of the evangelists. Before the newly-wedded Mary and Joseph came together, Mary "was found to be with child through the Holy Spirit" (ἐκ πνεύματος ἀγίου, Mt 1:18). Luke uses the verb "overshadow" (ἐπισκιάσει) to describe the Holy Spirit's presence to Mary in the infancy narrative (Lk 1:35); the same word is used by all three Synoptic authors to describe the appearance of the cloud, the sign of the divine presence, to the disciples at the Transfiguration. The Spirit descended upon Jesus at the time of his baptism (Mk 1:10 and paral., Jn 1:32-33, Acts 2:33; 10:38) then he led him to the wilderness to be tempted (Mk 1:14 and paral.). In the synagogue in Nazareth, Jesus began his reading from the prophet Isaiah with: "The Spirit of the Lord is upon me, because he has anointed me to preach good news to the poor" (Lk 4:16ff). He performed exorcisms by the Spirit: "If it is by the Spirit of God that I cast out demons, then the Kingdom of God has come upon you" (Mt 12:28, Lk 11:20). He possessed the Spirit beyond all measure (Jn 3:34) and promised his disciples that the Holy Spirit, whom the Father would send in his name, would teach them all things and would help them recall all that he, Jesus, had said to them (Jn 14:25-26).

The birth of the Church, like the birth of Jesus, was of the Spirit. The Holy Spirit sanctified the twelve apostles on the day of Resurrection (Jn 20:22) and enabled them to proclaim the gospel. And on the day of Pentecost, the Holy Spirit filled all the brethren, all the Church (Acts 2:4). Mary, the mother of Jesus, and "his brothers," the twelve and other women, a group of persons "in all about a hundred and twenty" (Acts 1:14-15) were all together in one place and "a sound came from heaven like the rush of a mighty wind, and it filled all the house where they were sitting" (Acts 2:2). At that moment, everything was sanctified—the people and the "temple" (τὸν οἶκον)—by the power of the Holy Spirit. After the birth of the Church, "the Spirit drove the apostles into the activities of preaching and teaching. Miracles were performed "in the name of Jesus Christ of Nazareth" Acts 3:6). Neither Peter nor Paul could resist the Spirit (Acts 10:46; 11:17; 16:6). The Church, filled with and led by the Spirit, said and did what Jesus said and did. Thus the second stage in the gospel's formation was brought about by the power and activity of the Spirit.

During the third stage, all the gifts of the Spirit (χαρίσματα) were given to the Christian community (1 Cor 1:7). No one could confess that "Jesus is Lord" except by being inspired by the Holy Spirit (1 Cor 12:3). Each person "in Christ," each member of the Body of Christ, was

> given the manifestation of the Spirit for the common good. To one is given through the Spirit the utterance of wisdom, and to another the utterance of knowledge according to the same Spirit, to another faith by the same Spirit, to another gifts of healing by the one Spirit, to another the working of miracles, to another prophecy... (1 Cor 12:7ff).

The Spirit recalled the words of Jesus, and men moved by the Holy Spirit spoke and wrote accordingly. The New Testament books and their authors were both inspired by the Spirit.

The gospels are not chronicles or archival documents, but inspired theological-historical writings. They are revelatory documents, to be read, preached and interpreted. They challenged and invited the Church and its members throughout the centuries "to continue in [Jesus'] word," to know the truth, for "the truth will make [them] free" (Jn 8:32). To the evangelist John, Christ was the incarnate truth (Jn 1:9, 14; 14:6). He who is Truth spoke truth and testified to truth (Jn 8:40, 45f; 16:7; 18:37). By whatever he said or did, he manifested God (Jn 5:19ff; 12:50). In the gospels we have the words and deeds of Christ vivified by the Spirit. Due to their inspiration and that of their authors, their power never diminishes.

V

Inspiration is always concrete. The same Spirit moves human beings to faithful accounts of the events of the life and ministry of Jesus. According to Origen, one of the greatest biblical scholars in the early Church, the evangelists wrote according to inspiration, yet at the same time they were able to express their own point of view (*epinoia*, which may be translated as "intention"). This insight into the nature of inspiration helped Origen in his attempt to explain the differences that exist between the Synoptics and the fourth gospel. In his commentary on the Gospel of John, Origen stressed the human aspect of the text, which is incompatible with the definition of inspiration as a mechanical dictation. The very attribution of the gospels to four specific human beings implies that the evangelists played an active role in their composition. To speak about the inspiration of the Holy Spirit means to recognize its "incarnate character." "Divine" and "human" are fully united, in inspiration no less than in the Incarnation.

Those who wrote the gospels were faithful participants in the life of the Church to which all spiritual gifts are given. Each member of the Church, as we have already seen, receives a particular gift of the Spirit. That received by the evangelists was the *charisma* of inspiration. It is true that we do not find the *charisma* of inspiration mentioned in Paul's letters, but it is also true that he never claims that his lists are complete. We must conclude, on the basis of what we understand from his discussions of spiritual gifts and their place in the Church, that if he had had to respond to a dispute regarding the inspiration of a biblical book, he would have included the charisma of inspiration. We may assume that the gift of inspiration was included among the gifts for the "common good," for the building up of the Church. The gift of inspiration was given to some members of the Body of Christ to provide the community with written gospels, which would bear permanent witness to the living Christ during the historical development of Christianity. Karl Rahner has argued that this *charisma* of inspiration was first of all a gift possessed by the Church and therefore should not be ascribed only to those who wrote the biblical books, but also to those who helped produce the "sources" which were incorporated in the inspired works.[15]

There are varieties of manifestations of the *charisma* of inspiration. No evangelist was more inspired than another, but each manifested differently the gift that was freely given to him. Mark's gift of inspiration did not change him into somebody else, but allowed him to make full use of it according to his personality. According to Vawter, "We should think of inspiration always as a positive divine and human interaction in

15 For K. Rahner's view on inspiration, see Bruce Vawter, *Biblical Inspiration* (Philadelphia: Westminster Press, 1972), pp. 110ff.

which the principle of condescension has been taken at face value. To conceive of an absolute inerrancy was not really to believe that God had condescended to the human sphere but rather that he had transformed it into something else."[16] The Bible as a whole testifies that the Word of God is mediated through the genuine human condition, including human limitations. Inspiration did not miraculously change the world view of the biblical authors into one acceptable to a modern scientific outlook. Their world view, like ours, was not absolute but relative; their language, like ours, was culturally conditioned. But the message and the reality that they conveyed through human language are not relative.

To make literal inerrancy a necessary component of the gift of inspiration is, after all, foreign to the New Testament message itself. The gospels bear witness to the Truth and to the power of God, not to their own freedom from error. They are free from falsehood or deception, but not from natural human errors. The evangelist Mark, for example, maintains that Abiathar was high priest during the reign of David (Mk 2:23-28), but according to I Sam 21:1-6, Ahimelech, not Abiathar, was high priest. This "error" had no effect on the meaning of the passage. The concept of inerrancy conflicts with the incarnational approach to the Bible, and with the New Testament concept of the synergetic activity of the Holy Spirit. The *charisma* of inspiration does not imply a new revelation which transports its recipient into a sphere entirely different from his own. The concept of inerrancy reveals more about our desire for absolute certainty than it does about the inspiration of a biblical book. God committed his message to human beings with human limitations. To cling to inerrancy, then, is to reject the reality of Christ's humiliation or *kenosis*.[17] The gospels are not "dictations from heaven," but records of the revelation of Christ, the Incarnate Word of God, written by his inspired disciples. Their human element is proved by the fact that it is the disciples themselves, and the Churches for which they wrote, who guarantee the truthfulness of their books.

16 B. Vawter, pp. 194f. The Bible records the mistakes of its authors, just as it does their inspired truths. "This is the higher inerrancy: the Bible testifies truthfully to the genuine human condition of the individual authors and the people through whom the word of God has been mediated." The concept of inerrancy demands "a notion of biblical truth fixed once for all in a single point of time, and, therefore, a notion of the word that is essentially lifeless." In the Bible the "word" has life of its own within the community to which it comes.

17 "There is a *kenosis* involved in God's committing His message to human words," writes R. Brown (*The Critical Meaning of the Bible* [New York: Paulist Press, 1981], p. 17).

6

Four Perspectives, One Image

Second-century tradition ascribed the first and fourth canonical gospels to two original disciples of Christ—Matthew and John respectively. It identified the author of the second canonical gospel as Mark and that of the third as Luke. Neither Mark nor Luke belonged to the group of the Twelve, but both were known to the churches of the first century and particularly to the three leaders of the Christian movement—Peter, Paul and James.

I

The Gospel of Mark is generally considered by modern scholars to be the oldest written gospel. Mark wrote his account of the life and teaching of Christ for a mixed community of Gentile and Jewish Christians. On the basis of Mark's explanation of Jewish practices (7:3f) and his translation of Aramaic expressions (3:17; 5:41; 7:34; 14:36; 15:34) for the benefit of his Gentile readers, some claim that his gospel was written primarily with Gentile Christians in mind.

According to early Church tradition, John Mark (Acts 12:12, 25; 13:5), a cousin of the apostle Barnabas (Col 4:10), accompanied Paul during his first missionary journey but later parted company with him (Acts 15:37). He was associated with the apostle Peter (1 Pet 5:13) and acted as his "interpreter." Mark produced this earliest gospel in Rome. Whether he wrote it before or after Peter's martyrdom (c. 64) cannot be ascertained, but it seems certain that it was written before the destruction of the Temple in Jerusalem in 70. The gospel fits in well with the situation of Christian persecution in Rome around this time.

The evangelist opens his narrative with the appearance of John the Baptist and the account of Jesus' baptism. After the descent of the Holy Spirit upon Jesus and his proclamation as the Son of God by a heavenly voice, the Spirit drives him out into the wilderness to be tempted by

Satan. Jesus' ensuing victory over Satan prepares the way for Jesus' later conquests over demonic powers, as 3:27 makes clear: "But no one can enter a strong man's house and plunder his goods, unless he first binds the strong man; then indeed he may plunder his house." After his victory in the wilderness and the arrest of John the Baptist, Jesus begins to proclaim that: "the time is fulfilled and the Kingdom of God is at hand; repent, and believe in the gospel" (Mk 1:15). Mark ends his introduction with this summary of Jesus' preaching.

The next section deals with the ministry of Jesus in Galilee, stressing conflicts with his opponents (1:16-8:21). We are told about both his exorcisms of unclean powers and about the opposition of the Pharisees in these chapters. While the demons recognize who Jesus is, the Pharisees do not. His debates with the Pharisees demonstrate a new attitude toward the law and community, which proved unacceptable to this religious group.

The chapters that follow (8:22-15:47) concentrate upon Jesus' disciples, who did not understand the meaning of his messiahship and his suffering. This part of the gospel includes an account of Christ's ministry in Judea (10-13). The resurrection account concludes the gospel.

Despite its simple structure, Mark's gospel is a complex piece of writing. While it provides historical and geographical data, its main purpose, to explain the significance of Jesus and his ministry, is Christological. To accomplish this task, Mark's tools included a new arrangement of the traditions about Jesus. An example of his technique is the literary device of interruption or intercalation, which is probably the most obvious characteristic of his presentation. Intercalation relates two stories in such a manner that one comments on the other (Mk 3:20-35; 5:21-43; 11:12-25). We may take as an example the interweaving of the stories of the fig tree and the cleansing of the Temple (11:12-25). After the evangelist narrates the cursing of the fig tree (11:12-14), he introduces the cleansing of the Temple (11:15-19), then returns again to the tree, which has withered (11:20-25). The first story helps us to see the significance of the second account, that is, Jesus' attitude to the Temple. Jesus curses the fig tree because it has borne no fruit. This points to the "withering" (destruction) of the Temple, which in God's eyes has borne no fruit either. Mark thus inserted the cleansing of the Temple in the midst of the story of the fig tree to reveal Jesus' real intention for entering the Temple—to drive out the merchants and to upset the tables of the money-changers. These actions are also symbolic; the cleansing of the Temple points to its destruction. If Christ had wanted only to convey the idea of the need for purification of the Temple, he could have symbolized it by pouring out water. Since he wanted to go further and to symbolize the destruction of the Temple, he upset the tables.[1] The story of the fig tree drives home the meaning of his actions. It was not the time for figs (11:13), and on this tree it would never be time. So it was with the Temple. The Temple had not become the house of prayer for all nations (Jer 7:11), and it would not be in the future. What is more, with the arrival of the Messiah and the reign of God, there is no need for the Temple, for Christ is now the source of God's salvation, the new Temple of God. The religious authorities in Jerusalem, who understood the meaning of Jesus' actions in the Temple, were ready to punish him, according to the Synoptic Gospels. By intercalating the two stories, Mark leads his readers to a better understanding of Jesus' attitude toward the Temple.[2]

Each of the gospels was written to serve a particular purpose, and each stresses its own theme. Mark's gospel emphasizes the necessity and the mystery of the cross of Christ. Those who desire to follow him must come to terms with the meaning of the cross and must be ready to share his destiny, to experience themselves the rejection and suffering he underwent. The cross of suffering will be transformed into the resurrecting cross, but there is no resurrection without the cross.

II

The Gospel of Matthew originated in Syria, probably in the city of Antioch, since its internal evidence suggests an area outside Judea and Galilee (10:18). The prevalent opinion is that it was written in the 80's or 90's of the first century. The author was familiar with Jewish Christianity and wrote for Christian Jews in the Hellenistic world outside

1 See E. P. Sanders, *Jesus and Judaism* (Philadelphia: Fortress Press, 1985), pp. 70f., 89f.
2 We probably should understand the cursing of the fig tree not as a punitive miracle but as a "parable in action," in which the actions of real life take on the meaning of a parable. The overturning of the tables should also be perceived as a parable in action, for it symbolizes the end of the Temple.

Palestine. Second-century tradition identified him as Matthew, a former collector of taxes and duties, and one of the Twelve. Modern critical scholarship rejects this, but it does support the idea that the gospel was written by a Jewish Christian. Certain scholars argue that the gospel, as it is known to us, could not have been written by the apostle Matthew, for it draws on the Gospel of Mark as its main source. If Matthew depended on sources available in Greek, then, according to this hypothesis, the author could not have been a disciple of Jesus. A modification of this theory suggests that Matthew, one of the Twelve, was associated with the Church which approved this gospel, and that he influenced it without having actually written it.

The structure of Matthew is more complex than that of Mark. While the gospel is Jewish in origin, its outlook is universal. We see this in the infancy narrative at the end (2:1ff) and in the command of the Risen Christ to the disciples at the end to go to all nations (28:16ff). The infancy gospel, the birth of the Messiah, is followed by the baptism and the temptations of the Son of God. The main structural characteristic of Matthew is its five clearly distinguished discourses. The first contains the Sermon on the Mount (5-7), presented in a fairly organized form. The Sermon on the Mount is followed by the collection of miracle stories (8-9) which were probably intended to show that Jesus is not only the Teacher of Israel but also the Messiah who performs the mighty works of God. This is followed by the second discourse: instructions for the mission of the Twelve (10). The third discourse consists of the parables of the Kingdom (13). The fourth is devoted to the author's community (18). This chapter is addressed to the disciples of Jesus. And the fifth is assigned to the end of the age and to the judgment (24-25). Each of these five discourses ends with the words: "And when Jesus had finished these sayings" (7:28, 11:1; 13:53; 19:1; 26:1).

Some scholars attempt to explain and illumine these five discourses with the help of the Pentateuch theory, that is, that Matthew gathered Jesus' teachings into five books according to the pattern of the Mosaic Pentateuch, the first five books of the Old Testament. This hypothesis is far from acceptance by many modern scholars, for Matthew contains seven books or sections, not five. The first book is the infancy narrative (1-2), as we have mentioned, and the account of the Passion and the

Resurrection of Christ (26-28) should surely be regarded as a seventh book. The beginning and the end of Matthew's gospel are not outside his main structure but are essential to a correct understanding of all the other parts. The very first word of the gospel, the beginning of the infancy account, is *biblos*, book.

It is more difficult to discern a single idea or theme conveyed by the structure of Matthew than it is in Mark. Some see the most distinctive theme of this gospel to be the concentration of the evangelist on Jesus as the promised Messiah. Others detect Matthew's emphasis upon Jesus, the Teacher of Israel, or upon Jesus the Son of God, and still others describe his "central truth" in terms of "the presence of Jesus," or that which in their reading of the gospel determines "Matthew's portrait of Jesus."[3]

It has been remarked that interpreters sometimes try to impose upon the gospel upon their perception of what would be the evangelist's "single idea." But it is important to realize that by preferring one of these themes as the unifying factor around which the gospel is structured, a scholar does not necessarily neglect the importance of other themes. In addition, we must be constantly aware that the evangelists were not preoccupied with one idea. Usually they employed many, since they found many in their sources and in the tradition of the Church. The structures of their gospels appeared in the process of telling the story of Jesus in their own way.[4] Matthew's gospel, like all the gospels, is kerygmatic in structure, concerned above all with presenting a portrait of Jesus the Messiah, the Son of Man and the Son of God, who is always present among us.

III

Luke, the author of the third canonical gospel, was the only Gentile by birth among the New Testament writers. He was Paul's travelling companion (Acts 16:10-17; 20:5-15; 21:1-18; 27-28; Col 4:14; Philem 24). Presumably he wrote his gospel and the Acts of the Apostles after the destruction of the Temple (70) and before 90. Both Luke and Acts are addressed to the "most excellent Theophilus" (Lk 1:3f, Acts 1:1), who may have been a potential or recent convert to Christianity. By exten-

3 Jack Dean Kingsbury, "The Gospel in Four Editions," *Interpretation*, 33:4, pp. 367ff.
4 Donald Senior, *What are They Saying About Matthew?* (New York: Paulist Press, 1983), p. 15.

sion, the gospel was written for Christians of Jewish and Gentile origin in the Hellenistic world, and it possibly originated in southern Greece or in the place of Paul's imprisonment.

The structure of Luke's gospel is simpler than that of Matthew's. In the preface, the evangelist recognizes his indebtedness to eyewitnesses of Jesus. He acknowledges the contribution of those who worked and (possibly) wrote before him and promises to write "an orderly account" (1:4). The preface is followed by the events that led to the birth of Jesus. Jesus' baptism, his genealogy, and the temptations (3:1-4:13) precede the account of his ministry in Galilee (4:14-9:50). The next section, the final journey to Jerusalem, which occupies about ten chapters (9:51-19:27), is the most distinctive feature of the gospel and constitutes Luke's contribution to our understanding of Jesus' teaching. Some of the best known parables of Christ are known only from this section. An account of Jesus' ministry in Jerusalem follows(19:28-21:38). As the others, this gospel ends with the account of Jesus' death and resurrection (22-24).

Luke's gospel concentrates on the universality of Jesus' message. Matthew's narrative also displays the universal character of the new message, but there is a difference between the two. Whereas Matthew reflects a Jewish Christianity which was enlarging its vision and becoming open to Gentiles, Luke gives us a vision of salvation which includes Gentiles, social outcasts, publicans, Samaritans, and women—an outlook in which all exclusionist tendencies disappear. Luke recounts how women followed Jesus (8:2-3) and how Anna was among the first to preach about Jesus "to all who were looking for the redemption of Jerusalem" (2:38). Jesus is proclaimed as the light to the Gentiles (2:32). Luke relates the events of Jesus' life to the universal empire, the Graeco-Roman world (3:38). Whereas Matthew linked Jesus to Abraham, the father of the Jewish nation, Luke links him to Adam, the father of the human race (3:23-38). The third evangelist, himself of Gentile origin and writing for Gentile-Christian churches, displays a deep love for the Old Testament and persistently reminds Gentile Christians of their historical origin in Jewish scripture. The Temple, of which he had been well informed, appears at the beginning and at the end of his gospel: Zechariah, the father of John the Baptist, is a priest in the Temple, and the gospel concludes with the return of the disciples to Jerusalem following the ascent of Jesus, after which they "were continually in the Temple blessing God" (24:53).

IV

Tradition identifies the evangelist John as the son of Zebedee, the brother of James, a member of the Twelve, and the disciple whom Jesus loved. It further locates the source of the fourth gospel in Ephesus. Both of these traditions have been questioned in contemporary New Testament scholarship.

The problem of the authorship of the fourth gospel proves to be even more difficult to solve than that of the Synoptics. Many Catholic and Protestant interpreters regard the Gospel of John as the work of several contributors. Rudolf Schnackenburg's monumental commentary on the gospel takes full account of the second-century Christian tradition about the author of the gospel and includes a detailed analysis of modern scholarship, and comes to the following solution: the gospel incorporated the Palestinian tradition which originated in apostolic times. This includes the eyewitness of John, who handed on the history of Jesus to his followers. Later, this received tradition was edited by an elder of the community who had access to other sources, including liturgical and kerygmatic material (6:31-58). In the last stage of authorship, the gospel received the support of an important church, presumably the church in Ephesus, as noted by ancient tradition. This church authenticated the final version of the gospel.

Jn 21:24, which reads "This is the disciple who is bearing witness to these things, and who has written these things; and we know that his testimony is true," may be paraphrased: "the beloved disciple is the witness to the basic tradition preserved here." John is the authority behind the gospel, but he is not the one who wrote it. He is the "author," not the "writer," of the gospel.[5]

5 *The Gospel According to St John* (New York: Herder and Herder, 1968), I, pp. 72 and 102f. The gospel is "essentially the work of the evangelist, who relied, however, on diverse traditions, and allowed his gospel to grow and mature slowly, but did not finish it completely" (p. 72). The theological emphases suggest a work of interpretation by the apostle and of theological shaping by the evangelist (p. 103). The designation of "the disciple whom Jesus loved," the Beloved Disciple, "would rather be due to his [John's] disciples, including the evangelist, who were accustomed to speak in this way of their master, John... Where the narrative goes back to

If this view on the growth of the Gospel of John is correct, the claim of the early Church is not dismissed but built upon. A similar interpretation may be drawn from the icon of the evangelist John in the Orthodox Church, which shows a Christian "scribe" at the feet of the apostle, recording his words. It implies that John is the source, but that the one at his feet is the "writer" of the gospel.

Modern scholars confess that we do not know with any certainty the historical circumstances under which the gospel was written. Since the discovery of the Dead Sea Scrolls, few have questioned the Palestinian origin of the tradition incorporated in the fourth gospel. Most scholars, at least at present, consider it to have been written before the end of the first century, after the destruction of the Temple. A few are even of the opinion that all four gospels were written before the fall of Jerusalem. We shall present the arguments concerning the dating of the gospels in the following chapter.

The structure of this last portrait of Christ differs from that in any of the Synoptics. It starts with a prologue that has no parallel in the first three narratives. The prologue is followed by the "Book of Signs," or miracle accounts (2:1-12:50). It is notable that the Gospel of John does not contain a single exorcism. In the fourth gospel the evangelist apparently concentrates on Satan himself and not on his army, on the source of the darkness which opposes the light. There are, therefore, no records of demonic possession, only references to possession by Satan himself (6:70). Passages such as 13:30 and 1:5 show the evangelist's preoccupation with the themes of light and darkness and with the conflict between them.

After the "Book of Signs" come the "Farewell Discourse" and the "High Priestly Prayer" (13-17). The passion, resurrection and first post-resurrection appearances of Christ in Jerusalem occupy the next three

the Apostle, he spoke of himself simply in the first person when he had to mention himself. His disciples, who noted his words and [related] his narratives, could no doubt have inserted his name; but it is also understandable that they did not use his name among themselves or that they chose respectfully to use a periphrasis" (pp. 103f).

In this gospel, John, the son of Zebedee, appears only in 21:2 and even here the name of John is omitted: Jesus appeared to "Simon Peter, Thomas called the Twin, Nathanael of Cana in Galilee, the sons of Zebedee, and two others of his disciples." We must reject the theory that the apostle John did not mention his name out of modesty, since his self-designation as the "Beloved Disciple" can hardly be called "modest."

For a summary of various views on the authorship of the fourth gospel, see Stephen Smalley, *John—Evangelist and Interpreter* (Exeter: Paternoster Press, 1978), pp. 66f.

chapters (18-20). In the last chapter we have a narrative of Christ's appearance in Galilee (21).

John emphasizes the Judean ministry of Jesus, whereas the events in the Synoptics take place mostly in Galilee. Jesus' ministry also spans a longer period of time in John than in the other gospels. Jesus visits Jerusalem more often than in the Synoptics: three feasts of Passover are mentioned (2:13; 6:4; 11:55). On the whole, the author appears to be more interested in other Jewish feasts than are the other evangelists. One feast, which may be the Jewish Pentecost, is unnamed (5:1). The Feasts of Tabernacles and Dedication, on the other hand, are explicitly mentioned (7:2; 10:22).

John's perspective, on the whole, is different from that of the Synoptics. It is founded on the premise that the Counselor (παράκλητος), the Holy Spirit, will remind the disciples of all that Jesus said to them (14:26). As the Holy Spirit is the "interpreter" of Jesus' history, so Jesus himself is the "interpreter" of God. "No one has ever seen God; the only Son [God], who is in the bosom of the Father, he has made him known" (ἐξηγήσατο, 1:18). This verb (ἐξηγέομαι) may be translated as "explain," "interpret" or "declare." The noun "exegesis" comes from it.

The most striking feature of John's gospel is Jesus' long discourses. The evangelist was undoubtedly a creative interpreter of the words and acts of Jesus in the light of his death and resurrection. Yet the actual words, parables and acts of Jesus are always what control this interpretation.

V

The difference between the portrait of Christ in the fourth gospel and those in the Synoptics probably derives from the author's use of independent gospel tradition. In the view of some interpreters, this provides readers with the key to a better understanding of the first three canonical gospels, for the evangelist interpreted gospel history at a higher level than did any of his predecessors. This interpreted history affirms the history of Jesus. It does not cover Christ with its layers of interpretation but allows him to shine through and above them.

Starting with the "beginning," with "the Word," who is not within history but is "with God" (1:1), John approached history from a vertical dimension, from the perspective of eternity. On the other hand, the other three evangelists approached history horizontally, from the perspective of unfolding time. Of course, neither approach excludes the others, but we can discern in John a preference for the vertical. John "takes the long line of history and bends it into a curve around his vertically understood Jesus," according to John Drury.[6] Jesus is thus the center of history, and everything else on the horizontal line of historical development is related to this center, to the Word of God that became man (1:14). In John, therefore, the words and deeds of Jesus during the course of his ministry reveal him as the incarnate Son of God.

This perspective is not conceptually alien to the Synoptic perspective. Where John differs from the Synoptic Gospels is in his emphasis and in his approach. John's emphasis on Jesus as the Divine Son is not contradicted by the Synoptics. All of the gospels proclaim a "high Christology." In Matthew's and Luke's accounts of the Annunciation, he whose coming is proclaimed is the Messiah, the incarnate God among men. In Matthew 1:22f we read, "Behold, a virgin shall conceive and bear a son, and his name shall be called Emmanuel (which means God with us)," and in Luke 1:32f: "He will be great, and will be called the son of the Most High, and the Lord God will give to him the throne of his father David, and he will reign over the house of Jacob for ever; and of his kingdom there will be no end." Mark presents the same mystery in his account of Jesus' baptism: "And when he came up out of the water, immediately he saw the heavens opened and the Spirit descending upon him like a dove; and a voice came from heaven, 'Thou art my beloved Son; with thee I am well pleased'" (1:10f). God did not adopt Jesus as his son at the baptism, but proclaimed that he was and always had been his son. Christ's baptism was God's manifestation, the Epiphany. "Mark's Christology is a high Christology, as high as any in the New Testament, not excluding that of John."[7] The Son of God, as Mark understands him, is a being not of this world. His divinity as well as his humanity are real. Each gospel affirms this in its own way.

Some commentators who have noted the distinct characteristics of the four gospels have been carried away into exaggerating them and

6 Alter and Kermode (eds.), *The Literary Guide to the Bible*, p. 422.
7 See Vincent Taylor, *The Gospel According to St Mark* (London: Macmillan, 1966), p. 121.

finding contradictions among them. As we have seen, differences in the gospels did arise from different historical situations in the early communities as well as from different traditions used by the evangelists in composing their books. It is worth emphasizing, however, that all four gospels bear witness to Jesus, that all four offer their readers a verbal portrait of him, and that in all four Jesus is presented as the fulfillment of the Old Testament hope. In this, John is equal to the Synoptics. In all four we perceive the blending of facts and their interpretation into one image. This is brought to perfection in the fourth gospel. All four gospels were inspired by one Spirit, yet each expresses itself in a different idiom. Their unique characteristics underline the intensity of the individual responses of their authors to God's final revelation, as well as the validity of their common inspiration. A great Christian Father of the fourth century, Basil the Great, stated that the Spirit does not deprive anybody of his reasoning power and freedom; only demonic possession does this. The gospels are our accounts of the free primary response of the disciples of Christ to what he was and to what God accomplished in him.

VI

Some object that the accounts of the life of Jesus were biased, and that, for this reason, they are of doubtful historical value. The evangelists did not conceal the fact that their gospels were colored by their experience of the resurrection. Without Christ's resurrection, neither the Church nor the gospels would have existed. The gospels record the facts of the past from the post-resurrection perspective, and for the evangelists there is no other possible perspective. Georges Florovsky has noted that "We can never remember even our own immediate past exactly as we have lived it, because, if we are really remembering and not just dreaming, we do remember the past occurrences in a perspective, against a changed background of our enriched experience."[8] The resurrection not only gave meaning to what preceded it, but it also transformed men and institutions. The cult of the Sabbath was replaced by the celebration on the day of the Lord's resurrection; Sunday and not the Sabbath became "the day which the Lord has made," and the crown of the week. Although they

8 Georges Florovsky, "The Predicament of the Christian Historian," in W. Leibrecht, ed., *Religion and Culture*, p. 150.

had been cowards during Jesus' final ministry in Jerusalem, after the resurrection the disciples become witnesses whom nobody could frighten. The rulers and elders of the people wondered at the boldness of Peter and John (Acts 4:13). Peter courageously proclaimed before the Sanhedrin that the followers of Jesus "must obey God rather than men" (Acts 5:29). This was a different Peter from the one whom Jesus strongly rebuked before the resurrection for being "not on the side of God but of men" (Mk 8:33 and paral.). What Paul wrote about his own life could have been applied to the members of the Twelve as well:

> But whatever gain I had, I counted as loss for the sake of Christ. Indeed I count everything as loss because of the surpassing worth of knowing Christ Jesus my Lord. For his sake I have suffered the loss of all things, and count them as refuse, in order that I may gain Christ and be found in him...that I may know him and the power of his resurrection, and may share his suffering, becoming like him in his death, that if possible I may attain the resurrection from the dead (Phil 3:7-11).

Although they were written in the light of his resurrection, the gospels preserved much that belonged to Jesus' pre-resurrection history. Yet this history was presented not as "pure" historical facts, but as a blend of acts and their interpretation. Only after the resurrection could such interpretation be made.

It is still the task of historical scholarship to find out, as far as possible, the history of Jesus. Scholars are helped in their research by the existence of four accounts of the teachings and works of Jesus, instead of just one. They can analyze and compare evidence from the primary sources and can try to see what derives from before and what from after the resurrection. An example of such a problem in historical research is Peter's confession. It is recorded by all four evangelists (Mt 16:13ff, Mk 8:27ff, Lk 9:18ff, Jn 6:68ff). Matthew, Mark and Luke differ in recording Peter's answer to Jesus' question, "But who do you say that I am?" According to Mark and Luke, Peter answered, "You are Christ" (Mk 8:29), or "The Christ of God" (Lk 9:20); but according to Matthew, Peter answered, "You are the Christ, the Son of the living God" (Mt 16:16). What did Peter actually say? Are we to accept Mark's and Luke's accounts, which are essentially the same, or are we to agree with Matthew, who adds the words, "the Son of the living God"? Mark and Luke indicate that Peter confessed that Jesus was the Messiah, whose coming was promised. In popular Jewish messianic expectation, the Messiah was not described as a divine being. Peter's confession in Matthew implies that at the time of the confession at Caesarea Philippi he and the other disciples had full knowledge of the mystery of Jesus' divine identity. This implication is inconsistent with Peter's refusal to accept the teaching of Jesus about his suffering, and with Jesus' subsequent rebuke of Peter, "Get behind me, Satan! You are a hindrance to me; for you are not on the side of God but of men" (Mt 16:23). Peter's objection to suffering and his rebuff come immediately after his confession. If this is so, then it can only indicate that Peter confessed him as the Christ, the fulfillment of the Old Testament, as Mark and Luke reported.

How then can we explain the words, "the Son of the living God"? The first evangelist who incorporated these words into his gospel did not distort or falsify what happened at Caesarea Philippi. By ascribing these words to Peter, he simply interprets Peter's confession in the light of the resurrection. The one whom Peter confessed as the Messiah was the incarnate Son of God. Peter's confession as recorded in Matthew forcefully brings out that the Jesus of history and the Christ of faith are one and the same. He whom the Church worships is no one else but the Jesus whom Peter confessed as the Messiah. Matthew added the meaning of the event as it evolved fully after the resurrection. He did not separate the history of Jesus from the history of the Lord in the Church. The former is fully understood in the light of the latter. The event was seen and its meaning was revealed only when it was seen from the climactic ending, which was simultaneously a new beginning. This has been called the double task of the evangelists: their simultaneous reporting of "what took place" and their conveyance of its meaning.

7

Closing the Gap

The gospels agree in the essential narrative, despite the differences we have noted. Together with the others, the fourth evangelist recorded the baptism of Jesus (1:32-34), the cleansing of the Temple (2:13-16), the miracle of the multiplication of loaves (6:1-13), walking on water (6:16-21), the anointing at Bethany with the entrance into Jerusalem (12:1-19), Judas' betrayal (13:21-30), the suffering, the crucifixion and resurrection of Christ, and his post-resurrection appearance.[1] Other parallels could be noted, but these are sufficient to make us aware of how much the evangelists had in common. Moreover, when their shared material is closely examined, it becomes apparent that John did not depend upon the Synoptics. It is important to stress that the fourth gospel is an independent source for the life and teachings of Christ.

I

Comparison of the gospel of John with the Synoptics shows that the fourth evangelist omitted many important events in the life of Jesus, which were presented in some detail by Matthew, Mark and Luke. The fourth gospel contains no accounts of the temptations, of the transfiguration of Christ, of the messianic confession of Peter, or of the three predictions of the passion; nor does it contain an account of the institution of the Eucharist or of the agony in the garden. As we have already seen, there are none of the exorcisms which are so frequent in the Synoptics. Closer reading and analysis of the gospel bring to light the real nature of these omissions.

Although John does not explicitly recount the temptations of Christ in the wilderness as Matthew and Luke do, they are indirectly reflected

1 Numerous introductions to the New Testament enumerate what the fourth evangelist has in common with the Synoptics and what he specifically incorporated in his gospel that does not have parallel in the others. This list, for instance, is given by A. Robert and A. Feuillet in their *Introduction to the New Testament* (New York: Desclee, 1965), p. 649.

in his gospel. The first temptation, to turn stones into bread (Mt 4:1ff, Lk 4:1ff), is suggested in the account of Jesus' discourse in the wilderness on the manna and on the true bread from heaven that gives life to the world (Jn 6:31ff). The temptation to display his miraculous powers is seen in the request made to Jesus by his brothers: "Leave here and go to Judea, that your disciples may see the works you are doing" (Jn 7:3ff). The temptation to rule over the kingdoms of the world is expressed concretely in Jesus' rejection of the crowds desiring to make him king after he performed the miracle of the multiplication of the bread. "Perceiving then that they were about to come and take him by force to make him king, Jesus withdrew again to the hills by himself" (Jn 6:15). The temptations of Jesus are therefore taken into consideration; what John omitted were not the temptations themselves, but a coherent narrative linking the three temptations together.

It has been argued that the fourth gospel does not recount the transfiguration and the agony in the garden: two events which are recorded by the Synoptics (Mk 9:2-8; 14:32-42 and paral.). In John, however, the glory of Christ is shown from the very beginning. "We behold his glory" (Jn 1:14). John presented the transfiguration of Christ not as one distinct episode in his life, but as something that could be seen in many events in his life and works, especially in his signs or miracles. Cana in Galilee was the place of his first sign, the first place where he "manifested his glory" (Jn 2:11). The same principle applies to parallels between John and Mark with regard to Jesus' agony in Gethsemane: Jn 12:27ff and Mk 14:34ff both depict Jesus' sorrow and trouble, his desire to avoid death, and his dedication to the will of his Father. Edwyn C. Hoskyns accurately described the intent of the fourth evangelist, when he commented that "the episodes of Transfiguration and Agony have not been omitted through ignorance or by an oversight. Rather, woven together in one consistent whole, they control the Christology of the Fourth Gospel."[2] The simultaneous glory and humiliation of Christ are presented as the very condition of his life. The ultimate moment of his humiliation, his death on the cross, is also a manifestation of his glory, his being lifted up (see Jn 12:33 and 17:5).

Like Mark, John has a theology of the cross. He presents God's son as

2 See his *Fourth Gospel* (London: Faber & Faber, 1947), p.81.

the one who "had come from God and was going to God" by death on the cross. He delivers three indirect predictions of the passion, all of which refer to the "lifting up" of "I" or the Son of Man (Jn 3:14; 8:28; 12:32-34). Nor does John overlook Peter's confession, which precedes the first prediction of the passion in Mark (8:27ff). He complements the Synoptic account by pointing out a motive for Jesus' question, "But who do you say that I am?" as well as the circumstances that prompted him to ask it. Peter's confession in the fourth gospel is linked with the feeding of the five thousand and with the people's attempt to make Jesus king (Jn 6:1-15). Resisting this temptation, Jesus separates himself and his disciples from the multitude. Many of his followers were disappointed, for they wanted him as their earthly king, the Messiah of the people's expectations. This moment of crisis is when Jesus asks his disciples, "But who do you say that I am?" And according to John it is indeed Peter who answers, "You are the Holy One of God" (Jn 6:68-69). In detailing the circumstances of Peter's confession, John probably followed "a fuller tradition."[3] Both in the Synoptics and in the fourth gospel, Peter is the one who replies for the disciples (Mt 16:13ff. and paral.). As the leader and spokesman of the group, he confessed Jesus' divinity.

John also refers indirectly to the institution of the Lord's Supper, although there is no straightforward account of it in this gospel. He refers to its occurrence in Jerusalem (Jn 13). There is more development of the meaning of the eucharistic words in this gospel than in any other. In particular, Jn 6:51-58 echoes the words of Christ reported by Paul in 1 Cor 11:24, the earliest written account of the eucharist. Like the Synoptics and Paul, John links the eucharist to the death of Christ and ascribes a redemptive character to it. While other accounts of the eucharist speak about "body" and "blood," the fourth evangelist uses the term "flesh." The Hebrew word basar, of which "flesh" is the more literal translation, stands behind both terms, "body" and "flesh." The technical sacrificial term "for many" (ὑπὲρ πολλῶν) used at the Last Supper: "This is my blood of the covenant, which is poured out for many" (Mk 14:24 and paral.), is paralleled in John by Christ's discourse on the living bread which shall be given "for the life of the world" (ὑπὲρ τῆς τοῦ κόσμου

---

3 C. H. Dodd, *Historical Tradition in the Fourth Gospel* (Cambridge: Cambridge University Press, 1963), p. 428.

ζωῆς, Jn 6:51) and in the discourse on the true vine, which is again eucharistic (15:13). In John the words of the institution, "This is my body" and "this is my blood," become "I am the living bread" (6:51) and "I am the true vine" (15:1). The Synoptics and John, therefore, share a common core of eucharistic tradition which is developed and expressed differently in each.

II

As we have seen, most scholars in the field of gospel research are committed to the two-source hypothesis as the solution to the "Synoptic problem," the problem of the literary composition of Matthew, Mark and Luke. There are, however, veteran exegetes who have raised challenging questions regarding the priority of Mark, its use by Matthew and Luke, as well as the existence of Q. Some Catholic scholars are committed to the theory of the priority of the Aramaic Matthew. According to this view, the apostle Matthew composed his gospel in the Aramaic language around 50, just before the appearance of an Aramaic collection of the sayings of Jesus. Soon after, both the gospel and the collection of sayings were translated into Greek. Supposedly, several Greek translations of the Aramaic Matthew came into existence within a relatively short period of time. Mark knew one of these and used it in composing his gospel, but he made little use of the sayings of Jesus found now in the first gospel, and no use at all of the special collection, since he was probably not acquainted with it. Then, after Mark's gospel was completed, an unidentified Christian (possibly a disciple of Matthew) thoroughly revised a Greek translation of the Aramaic gospel. In performing this task, he used Mark's gospel as a reference, put back the sayings that Mark had omitted, and added new material as well as sayings drawn from the special collection (Q). The result was the Gospel of Matthew. Luke, like the editor of the first gospel, used Mark, the collection of sayings, and his own special material that he had discovered through his research of the primitive gospel traditions.[4] This theory of the existence of the Aramaic Matthew is now taken more seriously by other scholars, who do not

---

4 "Introduction to the Synoptic Gospels," *Jerusalem Bible*, pp. 7-9. On the other hand, John L. McKenzie, along with many other scholars, finds the arguments for an Aramaic Matthew not "convincing" (in "The Gospel According to Matthew," *Jerome Biblical Commentary*, 43:13-14).

necessarily belong to the "catholic" tradition, but who give more attention to early patristic evidence than did their predecessors.

In his recent study, *The Roots of the Synoptic Gospels* (1986), Bo Reicke writes that the testimony of Papias, an early second-century Christian authority on gospel origins, "must be considered to be of unique importance as the earliest available evidence." Of the five books, *Logion Kyriakon Exegesis* (*A Commentary on the Reports About the Lord*, E. H. 3.39.1), we have only fragments. According to Papias, Matthew compiled the *logia* of the Lord in Aramaic and everybody translated them as well as they could. On the basis of Papias' account of the origin of the second gospel, Bo Reicke insists that the λόγια κυριακά should not be translated or understood simply as the "sayings of the Lord," but as "reports about the Lord." Papias noted that Peter "used to present the pieces of information (διδασκαλίαι) according to occasional needs, yet without delivery of any written compilation of the reports about the Lord (τὰ κυριακὰ λόγια) "(E. H. 3.19.115). Regarding Mark, Papias wrote that Mark depended upon Peter's utterances—what Christ said or did—and that on the basis of these utterances Mark compiled the λόγια κυριακά. Thus, according to Papias, the λόγια κυριακά in Mark included both the sayings of Christ and the accounts of his life and works. Reicke is not alone in supposing that Mark's concentration upon Capernaum, the home town of Peter, suggests that "the evangelist depends upon communications of Peter," since neither in Matthew nor in Luke do we find Mark's concentration upon Capernaum. In his account of Jesus' Galilean ministry, Matthew pays attention not only to Peter's native town, but also to some other places, and Luke's interest in Galilee is much less pronounced. With such divergences as these, how can we explain the common features of the Synoptics?

According to Papias, several persons translated Matthew into Greek. Our Matthew is thus seen as the product of translation, editing, and completion by several followers of the evangelist. While the Greek version of Matthew was receiving its final form, units containing the traditions about Jesus were already circulating in Greek. The independent use of these pericopes by the evangelists may explain to a considerable degree the similarities in their reports of Jesus' words and deeds. More similarities may have derived from personal contacts between the evangelists. Although there is no New Testament evidence for a personal relationship between Matthew and Mark, it is clear that Mark and Luke were in contact. Both of them were in the company of Paul, during Paul's imprisonment (Col 4:10,14; Phil 2:4). It is quite natural to assume that at this time Mark and Luke exchanged notes and information and made themselves more familiar with the earliest Christian traditions about Jesus.

The considerable amount of material common to Matthew and Luke cannot be explained by any personal contacts, for which we possess no evidence. As it is also improbable that Matthew and Luke both translated an Aramaic source for use in their gospels, it is more natural to infer that both used a Greek source. Some passages common to Matthew and Luke use the same words; some are worded differently but are arranged in a similar order. It is supposed that both types of common material came from a hypothetical written source, Q. But the Q theory does not easily explain all parallels in Matthew and Luke. We shall take as an example the parallel between the Sermon on the Mount in Mt 5:1ff and the Sermon on the Plain in Luke 6. The four beatitudes in Luke are given in the order that corresponds to that in Matthew. Despite this agreement in order, the wording is different in each gospel. If both evangelists had the same document at hand, why then did they differ in using it, not only in their versions of the beatitudes, but also in many other narratives assigned to Q? These differences have given rise to questions about whether Q was a single document. Some suppose that there were several documents at different times and in different places. Exegetes argue that after the "first edition" of Q was complete, additional sayings were incorporated into it. Matthew and Luke may therefore have used Q at different stages in its growth.

There is also doubt about the language and content. Was the language Greek or Aramaic? Did the content consist exclusively of the sayings of Jesus, or did it also include narratives? Scholars who have tried to reconstruct Q differ in their answers to these questions. It is now quite clear that we can never convincingly reconstruct Q. Nonetheless, this much disputed source has been retained as an essential component of the prevalent working hypothesis for the solution of the Synoptic problem, although there are those who hold the contrary view: that the literary history of the gospel formation may turn out to have a simpler and more complete explanation than the one envisaged by adherents to the two-source theory envisage.

Among gospel researchers, some deny that the parallels between Matthew and Luke come from the Q document. They point out that the two sermons, mentioned above, do not appear to come from the same source. Bo Reicke, for example, ascribes their similarities to the evangelists' links "with groups of believers representing living traditions of similar yet different kind." He affiliates Matthew with Peter and with other apostles, and Luke with Philip and with the people around him. According to this view, Luke did not depend on the Gospel of Mark and Q, but composed his gospel from material that he shared with Mark, from units of the tradition which were already circulating, and from information that he gathered in his contacts with the Hellenists, that is, Jewish Christians who spoke only Greek (Acts 6; 21:8-18).[5]

The two-source hypothesis now appears as rigid and biased towards literary borrowing. It is based on a linear succession of gospels: Mark-Matthew-Luke. Even if the priority of Mark is rejected, a horizontal line is still preserved. C. S. Mann, in his recent extensive commentary on Mark defends the thesis that Mark is the latest, not the earliest, of the Synoptics. He abandons, although reluctantly, the priority of Mark and posits the existence of an Ur-gospel, an original, principal gospel source. Matthew and Luke, according to this view, drew independently upon this most primitive gospel and were in turn drawn upon by Mark. With this book Mann revived some old theories regarding the origin and growth of the gospel tradition.[6] In the eighteenth century Johann J. Griesbach believed that Mark was a conflation of Matthew and Luke. Recently an American scholar, William R. Farmer, further defended this view, in his book *The Synoptic Problem* (1964), claiming that Matthew wrote first, that Luke used Matthew, and that Mark used both. But if Mark came after Matthew and Luke and if he used both, then a crucial question arises: why did he omit so much important material that was in his sources, such as the Sermon on the Mount or the parables of Luke? This attempt to reject Mark's traditional priority has been received with strong skepticism.

5 For this summary of recent discussions and views regarding the Synoptic Gospels, we are particularly indebted to Bo Reicke's *The Roots of the Synoptic Gospels*, especially pp. 155-188.
6 C. S. Mann, *Mark*, Anchor Bible, v. 27 (Garden City, NY: Doubleday, 1986).

In sum, the two-source theory in its classical formulation cannot continue to stand without modification or qualification. New approaches to the problem of gospel origins are significant, for three reasons. First, they pay more attention to the living tradition of the gospel and to oral translation of units of the Jesus tradition from Aramaic into Greek. Due to the presence of the Hellenists in Jerusalem (Acts 6-7), the primitive Christian community in Jerusalem was bilingual from the beginning. The oral tradition did not stop with the appearance of written gospel documents or sources. Second, these new approaches take patristic evidence, after evaluating it critically, as a solid starting point for their research. Third, they stress the importance of personal contacts or relationships between the evangelists and between the evangelists and the disciples of Jesus. The gospels were not written anonymously, but by prominent individuals within the Christian movement. All these emphases are valuable to the modern approach to the gospels, even though they are unavoidably based on assumption and speculation.

The Synoptic problem is not yet solved, but the new approach has introduced a more promising perspective toward a better understanding of the problem, if not of its solution. It is no longer possible to regard the formation of the gospels as an exclusively literary problem, or to consider them in a strictly linear succession. Rather, they passed through various stages, utilizing "overlapping traditions, both oral and written"; they grew up together and influenced one another.[7]

III

The discovery of the limitations of the two-source hypothesis has coincided with a new attempt to redate the New Testament documents. Until recently, it was the prevailing view that Mark was written some time between 65 and 70, before the destruction of the Temple in Jerusalem in 70, and that Matthew and Luke were written after the fall of Jerusalem, for they reflect the destruction of the city and the burning of the Temple by the Romans. In addition, these two gospels seem to reflect the life of the Christian Church in its struggle with the synagogue after 70. However, this dating scheme is by no means free of weaknesses and has recently been questioned.

7   John A. T. Robinson, *Can We Trust the New Testament?*, (Grand Rapids: Eerdmans, 1977), p. 76.

Among contemporary biblical scholars, John A. T. Robinson has dealt most systematically and extensively with this question. His central point can be stated as follows: The destruction of the Temple, which had such drastic consequences for the Jewish community, is in fact not reflected in the gospels. The gospels contain prophecies of the destruction, but no direct reference to the event itself. This point of view has been disputed by scholars who believe that the prophecies of the violent end of Jerusalem should be treated as vaticinia ex eventu, or "prophecies by hindsight." For example, they detect a reference to the destruction of Jerusalem in the parable of the marriage feast: "The king was angry and he sent his troops and destroyed those murderers and burned their city" (Mt 22:7). Similarly, Luke warns: "But when you see Jerusalem surrounded by armies, then know that its desolation has come near" (Lk 21:20). Many regard the details in these passages as specific enough to have been written after the event. Robinson, on the other hand, referring to the exegesis of these "prediction passages" by some leading New Testament scholars, argues that the imagery in these passages derives from that used in the Old Testament to refer to the fall of Jerusalem to the Babylonians in 587 B.C., and not from knowledge of the fate of the Second Temple in 70. Prominent among these exegetes is C. H. Dodd, whose analysis of Luke 19:42-44 and 21:0-24 has been independently confirmed by Bo Reicke.[8] Robinson expresses surprise that the evangelists would have left out any direct references to the fall of Jerusalem, and consequently assigns the gospels to the period between 40 and 65.[9]

8 Robinson, *Redating the New Testament* (Philadelphia: Westminster Press, 1976), p. 27. C. H. Dodd's exegesis of these verses in the Gospel of Luke led him to conclude that the language used by Luke or the language of the source he used comes not from recent events "but from a mind soaked in the Septuagint." According to Dodd, what colored the picture here is not Titus' capture in 70, but the Babylonian destruction of the Temple and Jerusalem in 586 B.C. "There is no single trait of the forecast which cannot be documented directly out of the Old Testament," concludes C. H.Dodd in his article, "The Fall of Jerusalem and the 'Abomination of Desolation'," published in 1947 and reprinted in his *More New Testament Studies* (Manchester: 1968), pp. 69-83.

9 J. A. T. Robinson distinguishes three stages in the development of the Synoptic Gospels: 1) the collection of sayings, such as Q, and special material of Matthew (M) and Luke (L), in the 30s and 40s of the first century; 2) the formation of "proto-gospels" in the 40s and 50s; 3) the formation of our Synoptic Gospels in the 50s and 60s. (See *Redating the New Testament*, p. 107).

IV

Scholars who claim that the Gospel of John was written at the end of the first century or even in the second century are usually those who see it as more of a theological than a historical document. Its highly developed theology suggests to them a much later date than the ones assigned to the Synoptics. They assume therefore that it could not depend upon the witness of the disciple who was closest to Jesus. This has changed in recent studies. The dean of biblical archaeologists, W. F. Albright, wrote that "the thought content" of the fourth gospel "reflects the period of Jewish history to which Jesus and John the Baptist belonged, and not of a later period."[10] In another essay he states that "we may rest assured that [the fourth gospel] contains the memories of the Apostle John—regardless of whether he died in Jerusalem or in Ephesus, though the latter is so well attested by tradition that it remains most plausible."[11] The documents discovered in the caves at Qumran (the Dead Sea Scrolls) supply us with evidence that language similar to the language of John was used by this extremely conservative Jewish group before the Roman destruction of Jerusalem. Before the discovery of the Dead Sea Scrolls, words such as "truth," "knowledge," "light" and "darkness" were taken by many to be sure signs that the Gospel of John is the most "Hellenistic" of the four. After the discovery, the scholarly estimation of its Jewish element moved in the opposite direction. John has been called the "most Jewish," preserving and transmitting historical material not in a Hellenistic but in a Jewish, Aramaic-speaking environment. Yet a closer look reveals that it is neither a "Hellenistic" nor a "Jewish" book. In a certain sense this gospel is the least Greek and the least Jewish of the four. Neither Greek nor Jew could have claimed that "the Word became flesh" (Jn 1:14). The essence of John's Gospel was alien to both Jew and Greek.

An inevitable consequence of the discovery of the Dead Sea Scrolls, then, has been reevaluation of the date John was written. Robinson argues that it was composed before 70, since this gospel, like Matthew and Luke, remains silent regarding the destruction of the Temple in

10 *Religion in Life*, 21, (1952), p. 550.
11 "Discoveries in Palestine and the Gospel of St John," in W. D. Davies and D. Daube, eds., *The Background of the New Testament and its Eschatology* (Cambridge: Cambridge University Press, 1956), p. 171.

Jerusalem. When John records Jesus' words about the destruction: "Destroy this temple, and in three days I will raise it up" (Jn 2:19), Robinson sees them as a "prophecy of what God would do in the resurrection," and not as a prophecy of the Roman destruction of the Temple: "It is in fact remarkable that there is nothing in John corresponding to the detailed prophecies of the siege and fall of Jerusalem."[12]

What is most important about the early dating of the gospels is that it tries to show that they were written within the framework of Judaism before 70, that is, before the Jews and "Jewish-Christians" began to travel divergent paths. We should keep in mind that Judaism before the destruction of Jerusalem was not monolithic, and that several groups were able to coexist within the synagogue even while disagreeing and fighting with each other. Thanks to Paul's letters, we know more about this period than about the decade from 80 to 90, which, in the words of Robinson, we were prone to assume as "a depository because we knew remarkably little about it."[13] Many of the twenty-seven books of the New Testament have been assigned to this period, and the struggle between "the synagogue" and "the church," the expulsion of the Jews from their synagogue because of their belief in Christ, are all explained as occurring in the eighties of the first century. Due to questions about the dating of the gospels, these conclusions can be reevaluated.

V

To illustrate how the dating can affect our interpretation of a gospel passage, let us see how two New Testament scholars who hold different views on the date of John interpret the healing of the blind man in chapter nine. Let us first summarize the account of this healing. A man blind from birth is healed by Jesus and shows himself to his neighbors, who are astonished. He tells them of Jesus, who anointed his eyes with clay and sent him to wash in the pool of Siloam. Since the miracle occurred on the Sabbath, the Pharisees take notice and request the man to appear before them and to repeat his story. The Pharisees then interrogate the man's parents, since they "did not believe that he had been blind and had received his sight" (9:18). The parents confirm that the healed man is their

12 *Redating the New Testament*, pp. 276-277.
13 *Can We Trust the New Testament?*, pp. 84-86.

son, that he was born blind, and that they do not know who opened his eyes. They also add that since their son is of age, he should speak for himself. They say this "because they [fear] the Jews, for the Jews had already agreed that if any one should confess him to be Christ, he was to be put out of the synagogue" (9:22). True to their promise, after the son is interrogated for the second time, "they cast him out" (9:34).

This passage is often cited in discussions concerning the dating of the gospel of John. J. D. G. Dunn, who expresses the view of the majority of New Testament scholars, and who accepts the view that John was written after 70, argues that the passage reflects the breach between Christians and "the Jews" which took place in the eighties of the first century, that is, almost twenty years after the destruction of Jerusalem. Dunn links the term "Jews" and the expulsion of the healed man from the synagogue to the formal decision of the Jewish authorities in the eighties to treat as heretics those who confessed Jesus to be the Messiah. Before 70, he contends, there were no expulsions from the synagogue of any Jews who held this belief. He dismissed as irrelevant the conflict between Stephen and the Jewish authorities, and Stephen's death, which happened a few years after the death and resurrection of Jesus, for this was a conflict which involved the Temple.[14]

For J. A. T. Robinson, by contrast, any link between John 9:22 and the official ban against the Nazarenes (Christians) of the late eighties "is very tenuous" and contains "no specific reference to excommunication." Expulsions took place even before the destruction of the Temple, at a time when all the various Jewish groups still considered themselves to be part of Judaism. Paul, for example, was expelled from the synagogue for preaching Christ. Robinson also refers to a passage from 1 Thessalonians, which may have been written as much as twenty years before the destruction of the Temple and therefore qualifies as one of the earliest New Testament documents. Paul addressed the persecuted Christians in Thessalonica as follows: "For you, brethren, became imitators of the churches of God in Christ Jesus which are in Judea; for you suffered the same things from your own countrymen as they did from the Jews" (1 Th 2:14). The term "the Jews" is used here in much the same way as it is used in John, referring not to the Jewish people but to "external authorities." Expulsions took place in the Qumran community, a fact recorded

14 *The Evidence for Jesus,* pp. 41-43.

by Josephus[15] and cited by Robinson in support of his argument.[16] Since he had received report of a man who was "living with his father's wife," Paul requested in his letter to the church in Corinth (54-55) that "he who has done this be removed from among you" (1 Cor 5:1-3). And how are we to understand the "great persecution" against the Hellenists after the death of Stephen, if not as a persecution for religious reasons, and their scattering "throughout the region of Judea and Samaria," if not as expulsion from the city and also from the synagogue to which they belonged (Acts 7-8)? In sum, it is clear that Jewish groups undoubtedly practiced expulsion both before and after 70, although attempts to date the gospel by means of such a reflection of historical realities in its terminology are far from conclusive.

The dating of any gospel is difficult,[17] but the attempt must be made because it bears so strongly on the interpretation. Robinson did not succeed in proving that everything in the New Testament was written before the destruction of the Temple. In connection with Jn 9:22 he admits that "there is no compelling reason to assign it to a situation at the end of the first century," but there is also no reason to deduce that it reflects a situation before the destruction of the Temple. What he indirectly proved is the growing conviction that the gospels, whether they were written at the end of the first century or before the Jewish-Roman War, contain a faithful record of the earliest traditions about Jesus. Robinson's real purpose was not to prove new dating of the New Testament, but to challenge the scholarly establishment and the "established dates" for the gospel. The importance of his book lies precisely in his questioning. He admits this in his introduction: "Indeed I am happy to prefix to my work the words with which Niels Bohr is said to have begun

---

15 *The Jewish War* II.8.8.

16 *Can We Trust the New Testament?*, pp. 84-86.

17 Robinson, for instance, argues that Mt 17:24-7, with its reference to a Temple tax, "clearly points to a pre-70 milieu." After 70 this tax "had to be paid to the temple treasury of Jupiter Capitolinus in Rome and would have had no bearing on the Jewish question" (Redating the New Testament, p. 104). John P. Meier sees this pericope in a different light. He agrees that this unit "circulated in the oral tradition at a time when the Temple tax was still a burning question for the early Jewish Christians," but he locates its time of writing and its incorporation into the Gospel of Matthew around 90. For him, this pericope even at the end of the first century "retains its important theological message about the freedom of sons, limited not by legalism but by a living concern" (see his *Christ, Church and Morality in the First Gospel* [New York: Paulist Press, 1979], p. 127, fn. 132.)

his lecture-courses: 'Every sentence I utter should be taken by you not as a statement but as a question'." And he concludes his book by expressing the hope that it will be "an irritant and incentive to further exploration, and, I should like to think, to the opening up of fresh questions."[18]

The debates over the origin of the Synoptic Gospels, over John's independence from them, and over the redating of the New Testament give us new insights into the traditions incorporated by the evangelists into their writing. Mark's gospel may still be regarded as the "earliest" due to its Petrine origin, and John's as the "latest," but not so late as had been thought before. John may have been the last to be written, but it bears witness to traditions as old as those of the Synoptics, if not older than theirs. The gap between oral and written traditions is now closing, for more attention has been given to the role of original witnesses in the early church.

Those whom Jesus chose became his witnesses. The Twelve were witnesses of Jesus and of his ministry "beginning from the baptism of John until the day when he was taken up," and they testified particularly to his resurrection (Acts 1:22). On the day of Pentecost, Peter declared on behalf of all of the disciples that "this Jesus God raised up, and of that we are all witnesses" (Acts 2:32).

We must distinguish here between the Twelve as eyewitnesses (αὐτόπται, Lk 1:2) and as witnessess (μάρτυρες, Acts 2:32) after the resurrection and Pentecost. As eyewitnesses of Jesus, they listened to his teaching and were willing to detach themselves from the "world," to follow him (Lk 14:25). There were other eyewitnesses of Jesus, however, who preferred to remain within the world, rather than to follow him. They "drew back and no longer went about with him," for they found his sayings hard to listen to (Jn 6:52ff). Not every eyewitness is necessarily a witness. As *martyres*, the Twelve testified to the events of the public ministry of Jesus and were thus responsible for transmitting the history of Jesus as well as for its interpretation. Above all, they testified to his resurrection and to its significance: they were *martyres* to the fact that the Risen Lord and Jesus were identical. Their testimony is the foundation of the gospels. Recent historical research points to the importance of these direct witnesses.

18 *Redating the New Testament*, pp. 12 and 357.

8

History and Chronology

The evangelists arranged their sources in a way that would convey to us the true image of Christ and the meaning of the events related to his life and mission. In some places they did this by leaving events in their proper chronological context. In other places they did this by taking an event out of its chronological context and placing it elsewhere to bring out its full significance. Chronological accuracy is strikingly present in the Passion accounts: all four gospels agree on the order of events in those days. It is probable that this agreement reflects careful preservation of the proper order of the events of the cross by the earliest Christian communities.

Throughout history doubts have been raised about Christ's death and resurrection, either because they seem implausible or on the basis of contravening evidence. Some recent questions have been raised, for example, over Jesus' trial before the Sanhedrin, questions which must be taken into account if we are to evaluate the gospels as a historical record.

I

It is sometimes difficult to designate at what point certain events occurred in the public ministry of Jesus. It is even more difficult to indicate at what point he pronounced a certain saying. Still, the gospels record the most important events of his life in their historical sequence. His baptism comes before his temptation; the transfiguration follows the confession of Peter; and both precede Christ's last journey to and ministry in Jerusalem. The chronological order of the passion may be better verified than that of any other sequence of events, since the passion story is a unified narrative. On the whole, there is a sense of historical movement in the ministry of Jesus as presented in the gospels, a definite sequence of events.

The problem of chronology in the gospels is not a minor one. Those critics who believe that the gospels are solely the creation of the community are usually skeptical about drawing up any chronological outline of the life of Jesus. On the other hand, critics who view the primitive *kerygma* as the basis of the gospels ascribe more significance to gospel chronology. For them the apostolic proclamation has a chronological outline: "The Word which was proclaimed throughout all Judea, beginning from Galilee after the baptism which John preached: how God anointed Jesus of Nazareth with the Holy Spirit and with power; how he went about doing good and healing all that were oppressed by the devil, for God was with him. And we are witnesses to all that he did both in the country of the Jews and in Jerusalem. They put him to death by hanging him on a tree; but God raised him on the third day and made him manifest..." (Acts 10:37ff). C. H. Dodd claims that the chronology of Mark is the most reliable: "Although it is hazardous to argue from the precise sequence of the narrative in detail, yet there is good reason to believe that in broad lines the Marcan order does represent a genuine succession of events within which movement and development can be traced." Subsequent criticism of this position did not cause Dodd to change his judgment on the framework of Mark's gospel in any substantial way.[1]

The chronological context of an event often draws out its meaning. The historical accounts reinforce theological truth. For example, the theological meaning of the account of the temptation of Jesus can be fully understood only when the temptation is considered in light of his baptism which immediately precedes the temptation. At Jesus' temptation, the devil tried to lure him into being a messiah, who would dispense with suffering and who would take a short cut to paradise. But Jesus declined to take a road that would remove him from suffering or separate him from the people for whose salvation he was baptized. In the temptation, therefore, Jesus revealed his divine role, announced at the baptism, not in terms of alien splendor, but in terms of the suffering Servant of God in Isaiah 53.

The theological and spiritual significance of an event may be revealed by the events which follow it. The baptism of Jesus, for example, not only

---

1 "The Framework of the Gospel Narrative," in *New Testament Studies* (Manchester: Manchester University Press, 1953), p. 11. Also see his *Historical Tradition in the Fourth Gospel* (Cambridge: Cambridge University Press, 1963), pp. 233-4, fn. 2.

    Martin Hengel writes: "The chronological sequence of events was not of decisive interest." Yet "the construction of a narrative framework presupposes fixed reminiscences of a fixed tradition" (see Acts 10:36-40). He also stresses that due to "the overwhelming impression which Jesus made," it was difficult to arrange some events and above all his sayings in a chronological or geographical order. But "the last days in Jerusalem are an exception here" (see his *Acts and the History of Earliest Christianity* [Philadelphia: Fortress Press, 1980], pp. 23f).

points out his suffering, but also sums up in one event the whole ministry of the Son of God, who is at the same time the servant. The meaning of Jesus' baptism does not become clear at once, but gradually, in the course of his life, death, and resurrection. The opened heaven, the descent of the Spirit, the voice of the Father, the coming of the Messiah "all indicate that the last times have dawned, redemption is about to appear." Thus the baptism is not simply the acceptance by Jesus of his death, but "the dawn of the new creation, the promise of life from the dead."[2] Christ's rising from the water anticipates his ascension; the same term, "going up" (anabaino), is used seven times with reference to Christ's ascent (Jn 1:51, 3:13, 6:62, 20:17; Acts 2:4; Rom 10:6; Eph 4:8-10).[3]

Chronological order is not always paramount in the gospels, however. Preference is often given to a topical arrangement. The Sermon on the Mount, for example, contains sayings which were pronounced on various occasions, and which probably belonged to different periods of the ministry of Jesus. The same applies to the parables (Mt 13) and to the miracles. It is quite obvious that the healing miracle, which immediately follows the Sermon on the Mount and which opens a series of miracles in Mt 8-9 does not belong there chronologically. "When he [Jesus] came down from the mountain great crowds followed him; and behold a leper came to him," asking to be made clean. Jesus "stretched out his hand and touched him, saying, 'I will; be clean'." The miracle account ends with the warning of Jesus, "See that you say nothing to anyone..." (Mt 8:1ff). Two difficulties indicate that the original context of the miracle is lost. The first is that lepers lived in colonies which were separated from the people, and in our story the leper approached Jesus while he was with great crowds. The second is that if the leper was healed while the crowds were watching, then Jesus could not have said, "See that you say nothing to anyone." The story is chronologically inconsistent with its setting.[4]

Topical arrangements of the works and words of Jesus were used in order to reach audiences who were not necessarily concerned with the sequence of events or with their context, but with the meaning of what

2 G. R. Beasley-Murray, *Baptism in the New Testament* (London: Macmillan, 1962), p. 61.
3 G. W. H. Lampe, *The Seal of the Spirit: A Study in the Doctrine of Baptism and Confirmation in the New Testament and the Fathers* (London: SPCK Press, 1951), p. 43.
4 See Xavier Léon-Dufour, *The Gospels and the Jesus of History* (London: W. Collins Sons, 1966), p. 163f.

Jesus said and did. The evangelists were concerned with relating everything to the ultimate revelation of God in Christ. Origen wrote that the evangelists should not be condemned for rearranging their material,

so that they speak of a thing which happened in one place as if it happened somewhere else, or of what took place at one time as if it had happened at another time, and introduce certain changes into the words actually spoken. Their intention was to speak the truth where it was possible both materially and spiritually and, where it was not possible to do both, they preferred the spiritual to the material. Indeed, spiritual truth was often preserved in what might be described as material falsehood.[5]

The story of the cleansing of the temple in the gospels (Mt 21:12-13, Mk 11:15-19, Lk 19:45-48, and Jn 2:13-25) has a different chronological setting in the Synoptics than it does in the fourth gospel. John placed it at the beginning, whereas the Synoptics ascribed it to the end of Jesus' public ministry, shortly before his crucifixion. By making it part of the Passion week, the Synoptic evangelists most probably remained faithful to the event's original chronological context. John may have moved the cleansing of the temple from the end to the very beginning of Jesus' public ministry in order to emphasize its symbolic value, to bring out the shadow of the cross which from the beginning lay over Jesus' proclamation of the gospel. At an early point in his ministry, Jesus inveighed against the religious authorities in Jerusalem and against their business transactions by claiming lordship over the temple: "Take these things away, you shall not make my Father's house a house of trade" (Jn 2:16). The evangelist reinforced this claim by recording that Jesus' disciples remembered that it was written: "Zeal for thy house will consume me" (Jn 2:17, a reference to Ps 69:9). The disciples understood that Jesus' zeal for the temple would lead to his death.[6] When confronted by the Jewish authorities in the Temple with the question: "What sign have you to show us for doing this?" Jesus responded by speaking of the temple of his body: "Destroy this temple, and in three days I will raise it up" (Jn 2:19). After his resurrection, his followers remembered and believed "the scripture and the words which Jesus had spoken" (Jn 2:22). John, therefore, links the cleansing of the temple to Jesus' death. The same connection is present in the Synoptics. When Jesus finished his teaching

5 In *Comm. in Ioann.* X,5, quoted by R. L. P. Milburn, *Early Christian Interpretation of History* (London: Adam & Charles Black, 1954), p. 49.
6 D. Moody Smith, "John," in *Harper Bible Commentary*, James L. Mays, ed. (San Francisco: Harper & Row, 1988), p. 1050.

in the cleansed temple, the chief priests and the scribes who heard him "sought a way to destroy him" (Mk 11:18, Lk 19:47).

Any attempt, ancient or modern, to solve the problem of the cleansing of the temple in the Synoptics and in John by positing two cleansings—one at the very beginning of Jesus' ministry and another at its end—has proven unsuccessful and futile. Such harmonizations have minimized the historical importance of the cleansing of the temple as a decisive event in Jesus' life and teaching and have obscured the theological meaning of the event as presented in John. Apparently, the fourth evangelist detached the cleansing of the temple from its "chronological context" to reveal "its theological significance."[7] This act makes concrete the words of the Prologue: "He came to his own home, and his own people received him not" (Jn 1:11).

II

As we noted above, the gospels display unusual agreement in their ordering sequence of the events of the Passion. The Last Supper, Gethsemane, the arrest, the trials, the crucifixion and death, the burial, the discovery of the empty tomb, and the post-resurrection appearances appear in one continuous narrative in all four gospels. In John, the Last Supper is reflected in several chapters (13-17). The passion narrative proper then begins: "When Jesus had spoken these words, he went forth with his disciples across the Kidron Valley, where there was a garden, which he and his disciples entered" (Jn 18:1). Obviously this garden is Gethsemane, named in two of the Synoptic Gospels (Mt 26:36, Mk 14:32). The agreement between John and the Synoptics over the events of the Passion is significant, for it implies that the fourth gospel contains an early tradition, as early as the Synoptics' sources, and that the passion events were proclaimed as a unit from the inception of the primitive Church in Jerusalem. It follows that the order of the events of the Passion week was not the creation of the evangelists but came from traditions which were rooted in and followed the order of the events of the life of Jesus.

Some interpreters of the Passion narratives have questioned the chronology, historical precision, and trustworthiness of the evangelists. To

7 E. Hoskyns, *The Fourth Gospel* (London: Faber & Faber, 1947), p. 126.

illustrate their criticism, we shall discuss the date of the Last Supper, the trials of Jesus, and the question of responsibility for his death.

Certain events in the gospels cannot be dated. Attempts to do so are usually individual exercises without much evidence from either the gospels themselves or contemporary sources. Still, the meaning of the Last Supper depends much upon its time (the Passover) and place (Jerusalem). This particular event is dated by all four gospels, although there is a disagreement between the Synoptics and John about the exact day.

The gospels agree that the Last Supper took place on Thursday evening (Friday) and the crucifixion on Friday. But they disagree as to whether or not the Last Supper was a Passover meal. According to the Synoptics, the Last Supper was the Passover meal and occurred on the day of Passover. The Jews reckoned a day from sunset to sunset, and the Passover meal started after sunset. The slaughter in the temple of the lambs eaten at the Passover meal took place on the previous day. According to the fourth gospel, the Last Supper, with the institution of the Eucharist occurred also on Thursday evening (Friday), and the crucifixion happened later on Friday. But this Friday was not the Passover day, Nissan 15 in the Jewish calendar, but Nissan 14, the day of the slaughtering of the paschal lambs. The crucifixion in John took place, therefore, on the eve of Passover. Those who brought Jesus, early on Friday, from Caiaphas to Pilate "did not enter the praetorium, so that they might not be defiled, but might eat the passover" (Jn 18:28). It was "the Day of Preparation," and the Sabbath that followed "was a high day" (Jn 19:14, 31). On the basis of the evidence of John, the Passover in the year in which Jesus was crucified fell on a Saturday and not on a Friday.

Various solutions have been offered for this discrepancy between the Synoptics and the fourth evangelist. Some have thought that John's terminology is theologically motivated, that he synchronized Christ's death on the cross and the slaughtering of the lambs in order to show that Christ is the true paschal lamb "who takes away the sins of the world." Another solution to this problem, recently proposed by A. Jaubert,[8] is a new chronological order for the Passion week, in which the Last Supper took place on a Tuesday evening (Wednesday) and the crucifixion on Friday. This particular explanation is based upon two

8 A. Jaubert, *The Date of the Last Supper* (New York: Alba House, 1965).

Jewish calendars that were used in the time of Jesus. According to the solar calendar known to us from the book of Jubilees,[9] found at Qumran, the major feasts were celebrated on the same day of the week. This calendar was probably used by all Jews up to 152 B.C. In that year, the Maccabees succeeded to the high priesthood and adopted the lunar calendar used in the Hellenistic world. The feast of the Passover falls on a Wednesday if it is celebrated according to the solar calendar, but not if it is celebrated according to the lunar calendar. Thus, according to Jaubert, Jesus may have used the Qumran solar calendar and celebrated the Last Supper on Tuesday evening. This theory allows three days, not one day as the gospels do, for the arrest, trial and crucifixion.

Although some have found this chronology helpful, others have criticized it for being out of harmony with the circumstances and atmosphere of the passion narratives. The high priests wanted Jesus arrested, but they wanted to avoid unrest among the people. Everything had to be done quickly and efficiently. If we allow three days for the trial, trouble with the crowd could not have been avoided. Jaubert's theory raises another difficulty: Is it reasonable to claim that Jesus celebrated the Passover according to the Qumran solar calendar and all the other feasts according to the Jerusalem calendar? He visited Jerusalem on the holy days, as did other non-Qumran Jews. There is not the slightest indication that Jesus was ever reproached for following the "heretical" calendar of the Qumran community. If Jesus ever followed the Qumran calendar, we would expect that his opponents would have used this deviation from the practice in Jerusalem to attack him and to try to isolate him from the masses. There was no opportunity to criticize Jesus on this point, for he was in Jerusalem even for the feast of the Dedication of the Temple (Hanukkah), as recorded in Jn 10:22. This feast commemorates the reconsecration of the Temple at the time of the Maccabean Wars (165 B.C.), after it was desecrated by Antiochus Epiphanes IV. It did not enter the Essene solar calendar, for the Essenes hated and rejected anything

9 The book belongs to the Jewish Apocrypha. Several copies of Jubilees were found at the Qumran library. It is probable that the Qumran group regarded it as a part of their Bible. The book was composed not long before 105 B.C., and it is possible that its composition followed the introduction of the lunar calendar in the Temple. This decision may have given rise to the separation of the Essenes from Jerusalem and from its priesthood. In Jubilees we have polemics against the lunar calendar, along with emphasis upon the supremacy of the Law and the Sabbath.

that might remind them of the Maccabees, even if it had to do with rededication of the Temple.[10]

Other theories have been propounded to reconcile the Synoptics and the fourth gospel, to avoid choosing one account over the other. One offers as a possibility that the Galilean Jews ate the Passover one day earlier than did the Jews of Jerusalem. Another considers it possible that the Jews in Jerusalem and throughout Palestine celebrated the Passover on Saturday in the year when Jesus was crucified, while the Jews who lived in the Diaspora observed the feast on Friday. According to this view, John's gospel gives the right date and chronology, whereas in Mark's gospel we have a chronology that was adjusted to the Church's tradition in Rome.[11] All these explanations are possible, but not probable. They cannot be supported by reliable evidence.

The trend among New Testament scholars today is to accept the Johannine chronology of the last days of Jesus' public ministry. Jesus had the Last Supper with the Twelve on Thursday evening, which was not the Passover day but the eve of the Passover, and he gave it a paschal coloring. He made it a meal "destined to commemorate and to replace the Pasch of Exodus."[12] This interpretation, which is based upon the evidence in John, does give a satisfactory explanation of the Synoptic claim that the Last Supper was a Passover meal. For Jesus and his disciples this was the paschal rite, during which the new rite, the Eucharist, was instituted. The atmosphere of the narrative in Jn 13 is that of the Passover. That it was held in Jerusalem after sunset (Jn 13:30), and that the participants were in reclining positions (Jn 13:23) also clearly indicate, according to John, that Jesus desired to make it the Passover meal.

Scholars have traditionally ascribed more historical value to the Synoptics, especially Mark, than to John. Whenever the first three and John's gospel disagree on some historical point, scholars have usually settled the question by taking the position of the Synoptics. Recently, however, high historical value has been ascribed to the Passion account in the

10 Raymond E. Brown, *New Testament Essays* (Milwaukee: Bruce Publishing, 1965), pp. 166f.
11 The first theory is linked with the name of Julian Morgenstern and the second was elaborated by M. H. Shepherd. (See Sherman E. Johnson, *The Gospel According to St. Mark* [New York: Harper & Bros., 1960], pp. 227f.)
12 A. Feuillet, "Some Major Themes of the New Testament," in A. Robert and A. Feuillet, eds., *Introduction to the New Testament* (New York: Desclee Co., 1965), pp. 794f.

fourth gospel. The tradition incorporated in John is being recognized as a tradition independent from, but as old and as authentic as those in the Synoptics.[13]

III

The succession of events between the Last Supper and Pilate's pronouncement of the death sentence receives full attention in all the gospels. The arrest of Christ took place at night, to avoid any commotion among the people. The readiness of Judas to lead soldiers to Gethsemane on Thursday night made this the most opportune time for the opponents of Jesus to seize him. Since everybody was busy on the eve of the Passover, there was little possibility of unrest among the people. From Gethsemane, according to John, Jesus was led to Annas, a former high priest (6-15 A.D.) whom the Roman procurator, the immediate predecessor of Pilate, had deposed, but whose influence upon the affairs of the Temple continued. Annas asked Jesus about his teaching and his disciples (Jn 18:12-14, 20-21). The real trial began as soon as Jesus was brought to the high priest Caiaphas and to the council. The climax of the inquiry came when Caiaphas asked, "Are you the Christ, the Son of the Blessed?" (Mk 14:61 and paral.). Jesus, who had been silent during the trial, then answered: "I am; and you will see the Son of Man sitting at the right hand of power, and coming with the clouds of heaven" (Mk 14:62 and paral.). Upon hearing Jesus' answer, Caiaphas "tore his mantle and said, 'Why do we still need witnesses?'" This symbolic act meant that he found Jesus guilty of blasphemy. "What is your judgment?" he asked the members of the Sanhedrin, and they "all condemned him as deserving death" (Mk 14:64).

Execution did not follow this judgment, however. What then was the purpose of this trial? Did it actually take place, or was it a creation of the early church, as some scholars claim, for the purpose of removing the responsibility for the death of Jesus from the Romans and putting it upon the Jews? Was Jesus found guilty of blasphemy, as the Synoptics

13 There are several additions in John to the outline of the life of Jesus in the Synoptics. According to John, Jesus did not start his public ministry in Galilee, but was active in Jerusalem and Judea before coming there. His first disciples came from among John the Baptist's followers (Jn 1:35-42). Before his death and resurrection, the ministry of Jesus in Judea spanned a longer period than the Synoptics suggest.

report? Did he blaspheme the name of God even from their perspective? For the law was clear: "He who blasphemes the name of the Lord shall be put to death; all the congregation shall stone him; the sojourner as well as the native, when he blasphemes the name, shall be put to death" (Lev 24:16). The term "name" stands for the revelatory name of God that he gave to Moses: "I am who I am," *YHWH* (Ex 3:14). This is the most sacred and most personal name of God in the Hebrew scripture. By blaspheming the name of the Lord, one pollutes the community, and it is the duty of the community to remove pollution by killing the pollutor. To those who follow the Mishnah (the collection of oral law complied around 200 A.D.), and apply it to the events of the thirties of the first century, Jesus was not, strictly speaking, a blasphemer, "for the blasphemer is not culpable unless he pronounces the name itself" (Sanh. 7:5). The Sanhedrin, therefore, could not have condemned him to death, for there was no blasphemy which would require such a sentence. And if the ruling body in Jerusalem had found him deserving of death, they would have stoned him.

It is on these grounds that the whole trial narrative has been rejected as historically unfounded. But the support for its historicity is still more compelling. According to Mark, Jesus said to Caiaphas: "I am; and you will see the Son of Man..." (14:62). Caiaphas, the gospel context implies, understood "I am" as the sacred name of God, inferring that Jesus was claiming God's prerogatives for himself. Why then did the Sanhedrin not execute the sentence? This question, to which we will return later in our discussion, is implicitly answered in the passion story of the fourth gospel. The Sanhedrin did not execute a death sentence (in spite of the "blasphemy" that had occurred) because it did not have the right to inflict capital punishment. "It is not lawful for us to put any man to death" (Jn 18:31).

The charges before Pilate brought against Jesus did not include a charge of blasphemy. The Jewish leaders probably knew that Pilate would not act as they wished on the basis of a purely religious offense. Accordingly, they produced political charges which in the last analysis governed Pilate's decision. They informed Pilate that they found Jesus "perverting our nation," that he was "forbidding us to give tribute to Caesar," and that he himself claimed to be "Christ a king" (Lk 23:2). All these charges had political overtones, but the last was the most explicit and dangerous, and Pilate paid more attention to it than to the first two. All four evangelists state that Pilate asked Jesus, "Are you the King of the Jews?" (Mt 27:11, Mk 15:2, Lk 23:3, Jn 18:33). Jesus responded that his kingdom was not of this world. In other words, he was not a king in Pilate's sense, an agitator, a rebel king, but the King who came into the world "to bear witness to the truth" (Jn 18:37-38).

Before Pilate pronounced a formal sentence, according to John, the leaders brought in for the first time the "religious charge" against Jesus. "We have a law, and by that law he ought to die, because he has made himself the Son of God" (Jn 19:7). The law to which they referred was the law dealing with blasphemy. After this, the decisive moment, a charge of political nature was again pressed: "If you release this man you are not Caesar's friend; everyone who makes himself a king sets himself against Caesar" (Jn 19:12). At this, Pilate "sat down on the judgment seat" and sentenced Jesus to be crucified.

IV

Some modern critics, both Christian and Jewish, have raised questions regarding the order and historicity of the presentation in the gospels of the trial of Jesus. Hans Lietzmann, in an influential essay (1931), started the modern debate about the historical value of this part of the Passion narrative.[14] Lietzmann argued that the record of the Passion week in Mark, the earliest among the gospels and the basis for the accounts in Matthew and Luke, is unreliable. Mark's report about Jesus' trial before the Sanhedrin, in Lietzmann's view, shows an anti-Jewish bias. This is based on Lietzmann's conviction that the Sanhedrin did in fact have the right to exercise capital punishment, and that therefore the trial could not have occurred. The Sanhedrin, he writes with some certainty, did not condemn Jesus on the count of blasphemy. If they had, then they would have had to execute him by stoning. If they did so in the case of Stephen (Acts 7:58ff), then why did they not do the same with Jesus? The Sanhedrin therefore did not try Jesus on religious charges, but simply handed Jesus over to the Roman authorities as a political rebel.

14 His views are summarized in *A History of the Early Church* (Cleveland: World Pub., 1953), v. I, pp. 59-60.

Some modern Christian theologians and New Testament scholars have adopted Lietzmann's views. Lietzmann may also have influenced those Jewish scholars who have recently focused on the trial and the responsibility for the death of Jesus. In his book, *On the Trial of Jesus* (1961), Paul Winter attempts to prove that the Jewish authorities were not directly involved, that their involvement was the result of Roman pressure, and that the Church and the evangelists distorted the facts to please Rome and to accuse Jerusalem. Using the method of form criticism to the extreme, Winter finds in the gospels not an account of a conflict between Jesus and his contemporaries, but an account of the Church in conflict with the synagogue at a considerably later period. When Christians and Jews came into conflict after the destruction of the Temple, Winter argues, the Church sought the good will of Rome to strengthen its position. Winter, like Lietzmann, avers that the Jewish authorities at the time of Jesus did have the right to inflict capital punishment and labels the gospel evidence about the first trial as untrustworthy. If the Sanhedrin sentenced Jesus to death, as they allegedly had the right to do, why did they not execute him?

Those Jewish scholars who have followed Winter have used other approaches to question this part of the Passion narrative. H. Cohn of the Israel Supreme Court, in his book *The Trial and Death of Jesus* (1971), defends Caiaphas and his father-in-law Annas as friends and not enemies of Jesus. He tries to remove their responsibility for the death of Jesus by asserting that they really strove to help Jesus and to save him from the wrath of the Roman authorities. Gaalyah Cornfeld does not support Cohn's view, but he states that "the Sanhedrin did not accuse [Jesus], but, on the contrary, tried to shield him from the high priest's charge." Cornfeld tries to justify this view of the Sanhedrin's friendly attitude towards Jesus with the Passion narrated by John.[15] According to Cornfeld, the Sanhedrin was not involved in any accusation against Jesus, nor did it accompany the priests of the Temple who led Jesus to Pilate. He notes that the evangelist John recorded neither any intervention by the Sanhedrin nor a trial before it. Instead, Jesus underwent an "informal inquiry."

The stipulation in the Mishnah against holding a trial on the evening

15 *The Historical Jesus, A Scholarly View of the Man and His World* (New York: Macmillan, 1982), p. 163.

of a Sabbath or a festival contradicts the gospel record of Jesus' trial at the Passover season. If a trial had been held then, a conviction would necessarily have waited until the day after the trial. Cornfeld uses this Mishnah regulation to throw doubt on the Synoptic account of Jesus' trial and conviction, which took place on the same day. He also cites the requirement that a trial in capital cases must be held "during the daytime and the verdict must also be readied during the daytime" (Sanh. 4:1). This contradicts Mark's account that Jesus was tried at night, "and as soon as it was morning the chief priests, with the elders and scribes, and the whole council held a consultation; and they bound Jesus and led him away and delivered him to Pilate" (Mk 15:1).

To put these arguments into perspective, we should note that the laws of the Mishnah were codified about two hundred years after the time of Jesus by the Pharisees, who were the only Jewish group of the first century to survivie the destruction of the Temple in 70 A.D. and the failure of the Bar Kochba revolt in 135. The Mishnah, therefore, contains the teachings of the Pharisees in the post-Temple period. There is no way of knowing whether the Mishnah reflects accurately the teaching of the Pharisees before the destruction of the Temple. We must remind ourselves that there was not a normative Judaism at the time of Jesus. Various groups and movements fought to promote their own vision of Judaism. Only under the guidance of the Pharisees did one view become a monolithic religious system in the later period, after 70. Moreover, the Sadducees, not the Pharisees, were Jesus' main opponents in Jerusalem, and Jesus was tried before a Sanhedrin in which the Sadducees predominated.

Some scholars have warned that the Mishnah contains legal material which originated only after the destruction of the Temple. It is almost impossible to know whether these "ideal laws" and precise procedures formulated in the Mishnah were applicable in the time of Jesus' trial. We know that Caiaphas and his ruling body considered Jesus a threat to their own interests, and that Caiaphas was willing to bring to an end Jesus' disturbing influence upon the people, to avoid the threat of destruction of the city by the Romans. Even if these regulations were in effect, the high priest might have considered the circumstances extraordinary enough to bend them.

The Passion according to John is more complex than Cornfeld seems to think. He built his argument on John's statement that Jesus was led first to Annas, who then "sent him bound to Caiaphas the high priest" (18:13-24) and that the trial before the council is not mentioned, although all three Synoptic Gospels record it (Mt 26:57-75, Mk 14:53-72, Lk 22:54-71). But we may counter this argument by noting that John did not need to narrate the trial, since he had already recorded the meeting of the Sanhedrin a few days before the Passover and Jesus' arrest, after Jesus raised Lazarus (Jn 11:45-53). The evangelist narrates that "many of the Jews" who had seen what Jesus did "believed in him." Some others, however, went to the "Pharisees and told them what Jesus had done. So the chief priests and the Pharisees gathered in council [the Sanhedrin] and said 'What are we to do? For this man performs many signs'" (Jn 11:45-47). After the discussion, which according to the gospel was not religious but political in nature ("If we let him go on thus, everyone will believe in him, and the Romans will come and destroy both our holy place and our nation" 11:48; "from that day on they took counsel how to put [Jesus] to death" 11:53). The evangelist did not repeat this in his passion narrative, because he wanted the reader to understand that the Sanhedrin had already plotted Jesus' death in connection with his public ministry.

Regarding the view that John does not implicate the Sanhedrin, we should also note that in Jn 18:28—"Then they led Jesus from the house of Caiaphas to the praetorium"—the word "they" seems to point to some members of the Sanhedrin. Later, the same people, "they," are described in the ensuing encounter with Pilate as "the Jews" (Jn 18:31, 38). This term, "the Jews," embraces much more than simply the chief priests. Raymond Brown has shown in his commentary *The Gospel According to John* (1966) that in some passages the fourth gospel speaks interchangeably of "the Jews" and of "the chief priests and the Pharisees." In Jn 18:3 "the chief priests and Pharisees" provide the police for Jesus' arrest, and in 18:12 they are "the police of the Jews." According to John 18:28-31, "they" or "the Jews" take Jesus to Pilate, while in Mk 15:1 this duty is performed by the members of the Sanhedrin. As we shall see, Brown also points out that in the usage of this gospel, the term "the Jews" often refers to the authorities in Jerusalem who are hostile to Jesus.

There is no doubt that the evangelist used this term to refer not only to the chief priests but also to "the Pharisees," the members of the ruling religious body.

Caiaphas' remark "that it is expedient...that one man should die for the people, and that the whole nation should not perish" (Jn 11:50) is a classical expression of "political expediency." We should not dismiss the fear with which the high priest and the council perceived political implications of Jesus' activity. The political risk made them even more determined to get rid of Jesus, as John made quite clear. The charges of blasphemy that played a crucial role in the Sanhedrin's condemnation of Jesus were recorded by John as well as by all the Synoptics (see Jn 5:17-18, 8:56-59, 10:25-31). Both political and religious factors are pivotal in John's gospel. The evangelist omits neither the Sanhedrin's supplication of Pilate nor the charge of blasphemy that is prominent in the Synoptic account of the trial.

The criticisms of Lietzmann and his followers have not remained unanswered.[16] A. N. Sherwin-White, a specialist in Roman history, argues vigorously and convincingly for the historicity and reliability of the trial accounts. He writes that only those states or cities that rendered particular service to the Roman state could rule their citizens un-restrictively as "free states" or "free cities."[17] Jerusalem was never considered a "free city." Consequently, while Jews were allowed to practice their religious beliefs, they were denied the right of capital punishment. In one specific case, however, the Sanhedrin had the right to execute even a Roman citizen—if he entered the Temple. A notice was posted at the entrance of the Temple: "No Gentile is to pass inside the wall round the Temple. If a man is caught doing so, it is his own fault, for death follows." This was a special arrangement between the Sanhedrin and the Romans, according to Josephus, which proves indirectly that the ruling religious authority in Jerusalem did not have the power to execute people in other cases.[18] Josephus wrote that James, the brother of the Lord, was

16 A good account and a selected bibliography of post-war discussion of the trial and passion of Jesus can be found in William Horbury, "The Passion Narratives and Historical Criticism," *Theology*, 75, 172, pp. 58-71.
17 A. N. Sherwin-White, *Roman Society and Roman Law in the New Testament* (Oxford: Clarendon Press, 1963), p. 36. The argument is developed in his article, "The Trial of Jesus," in D. E. Nineham and others, *Historicity and Chronology in the New Testament* (London: SPCK, 1965).
18 Josephus, *Jewish Wars*, VI.2.2, discussed in Sherwin-White, "The Trial of Jesus," pp. 107, 109.

executed illegally under the instigation of an extremist party within the Sanhedrin and without the approval of the Roman authorities. Sherwin-White adds that, like James, Stephen, the first martyr, seems to have been killed in a kind of lynching.[19] The Sanhedrin's lack of the power of life and death over its subjects did not mean that Jesus could not have been tried before this court, however. The Sanhedrin could condemn Jesus, but could not carry out the execution. The trial was held so that the Sanhedrin might announce that Jesus was a blasphemer, and that according to the law he must die. The Jewish religious authorities needed the trial to change the attitude of the people toward Jesus.

Sherwin-White stresses that there is nothing in the narratives of the passion or in the procedures described which makes them improbable according to Roman practice. He finds that the trial before Pilate and his final acceptance of the verdict under pressure are convincingly portrayed by John in his chapters on the trials and crucifixion (Jn 18-19).[20] Jesus underwent two trials, and at both he was found guilty. As a historian, Sherwin-White considers the gospels and the Acts to be exceptionally reliable sources and wonders why some New Testament scholars fail to recognize this.[21] In a more recent study, "The Historicity of the Sanhedrin Trial," E. Bammel undermines Lietzmann's and Winter's assertions regarding the right of the Sanhedrin to capital punishment by expressing the probability that "the Jews could at that time pass capital sentences, but were prevented from executing them."[22]

V

The Gospel of John has been called more anti-Jewish than any of the

19 *Ibid.*, 107ff.
20 *Roman Society and Roman Law*, pp. 46-47.
21 F. F. Bruce made a similar comment about the evidence for the New Testament writings, which is in his view "so much greater than the evidence for many writings of classical authors, the authenticity of which no one dreams of questioning…It is a curious fact that historians have often been much readier to trust the New Testament records than have many theologians." In a footnote he adds: "Historians like W. M. Ramsay, Ed Meyer, and A. T. Olmstead have protested vigorously against the excessive skepticism of some theologians in dealing with the historical writings of the New Testament" (*The New Testament Documents: Are They Reliable?* [Grand Rapids: Eerdmans, 1965], p. 15).
22 Published in E. Bammel (ed.), *The Trial of Jesus* (London: SCM Press, 1970), pp. 59-63. See also James Price, *The New Testament, Its History and Theology* (New York: Macmillan, 1987), p. 248, n. 89.

other gospels. This tendency, it has been claimed, accompanies John's effort to exonerate Pilate and to put the main responsibility for the death of Jesus upon the Jews. Some critics claim that the Jewish responsibility increases and Roman guilt decreases as one progresses from the earliest gospel (Mark) to the latest (John). Such an assertion is hardly supported by the evidence from the gospel itself.

John in particular distinguishes between the Jewish people and their religious authorities. John's four uses of the term "Jews" are outlined in modern commentaries. The first designates an ethnic national and religious group. Jesus told the Samaritan woman: "You worship what you do not know; we worship what we know, for salvation is from the Jews." Here the term is obviously used in a positive sense. Second, when the evangelist refers to the Jewish feasts, he writes "the Passover of the Jews was at hand" (Jn 2:13), or "now the Jews' feast of Tabernacles was at hand" (7:2). Again the term is used in an appreciative sense. Third, in the later chapters, the term "the Jews" may refer to those who believed in Jesus as well as to those who rejected him (11:45-46). But probably the fourth use is the most important, where, in the words of Raymond Brown, "the Jews" means "almost a technical title for the religious authorities, particularly those in Jerusalem, who [were] hostile to Jesus." The Gospel of John cannot be considered an anti-Semitic document on the basis of this usage alone. "The evangelist is condemning not race or people but opposition to Jesus," according to Brown.[23] In their attitude toward Jesus, the Jews were divided. There were those who were attracted to him, for "no man ever spoke like this man" (Jn 7:46ff; 10:19-21) and many of the Jews "believed in him" (Jn 11:45; 12:42). There was a division even among the Pharisees (Jn 9:13-16), and Nicodemus was a friendly voice in the Sanhedrin (Jn 7:50).[24]

The evangelist Luke distinguishes between the religious ruling authorities and the Jewish people themselves. Luke 22-23 brings out the contrast between how Jesus was mocked and beaten by "the men who were holding" him (22:63) and how, on the way to Golgotha, "a great multitude of people" followed him, along with women "who bewailed and lamented him" (Lk 23:27). When they reached the place of crucifix-

23 R. Brown, *The Gospel According to John* (New York: Doubleday, 1966), v. I, p. lxxii.
24 For other references in John, see W. Horbury, "Passion Narratives," p. 65.

ion, "the people stood by, watching; but the rulers scoffed at him, saying, 'He saved others; let him save himself, if he is the Christ of God, his Chosen One!' The soldiers also mocked him" (Lk 23:35-36). And when Jesus "breathed his last," then "all the multitude who assembled to see the sight, when they saw what had taken place, returned home beating their breasts. And all his acquaintances and the women who had followed him from Galilee stood at a distance and saw these things" (Lk 23:48-49).

The best known and most prominent Jewish New Testament scholar, David Flusser, has observed that in this passage the multitude of the Jewish people was with Jesus, and that the authorities were afraid to arrest him, for "they feared the people" (Lk 20:19); he adds that "it is therefore certain that the same Jewish people are three times referred to as sympathizing with Jesus."[25] Like John, Luke clearly distinguishes between "the rulers" and "the people," between those who showed hostility and those who displayed friendly concern.

Next we turn to Rome's responsibility for these events. John's Passion narrative (19:4, 6-7, 11f, 16) appears to lessen Rome's responsibility and underline that of the Jewish authorities. The pressure of "the Jews" upon the hesitant and fearful Pilate is the determining factor in this account of the condemnation of Jesus. But when we compare what the fourth evangelist writes about the relative responsibility of Romans and Jews for the death of Jesus with the earliest Jewish-Christian and Rabbinic sources, we cannot ascribe John's picture of the trial either to increasing hostility toward Jews in Christian circles or to the author's conscious effort to distort the facts and exonerate the Romans.

The earliest extant written Christian evidence regarding the responsibility for the death of Jesus is in 1 Thessalonians, written around 50, that is, before the gospels, where Paul mentions only "the Jews" as being responsible for the death of Jesus (1 Th 2:14-15). The earliest Rabbinic reference to the death of Jesus comes from the *Tannaim*, the rabbis of the second century who preserved the Jewish tradition codified in the Mishnah around 200 A.D. In the tractate Sanhedrin (43a), already discussed in the chapter on the Jewish and Roman evidence for Jesus, we again find, as in Paul, no reference to Roman participation in the

25 David Flusser, "The Crucified One and the Jews," *Immanuel*, v. 7 (1977), pp. 25-37.

sentencing of Jesus for "sorcery and leading Israel astray." The intensity of Paul's accusation against the Jews may be explained in part by his suffering at the hands of the synagogue authorities. The concern of the rabbis of the second century was "to explicate Jewish law, for which purpose the Romans would be irrelevant."[26] On the other hand, when the Roman historian Tacitus wrote (ca.115) that Christ "was executed by sentence of the procurator Pontius Pilate in the reign of Tiberius,"[27] he did not mention the role of the Jewish authorities, considering it irrelevant.

It is not an "anti-Jewish" attitude that John expresses in his passion narrative, but rather his sensitivity as a Jew to the failures of the religious leaders of his own people. His criticism of them never overshadowed his awareness of the responsibility of the Roman sovereign authority. His picture of Pilate is very unflattering. It is the image of a weak man, who has in mind only his own interest and position and who is afraid to do anything that could endanger his future. John placed emphasis on the image of Pilate as a man who could be intimidated. According to Josephus,[28] John's portrait of Pilate is accurate. Neither John nor the other evangelists exonerated the Romans. In all four Passion accounts the responsibility is shared by the religious authorities of Judaism and by the authority of the Roman occupying power, and it was Pilate who pronounced the sentence of death. This summary statement of the responsibility in the gospels is in accord with the primitive Christian proclamation. In his sermon on the first Pentecost, Peter told the "men of Israel" that they had used "lawless men" (heathens or Gentiles) to crucify Jesus (Acts 2:23). Josephus took the same point of view that "Pilate, at the suggestion of the principal men amongst us" condemned Jesus to the cross (*Antiquities* XVIII, 63f). The convergence of the earliest Christian and Jewish evidence points to the mutual complicity of Jewish and Roman authorities in the death of Jesus.

The Romans, of course, bore the primary responsibility for the death of Jesus. There is no suggestion to the contrary in any of the passion gospels. They alone had the right to inflict capital punishment. The

26 F. F. Bruce, *Jesus and Christian Origins Outside the New Testament* (Grand Rapids: Eerdmans, 1974), p. 57.
27 *Annals*, XV, 44.
28 *Antiquities*, XVIII.III.1; B.J.IX.2-3.

Sanhedrin had lost this authority most probably after the death of Herod the Great and the very unsuccessful brief rule of his son Archelaus in Judaea, about twenty-five years before the crucifixion. Caiaphas, with at least some of the members of the Sanhedrin, cooperated with the Romans in order to protect the privileges that remained to them, particularly those which applied to the Temple. The Temple was not simply a religious center but constituted "an economic unit." At the time of Christ, the Temple's economic activities were considerable. A great number of animals had to be provided for sacrifice. About 7000 priests and Levites were supported by the Temple's activities, as were scribes, incense makers, bakers, the Temple security police, and so on. This was a powerful pressure group: at any time the Temple authorities could organize their own crowd to support their own policies. We should also not forget the merchants and traders whose livelihood depended upon the Temple's purchases, nor the upper levels of the priestly families who accumulated enormous wealth and exploited the others under their supervision.[29] All this was known to the military authorities in Palestine, but they were tolerant toward these leading Temple families who supported and cooperated with the Roman rulers. Caiaphas, the high priest at the time of the crucifixion, held this office for eighteen years (18-36 A.D.). In those turbulent times, this was an unusually long period of service in this post. Only when Pilate left Jerusalem did Caiaphas lose this position. Cornfeld suggests that the reason for Caiaphas' longevity in this post lies in his personality: "[he] knew how to act in complete accord with the Roman governors of Tiberius' reign." During all these years of holding the office of high priest, Caiaphas presided over the Sanhedrin and undoubtedly was capable of exercising considerable influence over it. The Sanhedrin "certainly maintained the right to direct the Temple affairs," and determined policy in the religious and ritual life of the Jewish people.[30] Caiaphas could not have dealt on his own with the case

29 G. Cornfeld, *The Historical Jesus*, pp. 117f.
30 Jacob Neusner, *Judaism in the Beginning of Christianity* (Philadelphia: Fortress Press, 1984), p. 31. In the same context, Neusner writes that the Sanhedrin "acted with a measure of freedom to determine internal policy in religion, ritual, cult, and local law. The Sanhedrin lost authority to inflict capital punishment, it is generally assumed, shortly after Judea become a part of the Syrian provincial administration. Whether, in fact, it had administered the death penalty in Herod's reign is not entirely clear. The court certainly maintained the right to direct Temple affairs" (pp. 30-31).

of Jesus of Nazareth. Since Jesus had such a large following in Jerusalem, Caiaphas needed the support of the council, and, according to the gospels, he received it.

Modern critics have not succeeded in freeing the Sanhedrin from their responsibility for Jesus' death. From what we know of Jewish institutions, movements and Roman power at the time of Jesus, we see no justification for a radical reinterpretation of the gospel record, of the role of the high priest and of the Sanhedrin in the trial of Jesus. The modern tendency to exonerate even Caiaphas rejects completely the earliest Christian and Rabbinic traditions. Several factors lie behind these efforts. In part, they are due to the anachronistic application of Mishnaic laws to the trial of Jesus. In part, they represent a reaction to the unfortunate fact that the passion narrative, misunderstood and misrepresented, often inspired anti-Semitic violence against Jews in some Christian communities. Above all, they cannot be separated from the impact of the tragic experience of European Jews during the Second World War. Christian-Jewish relations cannot benefit from radical reinterpretations and distortions of the gospel accounts, but only from a dispassionate analysis of the gospel evidence and of the history of the time. They will benefit as well from the knowledge that the gospels are free from any form of anti-Semitism, as it is presently understood, and that on the basis of the gospel passion narratives, it is perverse to make a modern Jew or Jews of any period, for that matter, guilty of Jesus' death. They do not bear responsibility for the acts of Caiaphas and of the Sanhedrin. Any other conclusion, whether on historical or theological grounds, is absurd. The sequence of events in the gospels and the gospels' own interpretation of these events stand as the eternal witnesses to this truth.

9

Forging of the Canon

When the gospels were written, they did not incorporate all that was known about Jesus (Jn 20:30). They drew from a rich oral tradition which was passed on by the apostles and other eyewitnesses. The oral tradition continued to possess authority equal to that of the written gospels into the middle of the second century, and both oral and written traditions coexisted during that time.

In the late first or early second century there appeared a short Syrian document called the *Didache*, a treatise on Church practice and rules for the conduct of Christian communities. It contains many references, as we should expect, to the Gospel of Matthew, which took its final form in Syria. The treatise begins: "There are two ways, one of life and one of death; and between the two ways there is a great difference." Several echoes of the Sermon on the Mount follow: "Bless those who curse you," and "pray for your enemies" (*Did* 1.3); "If someone strikes you on the right cheek, turn to him the other one, and you will be perfect" (*Did* 1.4); and "Give to everyone who begs from you, and ask for no return" (*Did* 1.5). Did the author of the *Didache* have the written text of Matthew in front of him, or did he rely on parallel oral traditions? The first part of this treatise most probably does not depend on the written gospel, but on the author's memory of the Sermon. In the latter part, *Didache* 11-16, where other texts from Matthew appear, the author may have relied on the written text.

The early Christian fathers also drew from both oral and written gospel tradition. Ignatius of Antioch (martyred, ca. 110) knew material from two or three gospels, but whether it came from the written gospels or from oral tradition is difficult to ascertain. He may have written either from his memory of what he had heard from those who were in touch with the disciples of the apostles, or from his memory of the gospels which he had read.[1] Ignatius seems to have been particularly familiar with the gospels of Matthew and John. Justin the Martyr (ca. 100-165)

1 For a discussion of these possibilities, see Robert M. Grant, *Formation of the New Testament* (New York: Harper & Row, 1965), pp. 100-102.

both quoted from the written gospel and drew from the oral tradition. In his *Dialogue with Trypho* (47:5), he quoted Jesus as saying: "In what I find you, in this will I judge you." This particular saying does not exist in any of our four gospels and therefore was presumably derived from oral tradition. Justin ascribed to Jesus another saying not found in the canonical gospels: "There will be dissensions and squabbles" (*Dial* 35:3). The same saying is recorded in *Syr. Didasc.* VI,5; in the *Ps. Clem. Hom.* II,17 and XVI,21; and in the Coptic *Gospel of Thomas*, logion 16. These sources are independent of each other.[2] Probably, this saying referred to dissensions that accompany the work of false prophets (Mt 24, Mk 13).

Although Christian writers at the beginning of the second century considered oral tradition to be as authoritative as the written tradition, during the course of that century they tended increasingly to turn to the written gospel accounts. This subtle change was due to the spread of the Christian movement in the Hellenistic world, to the rise of heretical literature, and to the first tendencies toward creating a New Testament canon (as reflected in 2 Pet 3:15f). Formation of the canon became a major concern in the second century.

I

In addition to the gospels, which were written in the first century, a number of books written in the second century purports to tell of the life and teaching of Jesus. Most of these apocryphal gospels were written either to fill narrative gaps in the canonical gospels, often supplying imaginative material for this purpose, or to promote Gnostic teachings.

The apocryphal infancy gospels attempt to supply information about the childhood of Jesus lacking in the earlier gospels. *The Infancy of the Lord Jesus*, known also as the *Infancy Story of Thomas*, written in the second century, contains a story about the five-year old Jesus playing by a brook. "He made soft clay and fashioned from it twelve sparrows. And it was the sabbath when he did this." When a certain Jew complained to Joseph that Jesus was profaning the Sabbath, and after Joseph rebuked

2 J. Jeremias collected and analyzed those sayings of Jesus found outside the canonical gospels in *Unknown Sayings of Jesus* (London: SPCK Press, 1957). A selection of eleven sayings is furnished by the same author in "Isolated Sayings of Jesus," in Edgar Hennecke, *New Testament Apocrypha* (Philadelphia: Westminster Press, 1963), v. I, pp. 85-90.

him, the child Jesus clapped his hands and cried to the sparrows, "Off with you!", and the soft clay sparrows "went away chirping." Another story from this gospel tells how a child, who was playing with the young Jesus, fell from a window on the upper story of a house and died. The parents of the dead child accused Jesus of pushing the boy down. Jesus defended himself, but the parents insisted in their accusation. Then Jesus threw himself down by the body of the dead child, called him by his name and said, "Arise and tell me, did I throw you down?" The child came to life again and said, "No, Lord, you did not throw me down but raised me up."[3]

In this apocryphal infancy gospel, Jesus is not presented as the real child he was,[4] and his image in this literature has almost nothing to do with the way he is presented in Matthew's and Luke's infancy narratives. As a little child, he allegedly performed many wonders, according to the *Infancy Story of Thomas.* Those who believed that Jesus performed such miracles as a child might well have wondered why Jesus did not change stones into bread or throw himself from the pinnacle of the Temple (Mt 4, Lk 4), since the miracles which the devil demanded of Jesus during his temptation were precisely this kind of miracle. According to the apocryphal literature, Jesus displayed his divine power before the eyes of many, performing miraculous works just because he was challenged to do them.[5]

In these accounts Jesus has no human nature. In the apocryphal *Acts of John* (93), the apostle John tells his brethren that sometimes, when he would try to touch Jesus, he would have the sensation that he was laying hold of a material body, but at other times he would feel that the body of Jesus was not material but immaterial, as if it did not exist. "And oftentimes when I walked with him, I desired to see the print of his foot, whether it appeared on the earth; for I saw him as it were lifting himself up from the earth, and I never saw [a footprint]."[6]

3 For similar types of stories and miracles, see *The Account of Thomas the Israelite Philosopher Concerning the Childhood of the Lord,* in E. Hennecke, pp. 392-399. This infancy gospel is not related to the Gnostic *Gospel of Thomas.*
4 E. Hennecke, pp. 81-84.
5 See our article "Christ's Temptation in the Apocryphal Gospels and Acts," *St. Vladimir's Theological Quarterly,* 5:4 (1961), pp. 3-9.
6 Montague Rhodes James, *The Apocryphal New Testament* (Oxford: Clarendon Press, 1926), pp. 252-253. The original meaning of the word ἀπόκρυφος is "hidden." Irenaeus connected the word with "forged," and Tertullian with "false."

Much apocryphal literature replaced the historical incarnation ("The Word became flesh and dwelt among us…" Jn 1:14) with a non-historical "docetic" incarnation. The Word of God did not really become a human being, according to these apocryphal writers, but somehow entered our human existence without identifying himself with it. He only *appeared* ("appear" or "seem" is the meaning of the word "docetic") to be human, but in reality he was nothing of the kind. These apocryphal stories about Jesus are similar to the stories about the god Krishna in Hinduism, who is an *avatar* (descendent) of the Supreme God Vishnu.[7]

Some apocryphal gospels are difficult to characterize, for only fragments of them exist. Often these fragments are similar to material in the Synoptic Gospels. It is more probable that the authors of these apocryphal gospels were acquainted with the canonical gospels and drew upon them, than that they drew upon the oral tradition behind the gospels. The *Gospel of Peter*, for example, written around the middle of the second century, seems to depend upon the canonical gospels, although the events described in it are divorced from the Synoptic historical and geographical context. The main difference between this gospel and those of the Church, however, is in its apologetic tone. The testimony to Christ, which is the main characteristic of the four canonical gospels, is replaced by "direct proof of truth."[8] The New Testament books lack any description of the actual resurrection, but the *Gospel of Peter* contains this detailed account:

> Now in the night in which the Lord's day dawned, when the soldiers, two by two in every watch, were keeping guard, there rang out a loud voice in heaven, and they saw the heavens opened and two men came down from there in a great brightness and drew nigh to the sepulchre. That stone which had been laid against the entrance to the sepulchre started of itself to roll and gave way to the side, and the sepulchre was opened, and both the young men entered in…They saw again three men come out from the sepulchre, and two of them sustaining

7 Avatar "represents what the 'incarnation' would have been if it had followed logic, if the divine answer to the mystical aspirations of man were predictable. The disconcerting figure of the Crucified Christ reveals what the incarnation is when God makes it a reality" (Jacques-Albert Cuttat, *The Encounter of Religions* [New York: Declee Co., 1960], p. 58). The apocryphal gospels and Acts, which are products of human imagination and legend-making, provide good examples of what a docetic "incarnation" is.

8 E. Hennecke, p. 81. The *Protoevangelium* of James, written in the second century, displays a very free use of material contained in the infancy gospels of Matthew and Luke while using at the same time oral tradition, recounted in this writing, e.g., the birth of Jesus in a cave in Bethlehem. The *Protoevangelium* had considerable influence on the development of the Mary cult both in the East and the West.

the other, and a cross following them, and the heads of the two reaching to heaven, but that of him who was led of them by the hand overpassing the heavens. And they heard a voice out of the heavens crying, "Thou has preached to them that sleep," and from the cross there was heard the answer, "Yea."[9]

An account such as this was probably used for apologetic purposes, and to satisfy the people's curiosity.

II

When we read the apocryphal gospels after the New Testament books, we find ourselves in a completely new world full of wonders and legends. The apocryphal gospels markedly differ in literary form from the canonical gospels. The *Infancy Story of Thomas* is a poor source for a historical reconstruction of Jesus' childhood. These gospels are entertaining, however, and provide us with knowledge of the thoughts and hopes of some second-century Christians. We learn from them not about Jesus but about their audience, what they admired and what they thought.[10] Jerome sternly criticized apocryphal literature, yet he thought that some "gold" might be found in it.

A study of the Gnostic *Gospel of Thomas* for instance, may lead us to a better understanding of the way in which Jesus' sayings were transmitted, as well as of their editing in the light of Gnostic teachings. The *Gospel of Thomas* (not related to the *Infancy Story of Thomas*) was written originally in Greek, and a Greek version was known in Egypt in the second century. A fourth-century Coptic version, translated from Greek, was discovered in 1945 among other Gnostic writings at Nag Hammadi in Egypt. It consists solely of 114 sayings of Jesus, including some parables. This document has a Gnostic orientation. Some interpreters are of the opinion that the sayings of this Nag Hammadi document were based upon the Synoptic Gospels or their sources, which were then "edited in the light of gnostic beliefs."[11] A growing number of scholars argue that the *Gospel of Thomas* offers a Gnostic interpretation of Jesus' sayings, without knowledge of the New Testament gospels. *Thomas* should be considered an independent witness, which contains sayings

9 E. Hennecke, *Apocrypha,*pp. 185-186.
10 M. R. James, *The Apocryphal New Testament,* p. xiii.
11 C.K. Barrett, *The New Testament Background: Selected Documents,* revised and expanded edition (San Francisco: Harper & Row, 1987), p. 112.

that have parallels in the Synoptics, and not as "an eclectic excerpt" from them.[12]

Due to a lack of historical interest among the Gnostics, the *Gospel of Thomas* has neither a historical framework nor historical narratives. These omissions are due first of all to the fact that this gospel is a collection of sayings, a literary genre which particularly corresponds to Gnostic teaching. The book opens with the claim: "These are the secret sayings which the living Jesus spoke and which Didymos Judas Thomas wrote down," and the first saying reads: "And he said, 'Whoever finds the interpretation of these sayings will not experience death'." "The living Jesus" (the Risen Christ) speaks "the secret sayings." These opening statements express the Gnostic belief that after his resurrection, Christ was engaged in instructing chosen ones or a small group of his followers.[13]

Some of Jesus' sayings, as recorded in the Synoptics, were interpreted contrarily by the Gnostics. According to the Gospel of Matthew, Jesus said: "When you give alms, sound no trumpet before you" (6:2); and "When you pray, you must not be like the hypocrites" (6:5); and "When you fast, do not look dismal" (6:16). Jesus' use of "when" rather than "if" shows that he expected his followers to give alms, to pray, and to fast, and that he took these activities for granted. In the Gnostic *Gospel of Thomas*, when the disciples ask Jesus whether he wants them to fast, pray, and give alms, Jesus answers: "If you fast, you will give rise to sin for yourselves; and if you pray, you will be condemned; and if you give alms, you will do harm to your spirits" (Saying 14). When he is asked by his followers to pray and to fast, he answers: "What is the sin that I have committed, or wherein have I been defeated? But when the bridegroom leaves the bridal chamber, then let them fast and pray" (Saying 104). Since Gnostics believed that they never left the bridal chamber, they felt no need to fast or to pray.[14]

The Gnostic rejection of the world is reflected in Saying 56: "Jesus said, 'Whoever has come to understand the world has found (only) a corpse, and

12 James M. Robinson, ed., *The Nag Hammadi Library*, revised edition (San Francisco: Harper & Row, 1988). "Introduction to The Gospel of Thomas," by Helmut Koester, pp. 124-125, and the text of the gospel, pp. 126-138.
13 See the English translation of the *Gospel of Thomas*, with a commentary by Robert M. Grant and David Noel Freedman, in *The Secret Sayings of Jesus: The Gnostic Gospel of Thomas* (New York: Doubleday, 1960), pp. 115f.
14 *Ibid.*, p. 185.

whoever has found a corpse is superior to the world'." When his disciples ask: "When will you become revealed to us and when shall we see you?", Jesus speaks about ridding oneself of everything: "When you disrobe without being ashamed and take up your garments and place them under your feet like little children and tread on them, then [will you see] the son of the living one, and you will not be afraid." Gnostics could achieve their salvation only by denigrating everything that belonged to the world.

Were women considered worthy of this new life? They were, according to the Jesus of the *Gospel of Thomas*, but only on condition that they become male: "I myself shall lead her in order to make her male, so that she too may become a living spirit resembling you males. For every woman who will make herself male will enter the Kingdom of Heaven" (Saying 114). With reference to this saying, C. K. Barret observese that "the Gnostic [saw] the abolition of sexual distinction as the desirable end of the divine process, but in a very different way from Paul's 'neither male nor female'."[15] In Galatians and 1 Corinthians, Paul wrote specifically about the distinction between the sexes, as well as about their equality.

Some sayings have close parallels in the New Testament gospels. For example: "Jesus said, 'Whoever does not hate his father and his mother cannot become a disciple to me. And whoever does not hate his brothers and sisters and take up his cross in my way will not be worthy of me'" (Saying 55; Mt 10:37-38). This saying and others like it have given new impetus to the search for the historical Jesus. Did the author of the *Gospel of Thomas* derive some of his sayings, such as Saying 55, from the oral tradition, which started immediately after the death and resurrection of Jesus; or did he use a source similar to the hypothetical Q, supposedly used by Matthew and Luke?

Of special importance to New Testament scholars engaged in "Jesus research" is Saying 65: the parable of the Wicked Tenants, found also in Mk 12:1-12, Mt 21:33-46 and Lk 20:9-19. If Matthew and Luke used Mark, then two independent witnesses to this parable exist: the Gospel of Mark and the *Gospel of Thomas*. Let us compare them.

Saying 65 reads as follows:

15 C. K. Barrett, *Background,*p. 114.

He said, "There was a good man who owned a vineyard. He leased it to tenant farmers so that they might work it and he might collect the produce from them. He sent his servant so that the tenants might give him the produce of the vineyard. They seized his servant and beat him, all but killing him. The servant went back and told his master. The master said, 'Perhaps he did not recognize them.' He sent another servant. The tenants beat this one as well. Then the owner sent his son and said, 'Perhaps they will show respect to my son.' Because the tenants knew that it was he who was the heir to the vineyard, they seized him and killed him. Let him who has ears hear."

The structure of the parable in the *Gospel of Thomas* is more straight-forward than it is in Mark: first one servant comes, then another, and finally the son. It is also less developed than it is in Mk 12:1-9. Does this imply that Saying 65 is closer to the original than is Mark's version? Which one of them came from Jesus himself?[16] The answer to these questions cannot be drawn from the form of the parable, but only from an analysis of its key verse, to which other parts of the story lead and contribute its meaning. The parable's distinct triadic form, as it is reflected in the *Gospel of Thomas*, could have come from Jesus. However, its conclusion leads the hearer away from the cross. Hence we have the importance of the key verse in both versions.

In Mark, the key verse is: "And they took him and killed him, and cast him out of the vineyard" (Mk 12:8). In the *Gospel of Thomas* it reads: "They seized him and killed him." Mark used the words "cast him out of the vineyard" to show that Jesus considered his death "the ultimate disgrace" inflicted on the Son by the wicked tenants. By omitting these words, the author of the *Gospel of Thomas* reduced considerably the significance of Jesus' passion.[17] Mark's evidence, therefore, most proba-bly went back to Jesus himself, whereas dropping a part of the saying in the *Gospel of Thomas* reflects the difficulty which the Gnostics experi-enced in accepting the passion of Jesus.

The influence of Gnostic beliefs upon the transmission of Jesus' sayings and parables can be detected in many other sayings of Thomas. Omission of certain words, or introduction of additional material into the text, can fundamentally change the meaning and emphasis of the

16 For this comparison of the parables, I am indebted to James H. Charlesworth, *Jesus Within Judaism—New Light from Exciting Archaeological Discoveries* (New York: Doubleday, 1988), pp. 142ff.
17 *Ibid.*, pp. 142, 148.

story. Such is the case with the Lucan parable of the lost sheep (Lk 15:4-6). In the *Gospel of Thomas* the parable runs as follows:

> Jesus said, "The Kingdom is like a shepherd who had a hundred sheep. One of them, the largest, went astray. He left the ninety-nine and looked for that one until he found it. When he had gone to such trouble, he said to the sheep, 'I care for you more than the ninety-nine'" (saying 107).

Luke did not say that the one which was lost was "the largest," nor did he report that Jesus said to the sheep: "I care for you more than the ninety-nine." According to Luke's parable, the shepherd put the sheep on his shoulders and rejoiced, and when he came home he said to his friends, "Rejoice with me, for I have found my sheep which was lost" (Lk 15:6). In the Gnostic version, the lost sheep represents the Gnostic, or the kingdom which the Gnostic is looking for.[18] The parable, it appears, was reinterpreted by the Gnostics.

III

In addition to the *Gospel of Thomas*, several other Gnostic gospels were discovered at Nag Hammadi: *The Gospel of Truth, The Gospel of Philip, The Gospel of the Egyptians,* and *The Gospel of Mary.* What is their value as sources of knowledge about Jesus' public ministry?

The *Gospel of Truth* is a Gnostic text oriented towards Valentinianism. Some believe that Valentinus, a second-century Christian Gnostic, wrote it himself. He was known to the second-century father Irenaeus, who characterized Valentinus' views as "inconsistent," and accused him of adopting "the principles of the so-called Gnostic heresy" (*Adv. Haer.,* 3.11.9). The *Gospel of Truth* has nothing in common with the four canonical gospels. Its literary form is not that of a gospel, but that of a Christian Gnostic homily or meditation.[19] It lacks any historical account of Jesus. The Christian material in it is so transformed by Gnosticism, that it is almost beyond recognition. There is, however, one reference to the death of Jesus: "He was nailed to a tree; he published the edict of the Father on the cross" (20:25).

The *Gospel of Philip,* also a product of the Valentinian school, contains sayings of Jesus, followed by interpretations, as well as several

18 R. Grant and D. N. Freedman, *Secret Sayings,* p. 186.
19 J. M. Robinson, *Nag Hammad. Library, p. 38.*

sayings ascribed to Jesus but obviously Gnostic.[20] From the first group we may cite the following sayings as examples. First: "And the Lord [would] not have said, 'My [father who is in] heaven' (Mt 16:17) unless [he] had had another father, but he would have said simply '[My father]'" (55,33-35). Second: "He said, 'Go into your (sing.) chamber and shut the door behind you, and pray to your father who is in secret' (Mt 6:6), the one who is within them all. But that which is within them all is the fullness. Beyond it there is nothing else within it. This is that of which they say, 'That which is above them'" (68, 10-15). Third: "The word said, 'If you (pl.) know the truth, the truth will make you free' (Jn 8:32). Ignorance is a slave. Knowledge is freedom. If we know the truth, we shall find the fruits of the truth within us. If we are joined to it, it will bring our fulfillment" (84, 9-10). These are examples of canonical sayings colored by Gnostic interpretation. They are esoteric and were probably meant for the elect, the true Gnostics.

The Gnostic Gospels, particularly the *Gospel of Truth* and the *Gospel of Philip*, are valuable sources of information about the highly developed teachings of Christian Gnostics and about their distortions of early Christian teachings. They contain the teachings of Valentinus on theology, cosmology, anthropology and morality. The *Gospel of Truth*, in particular, reflects the basic religious experience of the Gnostics. In Gnosticism, the world was evil, created not by the "highest God" but by lower powers (demiurges), and salvation from it came through γνῶσις, ("knowledge"), or through an awareness that man's imprisoned spirit belongs not to this world but to the source of all being. The Gnostics' religion was rooted in their uncompromising contempt for and hostility toward earthly ties. Hostility to the world determined the Gnostic morality.[21]

The Gnostic attitude toward marriage typifies this mindset. Not all Gnostic groups feared that marriage ties would prevent one from attaining the truth. To Valentinus, marriage had value, but only for the pneumatic, the Gnostic, who was already saved. But those "from the world" who were united with women could not know the truth. The *Gospel of Philip* mirrors this teaching, making a distinction between "the

20 *Ibid.*, p. 139.
21 See Hans Jonas, *The Gnostic Religion*, second edition (Boston: Beacon Press, 1985), on Gnostic theology, cosmology, anthropology, eschatology and morality (pp. 42-47).

marriage of defilement" and "the undefiled marriage," which is "not fleshly but pure. It belongs not to desire but to the will. It belongs not to the darkness or the night but to the day and light" (82:4-10). Gnostics regarded themselves as "free men" who were tied to the world neither by fear nor by love, whose γνῶσις enabled them neither to "fear the flesh nor love it. If you (sg.) fear it, it will gain mastery over you. If you love it, it will swallow and paralyze you" (66:1-6).[22]

It is even less appropriate to apply the term "gospel" to *The Gospel of the Egyptians* and *The Gospel of Mary*, to consider them as sources for the life and teaching of Jesus. *The Gospel of the Egyptians* pertains to the life of Seth, not of Jesus. According to this gospel, Seth, a heavenly being, emanated from the Supreme God (or "the Great Invisible Spirit") and appeared on earth through a series of heavenly powers; and he was "the son of the incorruptible man Adamas."[23] If this tract is not significant to research into the origins of Christianity, it is valuable for its information on the origins of Gnosticism. Together with a few other documents discovered at Nag Hammadi, it has been used as evidence that Gnosticism was not simply a Christian heresy, but was originally an independent movement, which first emerged in the Hellenistic world among "syncretistic Jews."[24] This tract exercised great influence in the second

22 Robinson, pp. 140, 149, 158.
23 *Ibid.*, p. 208.
24 On the origins of Gnosticism see the essays in Charles W. Hedrick and Robert Hodgson, eds. *Nag Hammadi, Gnosticism, and Early Christianity* (Peabody, MA: Hendrickson, 1986). We should look for the origins of Gnosticism in the context of radical Judaism, in "the frustration of Jewish apocalyptic movements," in the despair of man's life in this world, which is full of evil, and in the challenge to and questioning of God's character and power by the existence of evil. The library discovered at Nag Hammadi may enable us to discover the secret of the origins of this movement, for Gnosticism was not simply a Christian heresy, as had been thought until the end of the nineteenth century (pp. 1-11). It has been frequently and justly noted that the major emphasis in Gnosticism is salvation through secret knowledge (γνῶσις), which is only for the elect. Now scholars agree that this type of salvation was already suggested in Jewish apocalyptic literature. The author of I Enoch, for example, ends his treatise with the following words: "Here ends the revelation of the secrets of Enoch" (I En. 108:15) and the author of 4 Ezra tells us that Ezra received secret knowledge (8:62; 14:24, 26, 46). J. H. Charlesworth concludes that in these books we encounter "many ideas later developed by the Gnostics" (pp. 77ff).

H. Jonas writes: "The violently anti-Jewish bias of the more prominent Gnostic systems is by itself not incompatible with Jewish heretical origin at some distance. Independently, however, of who the first Gnostics were and what the main religious traditions drawn into the movement and suffering arbitrary reinterpretation at its hand, the movement itself transcended ethnic and denominational boundaries, and its spiritual principle was new" (pp. 33f).

century. *The Gospel of the Egyptians* may originally have been a non-Christian Gnostic text, later appropriated by a Christian Gnostic group, who linked some aspects of the story of Jesus as Savior (depicting him as a mythic figure of heavenly origin, who comes into the world and performs the work of salvation) to that of Seth. This change of orientation occurred "through a sometimes extremely thin veneer of Christianizing."[25]

The Gospel of Mary Magdalene, which is just a fragment, starts with a dialogue between the risen Christ and his disciples. After Christ departs, the disciples are discouraged and they weep. Mary Magdalene then appears and exhorts them: "Do not grieve nor be irresolute, for his grace will be entirely with you and will protect you. But rather let us praise his greatness, for he has prepared us and made us into men" (9:15-20). Then Peter addresses Mary: "Sister, we know that the Savior loved you more than the rest of women. Tell us the words of the Savior which you remember—which you know (but) we do not, nor have we heard them." Mary then describes a special revelation that she received from Jesus, a gnostic myth of the soul's ascent to the realm of "silence" (17:1-5). When Mary finishes, Andrew and Peter express their doubts: "Did he really speak with a woman without our knowledge (and) not openly?" (17:10-20).

In its literary form this text is a dialogue. The confrontation between Mary and Peter and Andrew, at the end of Mary's description of the vision, undoubtedly reflects the confrontation between the "new revelation" (Gnosticism) given to Mary and the "old institutionalized religion" (orthodoxy) personified by Peter and Andrew.[26] The text, therefore, shows a confrontation between Gnostic ideas and second-century Christianity and contributes no knowledge about Jesus.

Elaine Pagels, a modern scholar of Gnosticism, recently discussed these texts in *The Gnostic Gospels* (1979), a popular account which gained wide circulation. Despite her expressed intention to write an historical account and "not to advocate any side but to explore the evidence," she did not maintain scholarly objectivity. The general tenor of her book encourages a one-sided enthusiasm for the suppressed Gnos-

25 J. M. Robinson, *Nag Hammadi Library,* p. 208.
26 *Ibid.,* p. 524.

tic cause, even though, at the end, she warns about the dangers of the Gnostic approach.[27] She leads the reader to conclude that the Church's beliefs in one God, the creator of heaven and earth, and in the bodily resurrection of Christ did not derive from Scripture or experience, but were promulgated to support and establish the authority of the bishops and the Church's teaching on apostolic succession in the second century.[28] Pagels attempts to explain the Church's belief that God, who created the world, "sent the Son into the world, not to condemn the world, but that the world might be saved through him" (Jn 3:17), in terms of a power struggle between competing Christian and Gnostic groups.[29]

Apparently, Pagels assumes that the Christian Gnostics represented a genuine alternative to the development of Christianity. This was not the view of the early Christians, who understood just how radically the Gnostics' beliefs about God, the world, and Christ differed from their own. Christians and Gnostics did not represent two theological possibilities, but two organically opposed groups. The Gnostic teaching was not a legitimate outgrowth of the Gospel of Christ, which was first lived and

27 See Raymond E. Brown's review of *The Gnostic Gospels*, in *New York Times Book Review*, Jan 20, 1980, p. 3.

28 Birger A. Pearson finds "The Politics of Monotheism" "one of the weakest chapters" in Pagels' book. "The early Christians would have been surprised to learn that this belief [Orthodox Christian monotheism] was being promulgated in order to bolster the authority of the bishops, as Pagels argues...One cannot account for that doctrine simply on those terms" ("Early Christianity and Gnosticism: A Review Essay," in *Religious Studies Review*, v. 13, n. 1 [1987], pp. 2-3).

We may add that the authority of the bishops in the Church was derived from their historical continuity with the apostles of Christ. The Gnostic groups claim the possession of truths which were handed over to them in secrecy by the apostles. The Church leaders pointed out that the apostolic tradition was not transmitted secretly but publicly.

29 Gedaliahu G. Strousa ("The Gnostic Temptation," *Numen* XXVII, 2 [1980], pp. 278-86) criticized Pagels' inclination to interpret theological positions, controversies, debates in the early Church "as disguised struggles between divergent social and political conceptions" (p. 279). Strousa argues that nobody can deny the importance of socio-political factors in any period of the Church's history, but no historian who overlooks the essential importance of the theological issue can be taken as a reliable guide in this complex world of the first century. Pagels sees that Gnostics rejected biblical monotheism, but she explains it as a consequence of their rejection of the hierarchical structure of the Church. Yet "she fails to mention" that "Marcion established throughout the world a Gnostic Church, with bishops, deacons, presbyters" and that in the third century, "Mani established, again on purely gnostic principles, a world church whose strong structures permitted his religion to survive for more than a thousand years." By rejecting Christian monotheism, the Gnostics rejected Christianity and created the basis for their own religion, which was a new religion.

then preached by the apostles, but it was an "alien factor" introduced to arrest and to change the course of Christian theological development and of corresponding institutions and to turn Christianity into its opposite.

If the Gnostic writings found in Nag Hammadi had replaced the canonical gospels, a split would have occurred within the concept of the Incarnation, producing a kind of spiritual Christ, whose resurrection would be an exclusively spiritual experience, and replacing the authoritative tradition of the Church with human self-knowledge.[30] To understand the Christian struggle against Gnosticism, nothing is more revealing than to read the five Gnostic Gospels and to compare them with Matthew, Mark, Luke and John. Whereas the New Testament gospels derived their structure from the early Christian *kerygma*, the Gnostics disregarded the historical framework and content of the canonical gospels. The Christian Gnostics were consequently free to use their so-called gospels as vehicles of basic Gnostic, rather than Christian, convictions, to reinterpret Jesus' words, and to create new sayings, which were often utterly different in form and spirit from the authentic words and teachings of Jesus. The portrait of Jesus that comes out of the Gnostic Gospels derived from the Gnostic vision of the Deity, the universe, and man's place in it. Christians who remained faithful to the Christ of history and experience rejected the Gnostic writings as divorced from both divine and human realities. The apocryphal writings mythologized and dehistoricized Jesus.[31] The Gnostic Gospels must be evaluated not only in content, but also within the context of the whole life and worship of Christian communities in the first two centuries. They must be weighed against the true origin of Christianity, the life and teaching of Christ.

30 In the opinion of Pheme Perkins, a scholar of New Testament and Gnosticism, "Pagels portrayed the Gnostics as the champions of individual creativity against an increasingly repressive and unimaginative orthodoxy." Pagels tends to present Gnostics as a people who were insisting on the rights of the "autonomous, creative human self." Perkins takes issue with this view and asserts that such a perception of the self "is largely the product of modern thought and presupposes a consciousness of self and world radically different from that of second and third-century people" (*The Gnostic Dialogue: The Early Church and the Crisis of Gnosticism* [New York: Paulist Press, 1980], p. 205).

31 The term μῦθος is used in the New Testament to signify "a divorce from the reality which had been historically manifested, and most of all in the incarnation (1 Tim 1:4; 4:7, 2 Tim 4:4; Tit 1:14, 2 Pet 1:16)," C. F. D. Moule, *The Birth of the New Testament* (London: Adam & Charles Black, 1962), p. 143.

IV

Not only did the Gnostics write their own books, but some of them also tried to control the formation of the Christian canon. This attempt began with Marcion's creation of his own canon (ca. 150) for the community that he organized after being excommunicated, with Valentinus, in Rome between 140 and 150. The Marcionite church existed for several centuries. Marcion denied that the Old Testament held authority for the Church, due to his overpowering belief that God, the Father of Jesus, was not the Hebrew YHWH.[32]

In his book *Antithesis*, of which only a few fragments remain, Marcion tried with utmost zeal to show that the God of the Hebrew Scripture is a God of strict justice, concerned only with punishing anyone who transgresses his law. Marcion claimed that Jesus was the Son, not of the Old Testament God, but of the Unknown God, the "good God" who is above Yahweh. He insisted upon the literal meaning of the Old Testament, rejecting the current use of the allegorical method to understand the relationship between the Old and New Testaments.[33]

Marcion also excluded a considerable number of the New Testament books from his canon, retaining only the Gospel of Luke and the Epistles of Paul. Many passages in Luke, however, were not to Marcion's taste. He omitted the first two chapters (the infancy narrative), thus making Jesus appear to come directly from heaven, an emanation from above which had nothing to do with the fulfillment of God's promise in

32 See Gilles Quispel, "Gnosticism," *The Encyclopedia of Religion*, M. Eliade, ed. (New York: Macmillan 1987), V:571.
33 On "Gnostic Allegory," see H. Jonas, pp. 91-97. Gnostic allegory had as its purpose the propagation of a specific Gnostic teaching, not the search for underlying connections between two different periods in the history of salvation, as was the case in the allegorical interpretation practiced by Origen and his Alexandrian school. The Gnostic approach undermined and distorted biblical tradition. One of the many examples of how a Bible story was radically transformed is the Gnostic allegorical interpretation of the serpent and its role in persuading Eve to eat of the tree. The serpent represented for some Gnostic groups the spiritual or pneumatic principle of Gnostic salvation, whereas God, the creator of this world, whom Adam and Eve disobeyed, appeared in Gnostic allegory (as in Gnostic theology) as a symbol of cosmic oppression. Marcion was an exception among the Gnostics. He did not indulge in allegorical fantasy, so cherished by other Gnostics. He avoided speculative thought and never claimed superior spiritual insight and knowledge. "He [made] faith and not knowledge the vehicle of redemption." Yet his idea of the unknown God, his dualism, and his "view of salvation as liberation from [an inferior and oppressive creator] are so outstandingly Gnostic, that anyone who professed them" must be considered a Gnostic (Jonas, p. 137).

history, as expressed in the Old Testament. Tertullian (c. 200) observed that Marcion "cut the Scriptures to pieces in order to adapt them to his own ideas."[34] Marcion's gospel was the good news of "the alien and good God, the Father of our Lord Jesus Christ," who came to deliver human-kind from enslavement by a cruel demiurge. Christ's role was of double significance, in Marcion's perspective: by freeing human beings from their wretched existence, he also saved them from the "just god" who created the world and the people of Israel. According to this rigid logic, Jesus' genealogy was wrong, for it linked him with the world's existence. Marcion eliminated the genealogy, references to the Old Testament in Luke, some of the parables, the entry into Jerusalem and the cleansing of the Temple. Marcion performed the same drastic surgery on the letters of Paul. He rejected the pastoral epistles for their preoccupation with the Church and its organization. Paradoxically, Marcion is known as the first great interpreter of Paul. "No one understood Paul till Marcion, and he misunderstood him."[35] But Paul, unlike Marcion, never rejected the God of the Old Testament, whom he called "the God and Father of our Lord Jesus Christ," nor did he reject either the world created by this God or the people of Israel.

In the view of some scholars, the work of Marcion forced the Church to create its own list of authoritative books, which would serve as the norm for its life and teaching. The question arises whether the Church would have had a New Testament canon without such outside pressures. A similar question may be raised about the doctrine of the Trinity, which took shape in response to the Arian controversies. In fact, the struggle with Marcion was not decisive in the formation of the New Testament canon, nor was the struggle with Arius in that of the doctrine of the Trinity. The canonicity of each book did not necessarily depend upon outside influences. The Church adhered to the books which it had

---

34 *De Praescr.* 38. According to Irenaeus, Marcion "mutilated the Gospel According to Luke, removing everything about the birth of the Lord and much of the teaching of the words of the Lord, in which the Lord is recorded as clearly confessing the creator of this universe as his Father...He also similarly cut up the Epistles of Paul, removing whatever the apostle said clearly about the God who made the world, that he is the Father of our Lord Jesus Christ, and whatever the apostle teaches by referring to the prophetic writings that predict the coming of the Lord" (*Adv. Haeres.*, I.27.2).

35 Comments by Harnack and others have been collected by Malcolm Muggeridge and Alec Vidler, *Paul, Envoy Extraordinary* (New York: Harper & Row, 1972), pp. 11-16.

always recognized, thus implicitly defining its canon. Similarly, the followers of Christ did not create a new faith in the doctrine of the Trinity, but gave authoritative expression to what it had always believed.

More than two hundred years passed after Marcion, before the final seal of canonical recognition was placed on the gospels. Certain criteria were used to determine which books belonged to the canon and which did not. The authoritative books had to have been written by the apostles themselves or by their disciples, their content had to have been of similarly apostolic origin, and usually they had to have been read in the context of public worship. Thus the authority of the gospels as proper liturgical texts preceded their canonization. The Church did not endow the New Testament with authority, but simply recognized its long-standing existence. The same spirit that guided the evangelists in writing their gospels, guided the Church through the whole process of refining the canon. Marcion, in his opposition to the Church's tradition, could not establish which books were inspired and which were not, since what is inspired (θεόπνευστος [2 Tim 3:16], which means literally "breathed into by God") cannot be the product of purely human impulse. Marcion's gospel was such a product. The gospels were not based upon man's insight, but upon the activity of God. Their authority, and that of all other parts of the New Testament, lay not in the books themselves, nor in the authority of the Church in which they were produced, but came from the Spirit of God, whose presence manifested itself in the life of the Church and in its members.

Marcion's canon was not only incomplete, but was also the canon of a Gnostic who used the Church's books, such as Luke, to produce his own image of Christ. In its long fight with Marcion and his church, the Christian communities adhered to all four gospels in order to preserve an undistorted image of Jesus. The spirit of Marcion can be encountered even in our own times, whenever religious leaders try to adjust Scripture to their own ideas.

V

In the last quarter of the second century, a question was raised as to why there should be four different accounts of Jesus' ministry, death, and resurrection. Why struggle with the difficulties and differences between them? Why not blend all four into a single harmonious narrative? Tatian, a Christian apologist from Mesopotamia, had the idea of producing one gospel narrative. Marcion had accepted only a revised version of the Gospel of Luke, but Tatian recognized all four gospels. His goal was a harmony, a continuous narrative. Accordingly, he composed the *Diatessaron* (ca. 175). The *Diatessaron* was used in some churches in the East, and the Syrian Church used it until the fifth century, when Rabbula, the Bishop of Edessa (411-435), replaced the "mixed gospels" with the "separated gospels." The existence of the *Diatessaron* proves that in the second century all four gospels were known. Its success in the Eastern churches of the early period was due to the fact that it presented the gospel narrative without the discrepancies that arise from a comparison of the four separate gospels.

The original text of the *Diatessaron* is lost. Whether Tatian wrote it in Syriac or in Greek is still debated. A page from the *Diatessaron* in Greek was discovered in the ruins of Dura Europus on the Euphrates, a Roman fortress destroyed by the Persians in the middle of the third century. Translations of Tatian's work from a much later period are preserved in Arabic and in Latin. On the basis of later versions of his work, we know that he began and ended the *Diatessaron* with verses from the Gospel according to St. John. This does not mean, however, that he followed the order of events as it is given in the fourth gospel. Often, Tatian must have found the order of the Synoptics preferable. Yet he considered the historicity of the account of the passion in the fourth gospel to be superior to the narrative of the first three;[36] on this particular point, modern gospel research supports him.

There is still a question as to whether Tatian displayed some Gnostic tendencies in the *Diatessaron.* According to Irenaeus, Tatian was a disciple of Justin Martyr in Rome. He left Rome after Justin's martyrdom and probably came under the influence of certain Gnostic circles including a group known as Encratites, who denied the sanctity of marriage and forbade the use of wine in the Eucharist. Some modern scholars are inclined to conclude that the *Diatessaron,* whenever it was written, was free of Gnostic tendencies. The ancient authorities, however, were of a

36 For a discussion of what we know of the *Diatessaron,* see Robert M. Grant, *The Earliest Lives of Jesus* (New York: Harper & Row, 1961), pp. 23-26.

different opinion. A well-known bishop of Cyrus, Theodoret (ca. 393-466), who was acquainted with Tatian's *Diatessaron* in Greek, wrote that Tatian omitted the genealogies that speak of Jesus as David's descendent according to the flesh, and that he did so under the influence of Gnostic teaching.

The *Diatessaron,* whether or not it was free of Gnostic tendencies, was not a divine-human work like the gospels, but simply a human document. The *Diatessaron* eliminated the diversity of the gospels and imposed upon them an unnatural uniformity inadequate to the divine matters it related. Any attempt at harmonizing two or more diverse accounts of the same event can capture only one aspect of its meaning. Sometimes it may not preserve the meaning of the records which are harmonized, but, quite to the contrary, may distort it completely. On the other hand, if the differences are preserved and the temptation to harmonize them is resisted, then many aspects of the meaning of the texts may be uncovered. Taken together, the four different accounts of the four witnesses offer us a full image of Christ. A harmonized gospel such as the *Diatessaron* cannot do this. This is why the Church finally rejected the *Diatessaron,* preferring the plurality of the gospels.

At the end of the second century, Irenaeus expressed the Church's perspective on the gospels by calling them the "foundation and pillar of our faith." The gospel was preached by those who "were clothed with the power from on high when the Holy Spirit came upon them, [and when] they were filled with all things and had perfect knowledge." Matthew, Mark, Luke, and John "handed down to us that there is one God, maker of heaven and earth, proclaimed by the Law and the Prophets, and one Christ the Son of God" (*Adv. Haeres.*, II.1). The heretics, on the other hand, according to Irenaeus, preached their own views and thus corrupted "the rule of faith." They did not have a saving message to proclaim. They opposed the living tradition of the Church, considering themselves wiser than the elders of the Church and even the apostles themselves. In Irenaeus' view, even if the gospels had not been written, we would still follow "the rule of tradition" which the apostles "handed down to those to whom they committed the Church" (*Adv. Haeres.* III.4).

Irenaeus stressed that the four gospels are really one gospel, "fourfold in form but held together in one Spirit." Those who "destroy the pattern of the gospel and present either more or less than four forms of the gospel (ἐυαγγέλιον τετράμορφον)" cut themselves off from the gospel and from the Church, from "the fellowship of the brethren." The Gnostics, in the view of Irenaeus, "bring forward their own compositions and boast that they have more gospels than really exist" (*Adv. Haeres.* III.8). He insisted that the Gnostic Gospels had nothing in common with the Church's gospels, the unity of which was guaranteed in their inspiration by the Holy Spirit.

Whereas the Gnostics distrusted the gospels and attempted to arrange the material in them to their own satisfaction, the Church defended its books as the expression of its faith and its life. It firmly rejected the idea of reducing the gospel to eliminate references to Jesus' humanity. The gospels were written to proclaim his true humanity as well as his divinity.

VI

Irenaeus accepted and defended all four gospels as canonical. The earliest list known to us of the New Testament books is the so-called Muratorian canon, which originated in Rome around 200. It mentions twenty-two books, among which are the four gospels and the epistles of Paul. The Epistle to the Hebrews and the catholic epistles (James, 1 and 2 Pet, and 3 Jn) are omitted. Athanasius, Bishop of Alexandria from 328 to 373, listed in his Festal Letter of 367 all twenty-seven books of the New Testament, concluding: "These are the springs of salvation, in order that he who is thirsty may fully refresh himself with the words contained in them. In them alone is the doctrine of piety proclaimed. Let no one add anything to them or take anything away from them."

The growth of the New Testament as an integrated collection of Christian writings started in the second century and ended in the fourth. Despite the fact that the New Testament itself contained evidence that a saying of Jesus was considered "Scripture" (1 Tim 5:8), early Christian writers hesitated to identify the first-century Christian writings, the gospels, and the Epistles of Paul, as Scripture. Only Jesus had authority for these early Christians, and when Clement of Rome (ca. 96) quoted the words of Christ, he introduced them, not as "what is written," but as "the words of the Lord Jesus" (I Clem 13:1-2). The Word of the Lord was above any other authority. They also hesitated to identify the words of Jesus as Scripture per se, for they already had the Old Testament as their Scripture. The apostolic writings were also considered authoritative, if not "Scriptural." Paul meant his letters to be read to all members of the Christian community. In his earliest extant writing, Paul concluded: "I adjure you by the Lord that this letter be read to all the brethren" (1 Th 5:27), and in one of his latest writings: "And when this letter has been read among you, have it read also in the Church of the Laodiceans; and see that you read also the letter from Laodicea" (Col 4:16). Even the "private" letter to Philemon was also meant for the Church in his house (Philem 2). Before his letters were accepted as "canonical," then, Paul had authority in the Church, and his writings to the various Christian communities in the Hellenistic world were viewed as the "rule of faith."[37]

The New Testament contains a diversity of writings,[38] but in the words of Günther Bornkamm, "There is hardly a single extra-canonical writing we know of that we would wish had been included in the New Testament canon."[39] The apocryphal gospels were rejected because they did not bear witness to the unifying center of Christ and to his work. The canon of the New Testament was necessary to keep the image of Christ free of an admixture of Gnosticism. A list of the books was indispensable so that Christians of all subsequent historical periods could learn about and relive the major events through which the Incarnate Lord manifested himself in human history.

37 On the formation of the canon of the New Testament there is an informative chapter by Raymond F. Collins in his *Introduction to the New Testament* (New York: Doubleday, 1987), pp. 1-40.
38 On the problem of the canon's diversity, see James D. G. Dunn, *Unity and Diversity in the New Testament—An Inquiry into the Character of Earliest Christianity* (Philadelphia: Westminster Press, 1977). The New Testament, as canon, "canonizes the unity of Christianity" as well as "the diversity of Christianity." It also canonizes "the range of acceptable diversity and the limits of acceptable diversity" (pp. 386f). The canon of the New Testament is closed, but, like the dogmas, it lives in the life of the Church. Yet there is a difference here. "The canon of Scripture forms a determinate body which excludes all possibility of further increase, while the 'dogmatic tradition,' in keeping its stability as the 'rule of faith,' from which nothing can be cut off, can be increased by receiving, to the extent that may be necessary, new expressions of revealed Truth, formulated by the Church" (Vladimir Lossky, "Tradition and Traditions," *The Meaning of Icons*, [Crestwood, NY: St. Vladimir's Seminary Press, 1983] p. 23). The canon of the New Testament as the record of revelation has a permanent presence and continuing influence that shapes the life of Christians.
39 Günther Bornkamm, *The New Testament—A Guide to its Writings* (London: SPCK, 1974), p. 4.

10

Who Do Men Say That I Am?

Who was Jesus? The answer to this question completely governs our interpretation of the gospels. What did the people who encountered him think of him? How did his disciples perceive him? How did Jesus respond to the titles with which his contemporaries defined him? And which titles and images did the earliest Christians consider adequate to the resurrected Christ? We now turn to the titles and descriptions of Jesus, given in the gospels and by the earliest Christian communities, to find an answer to the question of who Jesus was.

I

Jesus' contemporaries tried to understand who he was by identifying him with one of the figures associated with current Jewish messianic expectations. Some thought that he was John the Baptist, others that he was Elijah, and still others that he was "one of the prophets" (Mk 8:27 and paral.). John had been beheaded by Herod Antipas, son of Herod the Great, but "all [held] that John was a prophet" (Mt 21:26), "a righteous and holy man" (Mk 6:20). The prophet Elijah was expected to come again before the Messiah appeared. According to Old Testament tradition, two men, Enoch and Elijah, did not die. Enoch walked with God, and without experiencing death God "took him" (Gen 5:24). Elijah "went up by a whirlwind into heaven" (2 Kg 2:11). This tradition encouraged the belief that Elijah would return "before the great and terrible day of the Lord comes" (Mal 4:5).[1]

1 According to the Synoptics, Elijah had come in the person of John the Baptist. After the transfiguration, when the disciples asked Jesus, "Why do the scribes say that first Elijah must come?", Jesus told them "Elijah has come, and they did to him whatever they pleased, as it is written of him" (Mk 9:13). In Matthew's gospel the identification between John and Elijah is quite explicit: "And if you are willing to accept it, he is Elijah who is to come" (11:14). John the Baptist fulfilled the mission of Elijah (Lk 1:17, 76). There was no literal fulfillment, no literal return of Elijah (Mt 17:10ff, Mk 9:9ff), and therefore John the Baptist could say, according to the fourth gospel, that he was not Elijah (Jn 1:19f). In the Synoptics, it was not John who ascribed to himself the role of Elijah, but Jesus. He knew John's place in the history

Jesus was also identified with a prophet like Moses (Dt 18:15), "the prototype of the true prophet" (Dt 34:10-11), whom God would raise up at the last days. Thus Jesus' contemporaries thought that Jesus was that prophet, or John, raised from the dead, or that he was Elijah. He was viewed as one sign that the messianic age was about to come.

What these contemporary opinions had in common was the assumption that Jesus was a prophet. The gospels furnish ample evidence of this. During his ministry, some called him "a prophet, like one of the prophets of old" (Mk 6:15). After he raised the only son of a widow in Nain, those present glorified God, saying: "A great prophet has arisen among us" (Lk 7:16). When the people saw the miracle of the multiplication of the loaves and fishes, they said: "This is indeed the prophet who is to come into the world" (Jn 6:14). As a prophet, Jesus possessed the Spirit of God (Lk 4:18ff) and a gift of prophetic insight (Mk 2:8). Some of his acts could have been taken as prophetic—the cleansing of the Temple, for example. His attitude to contemporary Judaism was that of a prophet, in that he criticized its ritual and sacrifices and its neglect of the poor and of sinners. Some of his disciples saw him as "a prophet mighty in deed and word before God and all the people" (Lk 24:19), as the fulfillment of the messianic prophetic hope that God would raise up a prophet like Moses.

Moses' call, divine commission, and message to his people, and their deliverance from slavery in Egypt, were known not only to the learned, but to the common, illiterate people as well. The story of the Exodus, recited at public gatherings for worship and celebration, sank deep into their souls, lived in their memory, and fed their messianic expectations. They looked forward to the time when another Moses would deliver Israel from its new oppression, from the hated King Herod and the Romans who imposed him upon them. The new Moses would restore Israel's relationship with God and establish God's kingdom. Although the simple people did not leave written testimony to their universal messianic

of salvation, whereas the Baptist did not. There is another explanation for John's denial that he was Elijah. According to some speculations, "Elijah was an eschatological figure equivalent to the Messiah. It must be remembered that in Malachi 4:5 (Heb 3:23), Elijah precedes not the Messiah but the Day of the Lord. Elijah is not the Messiah's forerunner, but the Messiah's equivalent: he ushers in the Day of the Lord." For this reason the Baptist refused to accept "a role equivalent to messiahship" (C. F. D. Moule, *The Phenomenon of the New Testament* [Naperville, IL: A. R. Allenson, Inc., 1967], p. 71).

expectations, the first-century Jewish historian Josephus and some New Testament documents testify to them. These expectations lay behind the various prophetic movements and uprisings against Roman power in the first century, recorded by Josephus with pronounced hostility. Josephus labels the leaders of these movements "imposters and demagogues," who "under the guise of divine inspiration provoked revolutionary actions and impelled the masses to act like madmen." That these people were inspired by the heroes of their past history, and that they tried to follow the example of these heroes and to repeat their actions is clear from Josephus' descriptions: "They led [the masses] into the wilderness so that their God would show them signs of imminent liberation" (J.W.2.259). Josephus described a particular "charlatan" named Theudas, who in 45 A.D. "persuaded most of the common people to take their possessions and follow him to the Jordan River. He said he was a prophet, and that at his command the river would be divided and allow them an easy crossing." Fadus, the governor of Judea at that time, sent out a cavalry unit which prevented Theudas and his followers from crossing, by killing many "in a surprise attack" and beheading Theudas (Ant. 20.97-98). Apparently, his followers regarded Theudas as a new Moses. The parting of the waters corresponded to the parting of the Red Sea. The Theudas movement was inspired by the memory of God's deliverance of Israel under the leadership of Moses more than twelve centuries before. Moses had been the messenger and prophet of deliverance from Egypt. Theudas followed his example and persuaded his followers that he was the prophet of the oppressed people of the land and their deliverer from the yoke of the Romans. He was a prophet of action, like Moses.[2]

In the eyes of the common people Jesus was a prophet, but in the eyes of his opponents, the Temple authorities, religious leaders and the Romans, he was a false prophet. After they had him condemned for blasphemy, some members of the Sanhedrin struck him, saying: "Prophesy!" (Mk 14:65), and Luke narrates how the Temple police "mocked him and beat him." Having blindfolded him they asked him, "Prophesy! Who is it that struck you?" (Lk 22:63-64) Herod Antipas, to whom Pilate sent Jesus, also "with his soldiers treated him with contempt and mocked

2 For an illuminating account of prophets and prophetic movements in the time of Jesus, see Richard A. Horseley and John S. Hanson, *Bandits, Prophets, and Messiahs* (San Francisco: Harper & Row, 1985), pp. 160-187. They pay special attention to the social character of popular movements in the time of Jesus.

him; then, arraying him in gorgeous apparel, he sent him back to Pilate" (Lk 23:6ff). And the Roman soldiers "clothed him in a purple cloak...and...mocked him" (Mk 15:16ff). These robes, in addition to the crown of thorns put on Jesus' head, indicated that Jesus was accused of the political crime of claiming to be a king. The robes were the distinguished regalia of the Jewish and Hellenistic rulers. By mocking him, Jesus' opponents conveyed the idea that he was accused also as a false prophet.[3] Jewish and Roman authorities saw him as an imposter and the demagogue of a popular prophetic movement.

For those who supported him, however, Jesus was not just another prophet. The Spirit had descended on him and remained (emeinen) in him (Jn 1:32). The Spirit was with him not temporarily, as was the case with the historical prophets, but permanently. He was thus outside the "class" of the prophets. He proved this in the synagogue in Nazareth when he stood up to read from Isaiah 61:

> The Spirit of the Lord is upon me, because he has anointed me to preach good news to the poor. He has sent me to proclaim release to the captives and recovering of sight to the blind, to set at liberty those who are oppressed, to proclaim the acceptable year of the Lord.

He then revealed his identity and mission by saying: "Today this scripture has been fulfilled in your hearing" (Lk 4:18-21).

According to Matthew, Jesus was "greater" than the prophet Jonah, and his wisdom "greater" than the wisdom of Solomon (Mt 12:38-42; 13:16ff). He was also "greater" than John the Baptist (Mt 11:11, Lk 7:28). He never used the prophetic formula: "Thus saith the Lord," but introduced his sayings with *amen*, the word usually used to approve the words of somebody else and to end prayers. Jesus was unique in using *amen* only to confirm his own words: "*amen*, I say to you." John contains about twenty-five examples where *amen* is repeated: "*amen*, *amen*, I say to you," as if Jesus wanted particularly to stress the significance and revelatory character of his words.[4] For example, when Jesus says "*Amen*, *amen*, I say to you, you will see heaven opened, and the angels of God

---

3 J. Jeremias, *The Eucharistic Words of Jesus* (Philadelphia: Fortress Press, 1977), p. 79.
4 For the use and importance of *amen* in the sayings of Jesus, see J. Jeremias, *New Testament Theology* (New York: Charles Scribner's, 1971), pp. 35f; Martin Hengel, *The Charismatic Leader and His Followers* (New York: Crossroad, 1981), p. 69; X. Léon-Dufour, *Dictionary of the New Testament* (San Francisco: Harper & Row, 1980), p. 91.

ascending and descending upon the Son of Man" (Jn 1:51), he indicates that what Jacob saw in a vision (Gn 28:12) is now fulfilled in him: heaven and earth are bonded together by Jesus, the locus of God's revelation.

"Thus saith the Lord" was an introductory formula used by a prophet to indicate that his prophecy was not the product of his own insight or wisdom, but a message received from God. When Jesus introduced a saying with "*Amen*, I say to you," he spoke on the basis of his own authority and knowledge, which were rooted in his union with the Father, in his experience of the certainty of God's presence, and in the intimacy of his relationship with God.

Jesus was more than a prophet, more than Moses. In the Sermon on the Mount, he distinguished himself from Moses: "You have heard that it was said to the men of old, [by Moses] 'You shall not kill,'...But I say to you that every one who is angry with his brother shall be liable to judgment" (see Mt 5:21-48). The authorities, on the other hand, labeled him a false prophet and a dangerous political rebel. It is only by studying his own words against the background of contemporary understanding and interpretations that we may understand more clearly who Jesus was.

II

Jesus was called a prophet, but, as we have seen, his conduct was not that of a prophet. He was also addressed as "rabbi", yet this title could not fully describe him.

In all four gospels Jesus is called "rabbi" by his disciples. According to the evidence of Matthew and Luke, only Judas called him "rabbi"; but in Mark's gospel even the leading disciple, Peter, addressed him as "rabbi." He did so at the time of the transfiguration, after he confessed him to be the Christ. "Rabbi (master), it is well that we are here" (Mk 9:5). The reaction of Peter to Christ's transfiguration is recorded in two other Synoptic Gospels, but without the word "rabbi." Matthew used κύριε (Lord) and Luke ἐπιστάτα (master) (Mt 17:4, Lk 9:33).

According to the fourth evangelist, the two disciples of John the Baptist who followed Jesus asked him, "Rabbi, where are you staying?" and Nathanael, when he met Jesus, exclaimed, "Rabbi, you are the Son of God! You are the king of Israel!" (Jn 1:38, 49) The term "rabbi" is also used in this gospel for John the Baptist, although the people held that "John was a real prophet" (Mk 11:32 and paral.).

According to the gospels, then, the disciples of Jesus addressed him as "rabbi," which is equivalent to "teacher" and which is transmitted in the Synoptic Gospels as κύριε and ἐπιστάτα. In the fourth gospel it is interpreted as διδάσκαλος (teacher). In interpreting the gospel usage of "rabbi," we have to keep in mind that at the time of Jesus, "rabbi" did not have the meaning it acquired in Rabbinic Judaism after the fall of Jerusalem in 70. To address someone as "rabbi" during the public ministry of Jesus was to express a particular respect for him. Only later was the term "rabbi" used as a technical term applied to the ordained spiritual leader of a Jewish congregation.

In Jesus' time the scribes and lawyers were also addressed respectfully as rabbis. They were the scholars of the Torah, laymen who had acquired great knowledge of the law by being trained in the schools of famous teachers. What is surprising is that Jesus was called "rabbi," although he was not formally trained as a scribe. The people marveled, "How is it that this man has learning, when he has never studied?" (Jn 7:15). He possessed "learning" but not "the petty learnedness" of the scribes. He taught "as one who had authority, and not as the scribes" (Mk 1:22). His way of speaking and acting was not that of the scribes and lawyers of his time.[5] Lacking a permanent residence, he called his disciples to follow him from place to place, to abandon all possessions and to share in his suffering. He called his disciples, not to organize his own school and train them in the interpretation of the law, but "to send them out to preach, and have authority to cast out demons" (Mk 3:14-15).

Thus Jesus was respectfully addressed as a rabbi, but he had very little in common with the rabbis of his own time, and even less with the rabbis of the later period. Modern attempts to present Jesus as "the rabbi of Nazareth," to reduce him to categories which the "modern mind" would have no difficulty in understanding, are simply misleading, anachronistic, and confusing.

---

5 The section entitled "Jesus was not a 'rabbi'" in M. Hengel, *The Charismatic Leader*, pp. 42-50, contains a wealth of information on this subject.

III

"But who do you say that I am?" Jesus asked the Twelve. The emphasis here is upon "you" (ὑμεῖς), the disciples who were inside the circle of his followers. And Peter, as the leader of the group, answered, "You are the Christ" (Mk 8:29), that is, "you are the expected deliverer." This confession is the Christological watershed in the Gospel of Mark. At this point, those who were close to Jesus saw in him much more than those who did not follow him, for to the former he was the Christ. Without rejecting attempts to identify him with the messianic king of popular Jewish hope, Jesus nonetheless taught those around him the true nature of his messiahship by combining and transforming ancient messianic titles and traditions.

Messianic expectations in Jesus' time centered upon the coming of the Messiah (Gr. Christos; Hb. Mashiah) who would restore the nation of Israel to its previous grandeur as well as to its loyalty to God. The anointed one, Christ, would come from David's line, since God promised David that his throne would be established forever (2 Sam 7:12ff). Ez 37 contains a prophecy of the restoration of Israel: the divided land will be reunited and ruled by one king. "My servant David shall be king over them; and they shall all have one shepherd" (Ez 37:24). David would be king of the united Israel forever (Ez 37:25). In later developments, particularly during the Hellenistic age when Jewish nationalism under Roman rule was on the rise, this expectation acquired strong political overtones.

The term "Messiah" was used rather rarely in the Jewish literature which survives from the first century B.C. and from the time of Jesus. When Pompey conquered Palestine in 63 B.C. and made it a part of the province of Syria, however, a surge of intense popular messianic expectations took place. In the time of Jesus, the Messiah as the Son of David was eagerly expected. This did not necessarily mean that the Messiah would literally be a physical descendent of David, but rather that he would be God's beloved, sent to accomplish what David had accomplished.

The common people and the learned scribes and Pharisees shared the same hope, which was kept alive above all in their worship. From the Psalms, read constantly in their services, the people absorbed the words: "Thou hast said, 'I have made a covenant with my chosen one. I have sworn to David my servant. I will establish your descendants forever, and build your throne for all generations'" (Ps 89:3f). Every day they recited the prayer known as *Shemoneh Esreh*, "The Eighteen Benedictions." This prayer received its final form only after the fall of Jerusalem in 70, but it seems certain that Jesus and his disciples knew the first and last parts, which ask God to show his mercy on the people of Israel "and on the kingdom of the house of David, the Messiah of thy righteousness. Let the shoot of David sprout quickly, and raise up his horn with thy help." The Scripture, the daily prayers, the worship kept the hope of messianic deliverance alive.

After the conquest of Palestine, repeated rebellions against Roman rule took place. The distinguishing characteristics of these rebellions were chronicled in the two centuries following the conquest. Around the time of Jesus' birth, the royal palaces at Sepphoris and Jericho were destroyed by Judas, son of Ezekias, who "organized a sizable force," broke into the royal armories "at Sepphoris in Galilee...armed his followers, and attacked the others who vied for power" (J.W.2.56). An extreme zealot group took part in the bloody rebellion of 66-70. They were known as *Sicarii* (from *sica*, dagger in Latin), because they used daggers to murder "people in broad daylight right in the middle of the city. Mixing with the crowds, especially during the festivals, they would conceal small daggers beneath their garments and stealthily stab their opponents" (J.W.2.354-356). The last attempt by the Jews to remove the Romans from their land in 132-135 was led by Bar Kochba, whom Rabbi Akiba, the best known among the rabbis of this period, proclaimed "the king, the Messiah."

These outbreaks, which took place over a century and a half, had one common feature: the leaders were proclaimed to be kings or messiahs with the distinct mission of expelling the Romans from Palestine.[6] This specific coloration of contemporary messianic hope serves as a background for us to understand Jesus' messiahship. His society expected a national king who would fulfill the role of God's anointed. The crowds that gladly listened to Jesus disciples shared in this understanding and hoped for the restoration of the ancient glory of Israel.

Jesus, however, accepted the title of Messiah only if it was reinterpreted to his satisfaction. We see this reinterpretation in his symbolic

6 These "royal pretenders and messianic movements" are well described in R. A. Horsely and J. S. Hanson, *Bandits, Prophets, and Messiahs*, pp. 106-131.

acts, as well as in his statements. When Jesus entered Jerusalem seated upon an ass, the animal which symbolized peace, he let it be known that he was a king who would not use the sword, but would bring peace and establish a new relationship between God and men. The evangelists point to the tension between the people's messianic expectations and Jesus' offer to fulfill them. This conflict was reflected even in his greeting by the crowd. "Most of the crowd spread their garments on the road," and some shouted, "Hosanna to the Son of David! Blessed is he who comes in the name of the Lord! Hosanna in the highest!" (Mt 21:8ff). The crowds wanted a fulfillment different from that symbolized by Jesus riding on an ass (Zech 9:9). They expected Jesus to be a king like Jehu (2 Kg 9), before whom every one spread his garment, blew the trumpet, and exclaimed, "Jehu is King" (9:13). But Jehu was a revolutionary king who shed much blood. The people wanted Jesus to be a king who would not hesitate to use the sword to realize their nationalistic dreams.

The disciples of Jesus also shared this desire. Even though he confessed Jesus to be Christ, Peter could not understand Jesus' words about the suffering of the Son of Man. Neither Peter nor any other disciple associated suffering with the Messiah. Popular expectations, epitomized by the noble title "Son of David," did not ascribe suffering to the Messiah. Jesus came as the suffering Christ, as the expected one who revealed himself in an unexpected way.

Even on the day of Christ's resurrection, the disciples cherished the hope of national restoration. Two of them, still in despair after the crucifixion and not yet ready to believe the women who found the empty tomb and reported the angels' words that Jesus was alive, were going to Emmaus and "talking with each other about [the] things that had happened." On the way, the resurrected Jesus "drew near and went with them," although neither recognized him. Cleopas, one of the two, told the stranger about the condemnation and crucifixion of Jesus of Nazareth, which destroyed their hopes, for "we had hoped that he was the one to redeem Israel" (Lk 24:13ff). Only by faith in the resurrection could the error of this "nationalistic eschatology" be rejected and overcome. Some seem to assume that the question addressed to Christ just before his ascension, "Lord, will you at this time restore the kingdom to Israel?" (Acts 1:6), deals with nationalistic aspirations. Christ's answer: "It is not for you to know the time and seasons which the Father has fixed by his own authority" (Acts 1:7), indicates that the question involves the final consummation of all things, and not the political restoration of contemporary Israel.[7] Jesus thus corrected the messianic expectation of his disciples, leading them from their traditional beliefs to a new and higher understanding of the Messiah.

Only in the conversation with the Samaritan woman did Jesus accept the designation of Christ without qualification (Jn 4:25-26). In response to Jesus' words about worshipping the Father in spirit and truth, the woman said: "I know that the Messiah is coming (he who is called Christ); when he comes, he will show us all things." Then Jesus said, "I who speak to you am he." On the surface, the woman seems to express the Jewish messianic expectations. It is possible that the Samaritan understanding of the Messiah did not carry the political overtones of the Jewish understanding. The woman did not expect the son of David, but a prophet like Moses (Dt 18:15-22), since the Samaritans, descendents of the Northern Kingdom of Israel, followed a different royal line than David's.[8] According to John, Jesus' answer was: "I am" (ἐγὼ εἰμί),[9] and not "I am the Messiah." Even here, the term "Christ" was not adequate and could be misleading. The term "Messiah" had many applications. It was used for the anointed king (1 Sam 2), for the high priest (Lev 4), for

7 This point is clearly made by Richard J. Dillon and Joseph A. Fitzmyer, in "Acts of the Apostles," *Jerome Biblical Commentary*, 45:11. Only the Father knows "that day or that hour," Jesus told his disciples before the resurrection (Mk 13:32). Paul repeated this in his letter to the Thessalonians, "But as to the times and the seasons (τῶν χρόνων καὶ τῶν καιρῶν), brethren, you have no need to have anything written to you. For you yourselves know well that the day of the Lord will come like a thief in the night" (1 Th 5:1-2; Mt 24:43-44).

8 R. E. Brown, *The Gospel According to St John*, Anchor Bible Commentary (New York: Doubleday, 1966), p. 84; "John," D. Moody Smith, in *Harper's Bible Commentary*, James L. Mays (ed.) (San Francisco: Harper & Row, 1988), p. 1053.

9 R. E. Brown, *Jesus: God and Man* (Milwaukee, Bruce Publishing Co., 1967), p. 29. The use by Jesus of "I am" in the fourth gospel (Jn 6:20; 8:24, 28, 56; 13:19; 18:5, 6, 8) "appears to be a deliberate reference" to Ex 3:13-14, when God revealed his name to Moses as "I am who I am," which is the etymological meaning of the name Yahweh. For an understanding of the use by Jesus of the words "I am," we must refer to Is 43:25: "I, I am he who blots out your transgressions for my own sake, and I will not remember your sins;" Is 51:12: "I, I am he that comforts you;" and Is 52:6: "[my people] shall know that it is I who speak; here am I." Each of these is rendered as *ego eimi* (I am) in the Septuagint (see David M. Stanley and Raymond E. Brown, "Aspects of New Testament Thought," *Jerome Biblical Commentary* 78:58). The name "I am," or "I am he," is the name of God, and this name belongs to Jesus. It expresses not only his divinity, but also asserts the fullness of the divine presence in his human condition. "For in him the whole fullness of deity dwells bodily" (Col 2:9).

the prophet (1 Kg 19) and, in fact, for the foreign Persian king Cyrus (Is 45). Hence, Jesus' need to redefine and reinterpret this title in his own terms.

Jesus did not reject the title "Son of David," although he repudiated the popular conceptions of the Messiah's identity. When Bartimaeus, a blind beggar, cried out: "Jesus, son of David, have mercy on me," Jesus heard and healed him. Bartimaeus then joined the disciples and followed Jesus from Jericho on the way to Jerusalem (Mk 10:46-52 and paral.). But while teaching in the Temple in Jerusalem, Jesus still wondered how scribes who were not blind could say that Christ is the son of David, when David himself declared: "The Lord said to my Lord, sit at my right hand, till I put thy enemies under thy feet" (Mk 12:35-37 and paral., Ps 110:1). To Jesus, the Messiah was the Lord of David. In the Temple, then, Jesus again qualified the Messianic title, not because his opponents questioned his Davidic descent—there is no sign that they disputed it—but because the title "Son of David" was too narrow to convey his messiahship. Jesus removed all restrictions from the title. He was rooted in Israel and at the same time proclaimed himself the Lord of David.

As we mentioned above, Jesus transformed the popular Messianic expectations by predicting his suffering. His contemporaries looked for a triumphant, victorious Messiah, not one who would suffer and die. Jesus' predictions of his death confused and grieved his followers, but this did not lessen his determination. These predictions identified Jesus with the Suffering Servant spoken of by the prophet Isaiah (see Is 42:1-4; 49:1-6; 50:4-9; and 52:13-53:12). In some of these songs the Servant may be easily identified with Israel, but in others he has individual characteristics that transcend the historical nation and even the holy remnant which survived the Babylonian exile. In the first three songs, it is not always clear when the prophet identifies the Servant with the nation and when with the individual. The corporate aspect is the strongest in the first song, whereas in the second and in the third it is gradually reduced, so that in the third, the corporate personality is merged into the individual. The fourth song, by contrast, refers clearly to a person whose sufferings are not simply the consequence of his mission, but an essential part of it.[10]

10 See H. H. Rowley, *The Servant of the Lord and Other Essays* (London, 1952), pp. 50-53. According to this study, the first song is the closest to the "Israel passages outside the Songs." The thought of the prophet seems to be dominated by the "Collective Servant, Israel, destined to carry the light of true religion to all the world." In the second song, it is as if the prophet

Although Jesus was never called "the suffering servant," he fulfilled this role in his life. Like the Suffering Servant of Is 53, Jesus "was despised and rejected by men," "a man of sorrows" who "was wounded for our transgressions" (Is 53:3-5; see Mt 8:17). Like the Servant, Jesus was also "oppressed and...afflicted, yet...opened not his mouth" (53:7f). It was the will of God to bruise the Servant, to put him to grief; it was also the will of God that "he...see his offspring . . .[and] prolong his days" (53:10f). The days of the incarnate Son of God were "prolonged" by his resurrection, "because it was not possible for him to be held by [death]" (Acts 2:24). The course of events in Is 53—humiliations, condemnation, and then prolongation of life—are reflected in the three predictions of the passion (Mk 8:31; 9:31; 10:32ff), for in each of them Jesus refers to his future suffering, condemnation, and resurrection.[11]

The New Testament Christians, in coming to an understanding about the events of Jesus' life and ministry, considered Isaiah 53 fulfilled in Jesus, the suffering Messiah raised up and exalted at the right hand of God (Acts 2:32ff). The titles "Christ" and "Son of David," although incompatible with the figure of the Suffering Servant of God in the mind of Jesus' contemporaries, were in fact integrated in the life of Jesus and in the faith of the Church. To share in Christ's glory meant first of all to share in his suffering and death.

IV

In addition to the prophetic messianic hopes, there was another kind of messianic expectation in Jesus' time that was inspired by apocalyptic vision, an expectation epitomized by the title "Son of Man." Jesus used this title to qualify the title of Christ. Having been confessed as the Christ by his disciples, he "began to teach that the Son of Man must suffer many things" (Mk 8:31). When the high priest asked him, "Are

realizes that only "a purified Israel," the remnant, can fulfill this mission. Therefore, there will be not only a mission through Israel to all other nations, but also a mission to Israel. The third song refers to the suffering which the Servant will undergo in performing his task. Here, "It is not unmistakably clear whether (the prophet) is thinking of the collective Servant of an individual representative and leader." But in the fourth song the Servant "is unmistakably individual." Rowley adds, "It seems incredible to me that it can be other than a future figure" (pp. 50-53).

11 See A. Robert and A. Feuillet, *Introduction* (1965), p. 775; A. M. Hunter, *According to John: A New Look at the Fourth Gospel* (Philadelphia: Westminster Press, 1968), p. 92.

you the Christ?", Jesus answered, "I am; and you will see the Son of Man sitting at the right hand of Power" (Mk 14:61-62). The title "Son of Man" took precedence over the title of Christ in Jesus' teaching. It is of great importance that the term "Son of Man" appears in all four gospels, as well as in all the sources of tradition incorporated in the gospels, and that it is always used only by Jesus. There are eighty-two examples of this usage in the gospels. Whenever Jesus spoke about his suffering, passion, and death, he always referred to himself as the Son of Man. When he described his humble human condition, he again used this title: "Foxes have holes and birds of the air have nests; but the Son of Man has nowhere to lay his head" (Lk 9:58, Mt 8:20). This humanity is one aspect of the title's meaning. Another aspect is expressed in those sayings of Jesus that refer to his power to forgive sins, to his lordship over men and over their destiny, and finally to his second coming: "when the Son of Man comes in his glory, and all the angels with him, then he will sit on his glorious throne" (Mt 25:31). The first coming of the Son of Man was in humiliation, but the second will be in glory. The essential continuity between these two comings is preserved in the person who lived in utter poverty, who now sits "at the right hand of God," and who will come in the fullness of his glory. The title "Son of Man" therefore expresses both the humanity and the divinity of Jesus.

The gospels portray Jesus as one who instructed his followers by turning their attention to certain parts of the Old Testament that would lead them to a greater understanding of his role in God's plan of salvation. Of these, probably the two most important are Isaiah 53 and Daniel 7. Only one of the twelve verses in Is 53 is not used in the New Testament; the other verses are either quoted or alluded to not only in the gospels but in Acts, in the Pauline epistles, and in 1 Peter. As for Dan 7, there are references to this chapter in all the gospels, in the epistles of Paul, and in Revelation, as well as less direct references in other passages.[12]

The key verses in Dan 7 are the following:

I saw in the night visions, and behold, with the clouds of heaven there came one like a son of man, and he came to the Ancient of Days [God] and was presented before him. And to him was given dominion and glory and kingdom, that all peoples, nations, and languages should serve him; his dominion is an

12 C. H. Dodd, *The Old Testament in the New* (Philadelphia: Fortress Press, 1963), pp. 12, 14.

everlasting dominion, which shall not pass away, and his kingdom one that shall not be destroyed (7:13-14).

Verse 18 points out that the "one like a son of man" stands for "the saints of the Most High."

In all three passion prophecies in the Synoptic Gospels it is the Son of Man who "must suffer many things" (Mk 8:31), the Son of Man who "will be delivered into the hands of men" (Mk 9:31), and the Son of Man who will be handed over to "the chief priests and scribes" (Mk 10:33). In the fourth gospel the three predictions of suffering, while expressed differently than in the Synoptics, still speak about the Son of Man suffering.

And as Moses lifted up the servant in the wilderness, so must the Son of Man be lifted up (3:14).

When you have lifted up the Son of Man, then you will know that I am he, and that I do nothing on my own authority but speak thus as the Father taught me (8:28).

And I, when I am lifted up from the earth, will draw all men to myself (12:32).

In all three passages the Son of Man is to be condemned, then glorified. The verb ὑψόω (ὕψωσεν, lifted up) in this gospel refers both to the cross of Jesus and to his glorification, which will be accomplished in the resurrection and ascension. Like the other two, the last saying refers to the Son of Man, although not explicitly. The passage in which it occurs begins with: "The hour has come for the Son of Man to be glorified" (23), and ends with: "when Jesus had said this, he departed and hid himself from [the crowd]" (36). And the evangelist explains Jesus' words about his being "lifted up" as Jesus' attempt "to show by what death he was to die" (33). The crowd protested: "We have heard from the law that the Christ remains forever. How can you say that the Son of Man must be lifted up? Who is this Son of Man?" (34). Jesus' words about his own death confused them, since in their understanding the Messiah would remain forever (T. Levi 18:8).

As we have noted, only Jesus applied to himself the term Son of Man (except in the verse we just quoted). In the context of Dan 7, "one like a son of man" is a symbol or representative for the martyred, pious Israelites who suffered during the Maccabean revolt. In the gospels this expression came to mean "*the* Son of Man," an individual. After the fall of Jerusalem in 70, Dan 7:13 was messianically interpreted in Jewish circles (2 Esdras 13:3, 25-28). Even before the fall of Jerusalem, the Son of Man and the Messiah were already identified. 1 Enoch 37-71 describes the heavenly Son of Man.

1 Enoch is an essential source for an understanding of who the Son of Man would be, as well as for Jesus' understanding of himself. This apocalyptic document, according to scholarly consensus, was written before the destruction of Jerusalem in 70 and was therefore known to the contemporaries of Jesus. It describes the Son of Man, first of all, as a single heavenly figure, an individual and not a corporate personality. If in Dan 7, "one like a son of man" is a representative figure, in 1 Enoch he is clearly an individual. He is in the presence of the Lord prior to the creation of the world and throughout eternity. He is "the chosen one," the revealer of the Lord's wisdom to the righteous and to the holy ones. "He is the light of the Gentiles," and "those who dwell upon the earth shall fall and worship before him." The people "will be saved in his name," but the powerful and rich "shall be humiliated on account of the deeds of their hands." And no place will be found for them, because "they have denied the Lord of the Spirits and his Messiah." (1 Enoch 48:1-10). Here the Son of Man is God's chosen one and the Messiah. "Son of Man," therefore, existed as a title in pre-Christian Judaism. Not all that 1 Enoch attributes to the Son of Man, such as crushing the teeth of sinners,[13] corresponds to the portrait of Jesus; but on the whole, this document illumines our understanding of Jesus' messianic authority.

In Aramaic, the language of Jesus, however, the expression *bar nasha* can also mean simply a man, a circumlocution for "I" or "me," with no special significance. One could use this expression in order not to assert or to draw attention to oneself. One who uses it reveals and conceals himself at the same time. Jesus undoubtedly used this indirect manner of speaking. The gospels suggest that in some of Jesus' sayings "Son of Man" is used in this way. In these cases Jesus' use of the phrase directs the attention of his listeners to his human condition, to his unity with mankind. Those who follow Jesus are not to expect personal security, for he had none: "the Son of Man has nowhere to lay his head" (Mt 8:20). As he, the Son of Man, came not to be served but to serve (Mk 10:45),

13 There is a clear discussion of the Son of Man in 1 Enoch, in J. H. Charlesworth, *Jesus Within Judaism*, pp. 39ff, and the whole chapter in his book on "Jesus and the Pseudepigrapha," pp. 30-53, is important for historical research regarding Jesus and early Judaism.

so service must be a way of life for his disciples.

Sometimes in the Synoptic Gospels the same saying is preserved in two forms, with the "Son of Man" and "I." One of the beatitudes in Matthew says: "Blessed are you when men revile you...on my account" (5:11), and its parallel in Luke has "on account of the Son of Man" (6:22). At Caesarea Philippi, according to Matthew, Jesus asked: "Who do men say that the Son of Man is?" (16:13), but Mark (8:27) and Luke (9:18) have: "Who do men say that I am?" The "I" replaces "the Son of Man" in these sayings. Mt 10:33 and Lk 12:8 are other examples. "So everyone who acknowledges me before men, I also will acknowledge before my Father," in Matthew, contrasts with "the Son of Man also will acknowledge before the angels of God," in Luke.

There are, however, passages in which the title cannot be replaced by the personal pronoun, because there it is an explicit messianic designation. Again, they occur in all four gospels, such as "They will see the Son of Man coming in clouds" (Mk 13:26, Mt 24:30, Lk 21:27). When the high priest asks Jesus: "Are you the Christ, the Son of the Blessed?", Jesus answers: "I am; and you will see the Son of Man sitting at the right hand of Power, and coming with the clouds of heaven" (Mk 14:62, Mt 26:64, Lk 22:69). These sayings, like some others (Mt 25:31, Lk 17:24, 26; Jn 1:51), are transmitted "only in the Son of Man version."[14]

The Greek New Testament always translats the Aramaic expression *bar nasha* as ὁ υἱὸς τοῦ ἀνθρώπου (the Son of Man). Other possible translations—without a definite article, such as ἄνθρωπος (man) or υἱὸς ἀνθρώπου (a son of man)—were avoided. Some critics see the phrase "*the* Son of Man" as referring to Daniel's "son of man," a human figure who represents the martyrs of the Maccabean period. This figure stands here as a pattern for Jesus' public ministry, as one who "became obedient unto death." But in some other cases "the son of man" directs our attention to the transcendent "Son of Man" of 1 Enoch. Thus the very phrase "the Son of Man" as used exclusively by Jesus, signifies a figure who is both human and divine. By using the term in the third person, Jesus does not separate himself from "the Son of Man," but, instead, clearly distinguishes between his present humble life and his future glory as the Son of Man.[15]

14 J. Jeremias, *New Testament Theology*, p. 263.
15 *Ibid.*, p. 276.

The "Son of Man" in the gospels can designate either Jesus' human condition or his future glory, but it always underlines his messianic authority. This is because "the Son of Man" was recognized as a messianic title in Palestinian Judaism. The fourth evangelist made this connection more explicitly than did the others. In John, Jesus is the judge. The Father "has given him authority to execute judgment, because he is the Son of Man" (Jn 5:27). He is the Savior, for the Son of Man will give human beings eternal life (Jn 6:27). Finally, he is the exalted Lord of all as the Son of Man (Jn 8:28).

Yet neither the term "Messiah" nor "Son of Man" alone was sufficient to identify Jesus, to describe the nature of his ministry, or to convey the meaning of his person and his role in the history of salvation. Jesus therefore related himself also to the Suffering Servant of Yahweh and to the Son of Man in the visions of Daniel and 1 Enoch. He thereby combined two separate messianic expectations, the prophetic and the apocalyptic, bringing them together with the figure of the Suffering Servant of Isaiah 53. In contrast to the popular and apocalyptic conceptions of the Messiah, Jesus lived the role of God's anointed one through suffering. He thereby brought into existence a new people of God, which he personified, a new community which followed him and which shared his destiny.

Jesus' proclamation of the Kingdom of God points to a messianic self-consciousness which could not have been fully expressed by any current title or image. Jesus stood outside the circle of "popular messianic leaders."[16] Which of these would have resisted the third temptation of Christ in the wilderness: "All these I will give you, if you will fall down and worship me" (Mt 4:9)? On the contrary, after the miracle of the feeding, Jesus perceived that the people were about to make him king by force, so he withdrew "to the hills by himself" (Jn 6:15).

Jesus displayed a selective attitude towards the messianic hope, whether prophetic or apocalyptic. He rejected the nationalistic aspirations of both. He neither desired to be the ideal national king nor shared the hope of the apocalyptists that in the near future, God would destroy

16 M. Hengel, p. 59, and E. P. Sanders, *Jesus and Judaism* (Philadelphia: Fortress Press, 1986), p. 223.

the foreign empire and annihilate all the enemies of Israel. His apocalyptic title "Son of Man" went far beyond political considerations.

V

Jesus drew the attention of the people and of their leaders to his identity as the prophet, the Messiah, the Son of Man who came from the world that transcends this one (Jn 3:13f; 6:62). Yet the Gospel of Mark seems to imply that for most of his life Jesus tried to keep his messiahship a secret. When a man with an unclean spirit cried out, "What have you to do with us, Jesus of Nazareth? Have you come to destroy us? I know who you are, the Holy One of God," Jesus rebuked him by saying, "Be silent and come out of him" (Mk 1:24f). Jesus "cast out many demons; and he would not permit the demons to speak, because they knew him" (Mk 1:34). He ordered them not to proclaim him as the Son of God (Mk 3:11-12). After raising the daughter of Jairus, he strictly charged the witnesses of the event "that no one should know this" (Mk 5:43). After Peter's confession, he ordered the disciples to tell no one about him (Mk 8:30). Following the transfiguration, "he charged them to tell no one what they had seen, until the Son of Man should have risen from the dead" (Mk 9:9). On the basis of these and similar references in the gospel, Wilhelm Wrede (1901) and his followers took the radical position that Jesus never claimed to be the Messiah, and that he was identified as such by the community only after his death. In their view, the gospel accounts where Jesus tells those he heals and his disciples to remain silent are not the words of Jesus but of the early Church. The "messianic secret," they suggest, was inserted into the life of Jesus by the early Christian community to explain why Jesus was not known as the Messiah before the resurrection. Wrede also argued that Mark had "a considerable share in the creation" of the "secret," although it was primarily a collective accomplishment.[17]

17 A detailed account of Wrede's book (*The Messianic Secret in the Gospel,* 1901) is given in Albert Schweitzer, *The Quest of the Historical Jesus* (New York: Macmillan, 1961), pp. 330-48. R. Bultmann and M. Dibelius, the leading exponents of form criticism, have accepted Wrede's theory. Bultmann was also of the opinion that Jesus did not believe himself to be the Messiah. This opinion is a dogma of the Bultmann school and permeates much of Bultmann's interpretation of the gospel. For the disciples of Bultmann, the "messianic secret" does not belong to the life and teaching of Jesus, but is "the reflection and the interpretation of the post-Easter Church" (Gunther Bornkamm, *Jesus of Nazareth* {New York: Harper & Row,

If the "messianic secret" was the creation of certain circles in the early Church, then we should expect it to be reflected consistently in the gospels. However, such uniformity is lacking even in the Gospel of Mark. At the beginning of Mark, Jesus' baptism (Mk 1:9-11) symbolically sums up his mission as Son and Servant of God, his death, his resurrection and ascension. From the viewpoint of the scribes standing nearby, Jesus was arrogating divine prerogatives to himself by telling a man: "My son, your sins are forgiven" (Mk 2:5). Here and elsewhere Jesus did not conceal himself, but revealed himself. Jesus sometimes imposed "secrecy," according to Mark, but sometimes he did not (Mk 5:19). The "secret" had its origin in the evangelist's faithfulness to his sources, written and oral, which contained seemingly contradictory material regarding the messianic claims of Jesus. For the evangelists and for Jesus' disciples, the question of whether or not Jesus was the Messiah never existed. This does not contradict the gospel evidence that before the resurrection they were slow to understand his messiahship, contingent as it was on suffering and death. In order to perform his mission without being pressured by crowds, Jesus imposed silence on many occasions exactly because his messiahship transcended popular expectations. At the same time he could be freely recognized as the Messiah by those who supported him. There is no evidence in the New Testament documents that Jesus refused to claim to be the Messiah. His reinterpretation of the title did not prevent him from claiming it. He revealed himself on his own unexpected terms, a greater Messiah than that expected by the people.

Jesus was the suffering Messiah. At the transfiguration, Peter's confession at Caesarea Philippi and Jesus' prediction that the Messiah must suffer received divine confirmation. The essential link between Jesus' messiahship and his suffering and death was inconceivable and unacceptable to the disciples, as well as to the people of the time. Luke's account of the transfiguration reports that Moses and Elijah, who appeared with Jesus, "spoke of his departure which he was to accomplish at Jerusalem" (Lk 9:31). The Greek word for "departure" is *exodos*, which in the Lucan narrative points to Jesus' death. The meaning was that Jesus would perform another exodus, from Jerusalem, that through his death he

1960], p. 171).

would deliver his people from the slavery of sin. Thus the Messiah, at the moment of manifesting his divine glory, was revealed as the one who must suffer. After the transfiguration, Jesus continued to speak to his disciples about his passion, but the disciples were afraid to say or to ask anything, although they did not reject his words (Mk 9:31-32). When he described for the third time what kind of death he would endure, "his saying was hid from them and they did not grasp what was said" (Lk 18:34). A parallel account in Mark reports that immediately after the third prediction of the passion, James and John, the sons of Zebedee, requested to be granted seats in Jesus' glory, one at his right hand and one at his left. Jesus answered them: "You do not know what you are asking. Are you able to drink the cup that I drink, or to be baptized with the baptism with which I am baptized?" (Mk 10:35-38). This, again, pointed to his forthcoming suffering and death, to his acceptance of the cup of suffering (Mk 14:36).

Even after the third prediction of the passion, the idea of messianic suffering was foreign to the disciples. If there is a "messianic secret" in Mark, then it consists of the disciples' refusal to accept Jesus as the Messiah who must suffer, and not of Jesus' disclaimers to be the Messiah. The difficulty sprang from Jesus' unique identification of the Suffering Servant of the Lord with the Messiah.

VI

The title "Christ" or "Messiah," ambiguous in common usage during Jesus' public ministry, became one of the three titles considered by the early Church to be adequate to his identity and his accomplishment. After Jesus' death and resurrection, the term "Christ" no longer possessed nationalistic connotations. By confessing Jesus as the promised Messiah, the Son of David "according to the flesh" (Rom 1:3-4), the Christian community expressed its deep conviction that Jesus was the fulfillment of the history of salvation.

Yet to the early Christians, Christ's messiahship transcended the bounds of Israel and Judaism, and they confessed him also as "Lord." This was the second title. It was the most sacred name that the Church could give to the resurrected Christ.[18] The primitive Aramaic prayer in 1

18 The personal name of God in the Old Testament, Yahweh, consists of the four consonants YHWH, and is not spoken by Jews. Instead of saying Yahweh, a Jew would pronounce it as

Corinthians 16:22 contains the invocation "*Maranatha!*" which meant: "Our Lord, come!" The church in Jerusalem thereby ascribed to Christ the divine honor that had previously belonged to Yahweh alone. Some New Testament scholars, however, hold that the title κύριος was given to Jesus by the Hellenistic churches, not by the Jewish Christians in the primitive church at Jerusalem. But neither the gospels nor any other book in the New Testament reflect, directly or indirectly, any controversy between the mother Church and the Hellenistic Christian communities over assigning the title κύριος to Jesus.[19] It is true that practicing Jews would have been the most unlikely people in the Hellenistic world to acknowledge Jesus as the Lord. Only a uniquely extraordinary event could have led them to do so.

The third title given to Jesus by the early Church was "Son of God." This was applied to angels, to the king, to faithful Israelites, and in the New Testament to all men. "Blessed are the peacemakers, for they shall be called sons of God" (Mt 5:9,45). The Messiah is the Son of God (Mt 16:16). At both his baptism and transfiguration, a heavenly voice proclaimed him as God's Son (Mk 1:11; 9:7, and paral.). The theme of this divine Sonship occurs in all four gospels. "All things have been delivered to me by my Father," declared Jesus, "and no one knows the Father except the Son and any one to whom the Son chooses to reveal him" (Mt 11:25-27, Lk 16:21-22).

This was a much greater claim than any of the Old Testament prophets had made. The prophets "saw" and "heard" divine things but did not claim that they had full knowledge of God. Jesus, however, did claim such knowledge, on the unique basis of his union with the Father:

Adonai, "my Lord." This is due to the great reverence which the Jews have for the name of God. In the Septuagint the four sacred consonants were translated as κύριος (Lord). The first Christians called Jesus "Lord" (Acts 2:36, Rom 10:9, 1 Cor 12:3; 16:22; Rev 22:20f), thereby attributing to him the sovereignty that belongs to YHWH.

19 On this subject see Arthur W. Wainwright, *The Trinity in the New Testament* (London: SPCK, 1962), p. 87. This division between the primitive church in Jerusalem and the Hellenistic churches is highly questionable. Martin Hengel argues convincingly that the roots of the Greek-speaking Jewish-Christian community "extend back to the very earliest community in Jerusalem," and that "the first linguistic development of its *kerygma* and its christology must have already taken place there." He finds it difficult "to attribute particular theological views predominantly or exclusively to '*the* Hellenistic Diaspora' or to 'Palestinian Judaism'"; see his *The "Hellenization" of Judea in the First Century after Christ* (Philadelphia: Trinity Press, 1989), pp. 18, 28.

"I and the Father are one" (Jn 10:30). The theme of divine Sonship is very important in the Gospel of John. For the salvation of the world, God gave his only Son. The Father loves the Son and "shows him all that he himself is doing; the Son has power to give life, and to the Son all judgment is given" (Jn 5:20f). The Son glorifies the Father, for "no one has ever seen God; the only Son, who is in the bosom of the Father, he has made him known" (Jn 1:18).

Jesus did not use the title "Son of God" for himself, but rather spoke of himself as "Son," and addressed God as *abba* (an intimate form of "Father"). With *abba*, Jesus expressed his complete commitment and absolute obedience to the Father. With it he revealed his closeness to God, a sense of oneness with him that was quite different from that implied by similar passages in the Old Testament, and quite new to his contemporaries. It is definitely an exaggeration to claim that nobody but Jesus used the expression *abba* in addressing God: *abba* was sometimes used in this way in Jewish documents. What was unique to Jesus' usage was that he used it regularly and consistently.[20] The regular custom was to address God as *abinu* (*our* father, Mt 6:9). Jesus' use of *abba*, therefore, helps us to grasp something of his understanding of the relationship between God and himself. To him, the Father, the creator of the world, was not distant but permanently present. Only in this light can we understand the nature of the passion prophecies. Jesus did not seek martyrdom, but to accomplish the mission for which the Father sent him. He willed what the Father willed; he made the will of the Father his own: "The Son can do nothing of his own accord, but only what he sees the Father doing; for whatever he does, that the Son does likewise" (Jn 5:19). Jesus predicted his resurrection at the same time that he predicted his death. His life was a journey, coming from the Father and returning to the Father by way of the cross.

Christians, in turn, could address God as *abba* only after Jesus had completed his work of salvation and after the Spirit had come. Paul wrote in Romans: "For all who are led by the Spirit of God are sons of God. For you did not receive the spirit of slavery to fall back into fear, but you have received the spirit of sonship. When we cry, 'Abba! Father!' it is the Spirit

20 J. H. Charlesworth, *Jesus Within Judaism*, p. 134; J. D. G. Dunn, *Christology in the Making* (Philadelphia: Westminster, 1980), pp. 26f.

himself bearing witness with our spirit that we are children of God" (Rom 8:14-16). Man could not address God as *abba* through his own efforts. "God has sent the Spirit of his Son into our hearts, crying 'Abba! Father'" (Gal 4:6).

Some form critics have argued that the concept of "the Son" did not originate with Jesus but with the primitive Christian community. They support this assertion by stating that the term "Son" was not used in Judaism as a designation of the Messiah in a technical sense. This does not take into account the use of the "Son" in the parable of the Wicked Tenants (Mk 12:1-12), discussed above. There is also ample evidence from Jewish literature of the second and the first centuries before Christ, and from the first century A.D., that "Son" was used as a theological title. In this literature, God called Moses "my son," the righteous one shall be called "God's son," and the Messiah shall be God's Son. Josephus presented Moses as "a son in the likeness of God" (Ant. 2:232). The term "son" was used by Jews in Jesus' time to express a kind of legal adoption. The basic difference between Jesus' use of "Son" and its use in the Jewish parallels lies in the fact that Jesus used it about himself, while in the Jewish literature sonship is attributed to another, especially to the expected Messiah.[21]

There is no need therefore to point to the early church as the originator of the title. Rather, it derived from Jesus' unique relationship of intimate union with God the Father. Behind the Church's confession of faith lay the life and resurrection of Jesus, in the light of which the Church saw the meaning of the ancient prophecy of Nathan, that he would raise up David's offspring after him: "I will be his father and he shall be my son" (2 Sam 7:12-14).[22]

The earliest Christians identified Jesus as Christ, Lord and Son of God. The title Son of Man, however, entered none of the Church's credal statements, nor its early hymns. The early Christians found it inappropriate for missionary use. In the Hellenistic world, the title "Son of Man" was divested of its connotation of divine-human unity and it referred thereafter only to the humanity of Jesus.[23]

21 For all important references, see J. H. Charlesworth, *Jesus Within Judaism*, pp. 149-152.
22 M. Hengel, *The Son of God* (Philadelphia: Fortress Press, 1976), pp. 63-64.
23 Ignatius, *Eph* 20:2; Irenaeus, *A.H.* V.21.3; Justin, *Apology I*, 51.9.

Who was Jesus? The Church confessed him as Christ, the culmination of the history of salvation, the fulfiller of God's plan for his people. He was also the Lord, the *risen* Christ, who belonged not only to the past but who was permanently present in the community of believers as the center of their theological and liturgical life. Finally, Jesus was the Son of God, preexistent, incarnate, and exalted, according to the Church's creed. The hymn of *kenosis*, which Paul inherited from early Christian worship and incorporated in his letter to the Philippians (2:5-11), was structured upon these three stages in the life of Christ. The hymn speaks of Jesus as a heavenly figure "who was in the form of God, but did not count equality with God a thing to be grasped, but emptied himself, taking the form of a slave, being born in the likeness of man and found in human form. He humbled himself and became obedient unto death, even death on the cross. Therefore God has highly exalted him and bestowed on him the name which is above every name, that at the name of Jesus every knee should bow...and every tongue confess that Jesus Christ is Lord."[24] The Church fully understood Jesus' integration within himself of the roles of the "Lord" and the "Son of Man" who must suffer.[25] The inspiration for this hymn, therefore, was Jesus himself, his life, suffering and resurrection. The Church reflected upon the nature of his messiahship, followed Jesus in repudiating the popular messianic expectations, and confessed Jesus as the Lord, the victor, the true Messiah (Acts 2:34-35, 1 Cor 15:25, Heb 1:13).

---

24 In his book *The Son of God*, M. Hengel starts the discussion on the origin of Christology with Phil 2:6-8, stating that "the discrepancy between the shameful death" of Jesus and "the confession that depicts this executed man as a pre-existent divine figure [is] without analogy in the ancient world" (p. 1). The exaltation of the crucified Jesus "must already have taken place in the forties, and one is tempted to say that more happened in this period of less than two decades than in the whole of the next seven centuries, up to the time when the doctrine of the early church was completed" (p. 2).

25 There is "no reasonable ground for rejecting" the gospel evidence that Jesus "made that connection of the 'Lord' at God's right hand with the son of man in Daniel which proved so momentous for Christian thought" (C. H. Dodd, *According to the Scripture* [New York: Charles Scribner's Sons, 1953], p. 110).

11

Christ, Jews and Gentiles

Jesus spent his public ministry among his own people and addressed his message to them before it was sent to the Gentiles. Judaism at the time was not a monolithic system. Only after the fall of Jerusalem and the destruction of the Temple in 70 A.D. could it be identified exclusively with Rabbinic Judaism.[1] Before the catastrophe, various tendencies and groups existed within ancient Judaism. It was not a closed system. As the discovery of the Dead Sea Scrolls confirms, even the Essenes, while separated from the other groups, were subject to outside influences and were not isolated from the world surrounding them.

I

In Jesus' time approximately half a million Jews lived in Palestine. About six thousand of them belonged to the party of the Pharisees, about four thousand to the Essenes, and the Sadducees were less numerous than either group. In spite of such relatively small memberships, however, these religious groups exercised a powerful influence on Judaism. They differed from each other and often fought with each other, but none of them considered itself as being outside Judaism. As learned teachers and interpreters of the law, they shared an attitude of aloofness and of superiority toward the ignorant and illiterate masses. For the Pharisees, "this crowd who do not know the law are accursed" (Jn 7:49) and ritually

---

1 During the revolt of 66-70 A.D., both Jews and Jewish Christians had to leave Jerusalem and Palestine. The Jewish ruling authorities moved from Jerusalem to Jamnia, where a school had been founded before the fall of Jerusalem. Only after the fall, however, did the school and those who were associated with it take a leading position and exercise an all-powerful influence in consolidating Judaism after the tragic events of 70 A.D. Under the leadership of Rabbi Johanan ben Zakkai, the founder of the school at Jamnia, and later under Rabbi Gamaliel II, Judaism became suspicious of any internal diversity. The canon of the Hebrew scriptures was fixed, a uniform calendar was introduced, "a prayer was inserted in the synagogue service to make it impossible for Jewish Christians to join in the worship of Judaism" (W. D. Davies, *The Sermon on the Mount* [Cambridge: Cambridge University Press, 1966], p. 85). The codification of the oral law began, and Judaism as a whole was engaged in building "a fence around itself."

unclean.[2]

The Pharisees, described by the first-century Jewish historian Josephus, were "considered the most accurate interpreters of the laws." They "attributed everything to Fate and to God," and believed that every soul "is imperishable, but the soul of the good alone passes into another body, while the souls of the wicked suffer eternal punishment." But the Sadducees, according to Josephus, "[did] away with Fate altogether, and [removed] God beyond." They believed "that man has the free choice of good and evil, and that it rests with each man's will whether he follows the one or the other." They did not believe that the soul persists after death, nor did they consider penalties and rewards in the world to come. While the Pharisees were portrayed by Josephus as "affectionate to each other" and keen to cultivate "harmonious relations with the community," the Sadducees were "even among themselves rather boorish," and in their relations with other Jews they were "as rude as to aliens." By applying the term "Jewish philosophy" or "school" to these Jewish religious groups or movements, as well as to the Essenes and the "Zealots," Josephus tried to reach his readers in the Hellenistic world in terms that they would understand.[3]

The designation "Pharisee" probably comes from the Aramaic *perishayya*, meaning "separated ones," not in the sense of withdrawing from the world, but that in the world they chose to interpret and observe the Law, to organize their own religious fellowship (*havurah*) and to live a life of ritual purity. They tried to extend the applicability of the Temple laws to all aspects of life. They lived in the cities, separated from all others who did not keep the law as they did. They associated and ate with the ritually pure, trying to persuade other Jews in their cities to follow their example.[4] Messianic

---

2 R. Akiba was born among the *am ha-aretz* (c. 50 A.D.) and became a Rabbi in later life. Remembering his days as a member of the unlearned masses, he declared "that he would wish to bite a scholar 'like an ass.' 'Like a dog,' his disciples corrected him. But he replied, 'An ass's bite breaks the bone; a dog's does not.'" See C. K. Barrett, ed., *The New Testament Background: Selected Documents*, revised and expanded edition (New York: Harper & Row, 1989), p. 181.

3 *Ibid.*, pp. 157ff (Josephus, *War II*, pp. 119ff).

4 "One primary mark of Pharisaic commitment was the observance of the laws of ritual purity outside of the Temple, where everyone kept them" (p. 57). "Pharisaic table-fellowship took place in the same circumstances in which all nonritual table-fellowship occurred...this made the actual purity rule and food restrictions all the more important, for only they set the Pharisee apart from the people among whom they constantly lived," writes Jacob Neusner in *Judaism in the Beginning of Christianity* (Philadelphia: Fortress Press, 1984), pp. 57, 58.

expectations, which they cherished, were inseparable from the fulfillment of the law.

Jesus' understanding of the law brought him into conflict with the
casuistic Pharisees. In the Sermon on the Mount, for example, Jesus said:
"You have heard that it was said, 'You shall not commit adultery.' But I
say to you that every one who looks at a woman lustfully has already
committed adultery with her in his heart" (Mt 5:27f). By contrasting the
Mosaic commandment with his own pronouncement, Jesus did not
invalidate the law. Here, as well as in other antitheses, the expression
"*But* I say to you" (ἐγὼ δὲ λέγω ὑμῖν) is used not to oppose or abolish
God's commandment, but to proclaim the completion of the law by
Jesus' coming. The "but" (*de*) in the Sermon contrasts Moses and Jesus
and should be understood in the sense of fulfilling, not of abolishing the
law, as if Jesus had said: "You have heard that it was said...But I say
beyond that."[5] Even in the antithesis that deals with divorce (Mt 5:31-
32), Jesus did not "abolish" the Mosaic law but went beyond it. Moses
allowed a man to divorce his wife "for his hardness of heart," but Jesus
forbade this, for "from the beginning it was not so" (Mt 19:7-8). This
saying goes beyond the Mosaic requirements to consider the very structure of God's creation (Gn 2:24).

Jesus' demands exceeded the law. To fulfill the law means "to bring
it to completion" or to perfection. The law before Christ's coming was
σκιά (shadow), whose unfinished nature was revealed by the introduction of a new order, a new reality (see Heb 10:1). Jesus therefore
deepened and radicalized the Torah, cutting through the numerous
religious regulations of the Pharisees that had divided the people into
two religious classes: those who observed the ritual rules of purity and
those, the people of the land, who could not. The principle proclaimed
in Mk 7:15 was of universal importance: "There is nothing outside a
man which by going into him can defile him; but the things which come
out of a man are what defile him." By removing the legal discrimination
between clean and unclean, Jesus opened and prepared the way for
Gentiles to follow him as well.

Among Jesus' sayings referring to God's commandments and to the

5 See Franz Mussner, *Tractate on the Jews: The Significance of Judaism for Christian Faith*
(Philadelphia: Fortress Press, 1984), pp. 116f; E. P. Sanders, *Jesus and Judaism*, p. 260.

demands of the law, one was particularly striking and even shocking to pious Jews. One of his would-be disciples, when asked by Jesus to follow him, said "'Lord, let me first go and bury my father.' But Jesus said to him 'Follow me, and leave the dead to bury their own dead'" (Mt 8:21-22, Lk 9:59-60). Not to take care of one's dead parents was in effect to be in open disobedience to God and to his demands, since it conflicted with God's commandment: "Honor your father and your mother, that your days may be long in the land which the Lord your God gives you" (Ex 20:12). Nothing similar to this saying of Jesus can be found in Judaism, in the early Church, or in the piety of the Hellenistic world. What then does the saying reveal about Jesus' attitude to the law?

It appears that with this saying, Jesus was willing to put himself above both the law and pious custom. All attempts to remove its offensive character and its implication of antinomianism have proven inadequate. The saying has been applied to all those who are spiritually dead, those who "may indeed see but not perceive, who may indeed hear but not understand," those to whom the message comes but who close themselves to it. They are those who hear the gospel "but the care of the world" interferes with their response (Mk 4:11f). Jesus, however, referred here to those who are really dead. To overlook this is to miss the primary meaning of this saying: namely, Jesus' sovereign freedom with respect to the law.[6]

Two texts from the Old Testament shed light on Mt 8:21-22. The first is the account of the calling of Elisha (1 Kg 19:19-21), and the second comes from Jeremiah's life (Jer 16:5-7). The prophet Elijah, having returned from Mount Horeb, found Elisha, who was plowing, and he cast his mantle upon him. As Elijah was leaving, Elisha ran after him saying: "Let me kiss my father and my mother, and then I will follow you." Then Elijah responded: "Go, and return to me, for I have done something very important to you" (RSV). Jesus demanded more from his would-be disciple than Elijah asked of Elisha: total commitment, trust, loyalty, and detachment from all family ties. In Jer 16:5-7, God, in view of his impending judgment, commands: "Do not enter the house of mourning, or go to lament, or bemoan them; for I have taken away my peace from this people, my steadfast love and mercy," and "no

6 Martin Hengel, *The Charismatic Leader and His Followers*, p. 11.

one shall break bread for the mourner, to comfort him for the dead; nor shall any one give him the cup of consolation to drink for his father or his mother" (Jer 16:5-7). All these customs, as expressions of family piety, must be relinquished. This shows that the judgment is just around the corner, that "both great and small shall die in this land," and that normal mourning customs should be set aside. Jesus' saying works in a similar way. Here it is not only a question of judgement, but also of the would-be disciple's incorporation into the messianic community. The desire to enter the Kingdom of God puts aside all other pious desires, customs and requirements. It is no time to look back, for to follow Jesus and his demands takes priority over all other demands.

Again, with this saying Jesus did not abolish the law and its requirements of family duty and piety. Rather, he fulfilled it. His harsh, "shocking" saying should be seen in the light of the coming of the Kingdom of God. With the coming of Jesus, whose teaching is the incarnation of the pure will of God, family ties and obligations are to be seen in the light of his messianic sovereignty. When his mother and brothers asked for him, Jesus, looking at the crowd he was teaching, responded: "Here are my mother and my brothers! Whoever does the will of God is my brother, and sister, and mother" (Mk 3:31-35). The family is not abandoned but raised to a higher level through its relation to God and through its fulfillment of God's will as revealed by his incarnate Son. His followers never took Jesus' saying in Mt 8:21-22 as an excuse for avoiding their sacred obligation toward their parents, nor did they see in it a seed of "lawlessness"; rather, they saw it as an expression of Jesus' authority which transcended any other authority, whether of the prophets, the sages, or the rabbis.[7]

II

The Sadducees (Aramaic *zadduqaya*, from Zadok, Gr. Sadok, the high priest of David) were also interpreters of the Law. But above all, their main influence was in the Temple.

The Sadducees had no messianic hope, nor any belief in the resurrection of the dead (Mt 22:23). They accepted only the first five books of

---

7 For this discussion on Mt 8:21-22, I am indebted to M. Hengel, *The Charismatic Leader and His Followers*, pp. 1-16.

Moses (the Pentateuch) as their scripture and were suspicious of any new addition to it. The Prophets and the Writings, the other two parts of the Hebrew Scripture, were not dismissed outright, but they did not possess God's authority. The Sadducees rejected oral tradition and the "oral Torah." The law, for them, had to be interpreted and applied literally. It was this literal-mindedness which Jesus attacked, accusing the Sadducees of knowing neither the Scriptures nor the power of God (Mt 22:23-33 and paral.).

Rigid conservatives in interpreting Scripture, the Sadducees inflexibly resisted any changes in the ritual of the Temple. However, they were flexible in dealing with the Romans. The Gentile occupiers allowed them to worship as they pleased, and the Sadducees were ready to collaborate with them. Thus they were able to preserve both the Temple cult with all its riches, and their aristocratic status.

Jesus' cleansing of the Temple particularly offended the Temple priests and their circle. The Sadducees saw in this act an attack on everything related to the Temple, and on themselves as well.[8] They regarded it as an attack on the place of both God's revelation and God's forgiveness of the sins of the people. In their mind, there was no doubt that Jesus of Nazareth deserved death for this "cleansing." Consequently the Chief priest and the Scribes "sought a way to destroy him" (Mk 11:18).

The Sadducees understood the purpose of Jesus' prophetic action, but they were ignorant of his true identity and of his real reason for undertaking the cleansing of the holy place. The very action of overturning tables revealed the meaning of Jesus' work. It symbolized the arrival of the end of an age that the Temple in Jerusalem represented and the arrival of a new age, with a new Temple (Jn 2:19f). The old Temple would be replaced by the resurrected Christ, the new locus of God's revelation and forgiveness. Jesus did not see the Temple as an institution of enduring significance. His attitude toward it cannot be separated from his attitude toward the law, since, after all, the rites of the Temple were

8   E. P. Sanders writes that "had Jesus wished to make a gesture symbolizing purity, he doubtless could have done so. The pouring out of water comes immediately to mind. The turning over of even one table points toward destruction" (*Jesus and Judaism*, p. 70). Why did Jesus undertake this attack on the Temple? "The obvious answer is that destruction, in turn, looks toward restoration" (p. 71).

based on the Torah. Neither the Law nor the Temple therefore could be adequate or final for him. He saw beyond both the law and the Temple.

Whereas the Pharisees survived the destruction of the Temple by the Romans, the Sadducees lost all their power and influence after 70 A.D. They were influential among the priests and the rich, and the Pharisees among urban groups and the people of the synagogue. Before the fall of Jerusalem, the Sadducees had not kept in touch with new developments or with new religious ideas, and after the fall, when their system was destroyed, they were unprepared to cope with a new religious and political situation bereft of the Temple and the sacrifices. There was no messianic hope to sustain them, as there was for the Pharisees, and soon they disappeared entirely.

The third important Jewish religious group at the time of Jesus was the Essenes. The origin of the term Essene is uncertain. It might come from the Aramaic *hasayya*, meaning "pious one." The Essenes are not mentioned in the New Testament, but they were known to Jesus and to his followers. Who were they, where did they live, and what did they believe?

Like the Pharisees, the Essenes evolved from the *Hasidim,* "the pious ones" of the Maccabean period, who "chose to die rather than profane the holy covenant; and they did die" (1 Mc 1:63). The political ambitions of the Maccabees to establish themselves as a dynasty, the appointment of a Maccabee as high priest (which broke the Zadokite line of succession), and the introduction of the lunar calendar into the Temple forced many devout people to withdraw into the wilderness and to separate themselves from the priesthood in Jerusalem. The Qumran group attached great importance to the priesthood. By calling themselves the sons of Zadok, the Dead Sea ascetics wanted to stress that theirs was the legitimate priesthood, and that the priests of the Temple in Jerusalem were imposters. Josephus estimated that about four thousand Essenes lived in Palestine. Not all of them could have lived at Qumran, which produced the Dead Sea Scrolls. While some three hundred lived at this monastic establishment, the rest lived elsewhere, and a group of them even lived in a section of Jerusalem. It is probable that Jesus met some of these Essenes who settled outside Qumran, and that he talked with them.

The Essenes were inspired by "the belief in the end of days." They lived in the hope that the covenant which God established with his people would be "wholly fulfilled" at some future time. How much they were permeated by the messianic hope is reflected by their expectations of *two* messiahs—the priestly Messiah of Aaron and the political Messiah of Israel. The hope in the coming of two messiahs had its origin in the prophecy of Zechariah 4:14 ("these are two anointed [Messiahs] who stand by the Lord of the whole earth"), which refers to the High Priest and to a King who will come from the House of David. In the Qumran documents, the Messiah who comes from the priestly line appears to be more important than the Messiah who comes from the line of David. The Essenes were so preoccupied with the illegitimacy of the High Priest of the Temple in Jerusalem that they dreamed of reestablishing the legal priesthood. Therefore, they attached more importance to the priestly messiah. They also expected the coming of a prophet who would proclaim the end of the world.

The leader of the Qumran group was known as the Teacher of Righteousness (probably a priest of the Zadokite line). Biblical commentaries discovered at Qumran suggest that he was an inspired interpreter of Scripture, especially of the law. The Essenes were preoccupied with this. The reason for making a final break with Jerusalem was their conviction that the law was not observed fully and completely there. The Essenes based their community upon the law; with respect to the place of the law in the daily life of the people, they surpassed even the Pharisees. They have thus been characterized as "super-Pharisees." The Essene attitude toward the calendar was inseparable from their attitude toward the law. The Qumran members were known as "calendar specialists." They closely linked salvation to the observance of a feast according to the "right" calendar. Being extreme legalists, they were also extreme ritualists. Almost everything depended upon the right observances, according to the right calendar. It was essential for a member of the Qumran community to live according to the calendar. A modern critic has observed ironically that "nowhere [did Jesus say] 'Follow me and adopt my calendar.'"[9]

9 Ethelbert Stauffer, *Jesus and the Wilderness Community at Qumran* (Philadelphia: Fortress Press, 1964), p. 16.

The group thought of itself as the true Israel, as the community of the Covenant, as the Sons of Light who would survive all the tribulations that mark the end of this impure age. The Essenes therefore prepared themselves for a holy war at the end of time. Their preoccupation with this "imminent eschatological crisis" completely colored their outlook. The sect withdrew from the world to purify itself before the final event came to pass.

Jesus may have known some Essenes, and may even have praised their singleness of heart, their commitment to the God of Israel. Upon entering the Qumran community, they contributed all that they possessed to the common fund, referring to themselves as "the poor." Although there is no single explicit reference to the Essenes in the gospels, there is material that strongly suggests that Jesus was aware of the teachings of the Qumran sectarians.

An example of Essene teaching is the phrase: "Hate your enemy." Jesus said: "You have heard that it was said 'You shall love your neighbor and hate your enemy.' But I say to you, love your enemies and pray for those who persecute you, so that you may be sons of your Father who is in heaven" (Mt 5:43f). "Hate your enemy" is found neither in the Old Testament nor in Rabbinic literature. There are, however, texts in the Old Testament from which Jesus could have culled the expression "hate your enemy," such as Ps 139:21-22:

Do I not hate them that hate thee, O Lord?
And do I not loathe them that rise up against thee?
I hate them with perfect hatred;
I count them my enemies.

By contrast, we have explicit advice from the Hebrew sages to their youth in the period after the Babylonian Captivity:

If your enemy is hungry, give him bread to eat;
And if he is thirsty, give him water to drink;
For you will heap coals of fire on his head,
And the Lord will reward you.
(Pr 25:21-22; see Mt 5:44-45 and Rom 12:20-21)

Still, the psalmist did not exhort his contemporaries to hate their enemies, and what the sages asked for was less than loving one's enemy. They thought that hatred or vengeance could be overcome by acts of mercy. By being confronted with good, the enemy may be led to repentance, as Paul wrote to the Roman Christians: "Do not be overcome by evil, but overcome evil with good" (Rom 12:21).

The injunction to hate one's enemy occurs in the Dead Sea Scrolls, in the *Manual of Discipline*, also called the *Rule of Community* at Qumran:

> Everyone who wishes to join the community must pledge himself to respect God and man…to walk blamelessly before him in conformity with all that has been revealed as relevant to several periods during which they are to bear witness [to Him]; to love all the children of light, each according to his stake in the formal community of God; and to hate all the children of darkness, each according to the measure of his guilt, which God will ultimately requite (I, 3f).[10]

It is possible that Jesus had the Qumran sectarians in mind when he pronounced the saying recorded in Mt 5:43ff, and that he condemned their attitude of hatred toward their enemy.[11]

The Lucan parable of the Great Banquet (14:15-24) is probably another reference to Essene teaching and belief. When many rejected the invitation to share in God's kingdom, the householder said to his servant: "Go out quickly to the streets and lanes of the city, and bring in the poor and maimed and blind and lame." In the Qumran literature the following text is found: "Fools, madmen, simpletons and imbeciles, the blind, the maimed, the lame, the deaf, and minors, none of these may enter the midst of the community, for the holy angels [are in the midst of it]."[12] The Qumran community was a priestly sect of priestly origins. By contrast, all those whom the Essenes rejected were invited by Jesus into his kingdom.

There are other texts in the gospels which may be interpreted as being directed against the Essenes.[13] Matthew, for instance, ends the parable of the laborers in the vineyard with the words, "so the last will be first and the first last" (20:16). These words may be understood as spoken not only against the Pharisees, but also against the Essenes. The Qumran community was well organized, with a clear line drawn between the hierarchy and the other members of the community.

10 Theodore H. Gaster, *The Dead Sea Scriptures* (Garden City, NY: Doubleday & Co., 1964), p. 46.
11 W. D. Davies, *The Sermon on the Mount*, p. 83.
12 J. T. Milik, *Ten Years of Discovery in the Wilderness* (London: SCM Press, 1959), pp. 114ff. Milik adds that we have here an expansion of "priestly disqualifications found in the Pentateuch."
13 See W. D. Davies, *Christian Origins and Judaism* (Philadelphia: Westminster Press, 1962), p. 117.

The gospels differ from the Dead Sea Scrolls on several essential issues. In the Christian documents, the Messiah has already come: Jesus of Nazareth, whose death and resurrection are the source of salvation. The Teacher of the Qumran documents is not seen as a messianic figure. Whether this Teacher suffered martyrdom or not cannot be proved with any degree of certainty. If he did suffer at the hands of the "Wicked Priest," his death was not interpreted as the source of salvation by his followers. Various guesses have been made about his identity; one of them surmises that he was, if not the Messiah, then the forerunner of the Messiah. These guesses and alleged similarities between the Qumran leader and Christ of the New Testament have been proved to be over-stated. Even if the Teacher of Righteousness was crucified, this fact would not necessarily make him a counterpart of Jesus and of his suffering. Many Jews were crucified before and after Jesus. Judaism had its martyrs, and their cult is suggested in the gospel (Mt 23:29-31). An image of the crucified leader or Teacher, who would also be the Re-deemer, cannot be derived from the Dead Sea Scrolls. The Qumran convenanters expected a Messiah to come.

With the discovery of the Scrolls, our knowledge of the complex nature of Judaism in the time of Jesus is considerably increased. They have become indispensable for the study of New Testament background. From these documents, produced by the Jewish monastic group at Qumran, we learn about a Jewish religious movement that directly opposed the Jewish priestly establishment in Jerusalem, and, therefore, that Judaism was not a monolithic system. A variety of Jewish outlooks existed at the time of Jesus. Although there is nothing specific about Jesus in these documents, they contribute to our knowledge of Judaism as the context of Jesus' life and ministry.

IV

After describing the Pharisees, Sadducees and Essenes, Josephus turns to "the fourth philosophy," the Zealots. Soon after Herod's son, Archaelaus, was deposed in 6 A.D., certain Jews rebelled against Roman registration for tax purposes. They saw the census of Quirinius as a symbol of the Jewish subjugation to Rome. Their leader was "a certain Judas" who was "in league with the Pharisee Saddok." The nation, according to Josephus, was in a state of "unrest."[14] Josephus' reference to the event that followed the census has been taken by some scholars as evidence for the existence of an organized Zealot party with a definite political-religious program. Others interpret Josephus' report as a description of a group of people without a clear program or leadership that would distinguish it from existing Jewish parties or movements. According to these scholars, Josephus' "fourth philosophy" or "school" shared the Pharisees' view regarding the law. On the basis of a reevaluation of Josephus' text, they argue that the people, under the leadership of Judas and "the Pharisee Saddok," resisted Roman taxation without using arms. An organized party of Zealots therefore did not exist during Jesus' public ministry. The organized party originated in the Jewish-Roman War that led to the destruction of the Temple in 70 A.D.[15] Of course,* there were individual zealots who had a passion for liberty and who dreamt of liberating their people from the Roman yoke in Jesus' time. The possibility of violence was ever present during the Roman occupation of Palestine. In the wider meaning of the term, a Zealot might be one who was "zealous for God" (Acts 22:3), devoted to the law and ready to defend it. In the narrow sense of the word, the Zealots were identified as "militant patriots" who committed violent acts without belonging to an armed, organized opposition to Rome.[16] In view of this, it is justifiable to examine the problem of the relations between Jesus and the Zealots and to try to define what Jesus' attitude was toward them.

Two recent books about Jesus and the Zealots were both written according to the premise that an organized Zealot movement was alive in Jesus' time. S. G. P. Brandon, in his book *Jesus and the Zealots* (1967), defends with great skill and erudition the thesis that Jesus was a revolutionary. Brandon does not say that Jesus was a Zealot, but that he viewed the work and action of the Zealots, organized upon the principle of violent resistance to the Romans, with great sympathy and understanding. According to Brandon, Jesus' work was linked with the Zealots, and he agreed with their principles. Even if Jesus was not a Zealot, it is

---

14 *Antiquities* XVIII, 4,23-25.
15 See R. A. Horsley and J. S. Hanson, *Bandits, Prophets and Messiahs*, pp. 220ff; *The New Jerome Biblical Commentary*, 75:179.
16 J. P. M. Sweet, "The Zealots and Jesus," in E. Bammel and C. F. D. Moule (eds.), *Jesus and the Politics of His Day*, p. 5, fn. 8.

difficult to see any difference between the purposes of Jesus and those of the Zealots. Brandon attaches significance to the fact that there is no record in the gospels of any direct denunciation of the Zealots by Jesus.

To support the view of Jesus' close connection with the Zealots, Brandon concentrates on the events of the last week in Jerusalem, especially on the cleansing of the Temple. He gives much less attention to Jesus' sayings and teachings, assuming that the gospel report of the events was less distorted than that of Jesus' teachings. But in his interpretation of the cleansing of the Temple, Brandon distorts what most modern scholars would see as Jesus' intention. These would argue that the cleansing was not an act of violence but a prophetic act. To the ruling authorities this act appeared dangerous, not because Jesus used violence or was ready to use violence, but because he challenged their authority on their own ground—Jesus claimed the Temple for himself.

In Oscar Cullmann's book *Jesus and the Revolutionaries* (1970), a chapter is devoted to the "political question" of Jesus and the Zealots. Cullmann argues that Jesus did not join the Zealots, "for their goals and their methods were not his." Jesus never considered the use of violence as an option. His teaching to "love your enemies" (Mt 5:43) placed him above the political, revolutionary struggle in which the Zealots were involved. According to Cullmann, Jesus was a great disappointment for the Zealots, a fact which "may have played a part in Judas' betrayal of him."

According to Josephus, Cullmann points out, the Zealots shared the teachings of the Pharisees. It may be that Jesus did not attack the Zealots directly, as he did the Pharisees, because they shared the same religious precepts. Rather, the Zealots were indirectly included in Jesus' criticism of the Pharisees.[17]

Brandon's and Cullmann's views should be considered as two representative approaches to the question of the relationship between Jesus and the Zealots. Books written on the same subject, before or after these two books, are similar in substance. Hyam Maccoby (*Revolution in Judea: Jesus and the Jewish Resistance*, 1973) portrays Jesus as a Galilean, anti-Roman rebel. In his view, the gospels are a rewriting of history, and Jesus actually arrived in Jerusalem before the Passover to foment armed insur-

17 *Jesus and the Revolutionaries* (New York: Harper & Row, 1970), p. 67, n. 7.

rection there. Jesus' mission was not the salvation of man from sin but the liberation of his people from the Roman yoke. The fate of the disciples of Jesus, however, appears to undermine Maccoby's imaginative reconstruction of "revolution in Judea." After all, they, too, would presumably have been Galilean insurgents like him and should have been arrested with him.[18] But they were left free to organize their own community in Jerusalem.

After examining Jesus' actions and his message, Martin Hengel expresses a diametrically opposite point of view. He sees "the heart of the proclamation of Jesus" as "the conscious rejection of violence."[19] Jesus renounced violence (Mt 5:38-46, Lk 6:27-36). By rejecting the third temptation (Mt 4:9), Jesus renounced political, nationalistic messianism and the use of violence. One of Jesus' disciples was a Zealot (Lk 6:15), and another was a tax-collector (Mt 9:9), but both abandoned their former views or occupations and followed him. Their lives were molded by him.

Jesus was neither a Sadducee nor a Pharisee, neither an Essene nor a Zealot. He cannot be identified with any party of first-century Judaism. Rather, he addressed the people of Israel as a whole.

V

The chosen people of God had the privilege of hearing the words of Jesus and of witnessing his works before anybody else did. "Go nowhere among Gentiles," Jesus instructed the Twelve, "and enter no town of the Samaritans, but go rather to the lost sheep of the house of Israel. And preach as you go, saying, 'The Kingdom of heaven is at hand'" (Mt 10:5-7). To the Canaanite woman, a Gentile, who asked mercy for herself and for her sick daughter, Jesus answered "I was sent only to the lost sheep of the house of Israel" (Mt 15:24).

18 Hillel Halkin, "Jesus as Jew," in *Commentary* (September 1981), reviewed this book and asked these questions: "Why, when Jesus was arrested, were his disciples not taken into custody, too, if they were armed rebels like himself? Why, if his offence was insurrection, did the Romans prefer to have the Jewish religious authorities interrogate him first instead of dealing with him directly themselves? The way a Roman governor, especially one with a reputation for cruelty like Pontius Pilate, might have been expected to behave toward an insurgency in Jerusalem would have been to seize all its members as quickly as possible, pass summary judgment on them, and execute them to a man" (p. 78).

19 *Was Jesus a Revolutionist?* (Philadelphia: Fortress Press, 1971), p. 26.

Jesus and his disciples did not start with the conversion of other nations, but with their own people. They came from and went to Israel with their message. As was only appropriate, the Twelve began by teaching the people who had been set apart for God's special purposes, who had been called and elected, and with whom God had established his Covenant. From this people the disciples expected a positive response to the new works God was performing in their midst.

Yet this mission to Israel did not exclude either the Samaritans or the Gentiles from salvation, from experiencing the power of the age to come. To be a Samaritan was to be a member of an impure people. The term "Samaritan" was a term for the enemy (Jn 8:48). The Samaritan woman was surprised that Jesus, a Jew, asked a drink of her, "for Jews have no dealings with Samaritans" (Jn 4:7ff). To the lawyer's question, "And who is my neighbor?" Jesus answered with the parable of the Good Samaritan (Lk 10:29ff). On the way to Jerusalem, Jesus passed through Samaria, but the Samaritans "would not receive him, because his face was set toward Jerusalem." When sons of Zebedee asked for fire from heaven to consume the Samaritans, Jesus "turned and rebuked [them]" (Lk 9:51ff). A Samaritan was healed by Jesus and praised for his faith (Lk 17:11ff). Jesus manifestly did not exclude the Samaritans from his kingdom.

Neither did Jesus exclude the Gentile world. He eventually healed the daughter of the Syrophoenician woman, to whom he had previously said that he had been sent only to the lost sheep of the house of Israel (Mt 15:24ff, Mk 7:24-30). The centurion's servant was also healed (Mt 8:5ff and paral.). It was Jesus who declared that many Gentiles "will come from east and west and sit at table with Abraham, Isaac, and Jacob in the Kingdom of God," whereas the children of Abraham might lose the kingdom (Mt 8:11-12). The story of the Gerasene demoniac (Mk 5:1-20 and paral.) testifies to Jesus' activity among the Gentiles. The expressions "Go therefore to the thoroughfares, and invite as many as you find" (Mt 22:9) or "Go out to the highways and hedges" (Lk 14:23) in the Parable of the Marriage Feast, indicate that the gospel was offered to the Gentiles. He even takes a Gentile woman as an example of what will happen at the judgment (Lk 11:31, Mt 12:42).

In the Old Testament there are both positive and negative statements about the Gentiles. In the same prophetic books (Isaiah and Micah, for example) both attitudes toward the Gentiles can be found. The Gentiles will be saved; the Gentiles will be destroyed (Is 56:6-8; 45:22; 54:3). Micah predicted both the defeat of the Gentiles (Mic 5) and that many nations would come to the mountain of the Lord, where all would be secure (Mic 4). The rabbis also made both favorable and harsh statements about the Gentiles: "There are righteous Gentiles;" "there are no righteous Gentiles."[20] Jesus' attitude toward the Gentiles, by contrast, was consistently positive.

In its missionary work the apostolic Church extended Jesus' mission to the Gentiles. After the death and resurrection of Jesus, the dividing wall between the Jews and the "nations," which had already started to crumble during his public ministry, was abolished. The disciples were sent to "make disciples of all nations" (Mt 28:18-20), to preach "the gospel...to all nations" (Mk 13:10). To bear testimony to the Gentiles would not be an easy task. The disciples were warned about the consequences of their witness to Jesus, about their persecution for his sake (Mt 10:18). At the last judgment all nations would be present. The separation between "sheep" and "goats" would be made not on a racial or national basis, nor on the basis of privilege or merits, but on the basis of each man's relation to the Son of Man and to his neighbor (Mt 25:31ff). From this perspective, both Jews and Gentiles are under the judgment and mercy of God.[21]

Jesus came to bring into existence a new community, where Jews and Gentiles would worship together and share equally in gifts bestowed upon the Church of Christ. He came that he might reconcile both of them to God "in one body through the cross" (Eph 2:14f). The mission of Jesus to Israel, his acceptance of and his activity among the Gentiles, limited but significant, were the signs of his messianic authority and of the inauguration of the Kingdom of God.

20 See E. P. Sanders, *Jesus and Judaism*, pp. 212ff.
21 "Wherever Jesus speaks of the power, dominion, and kingdom of the returning Son of Man, the Gentile world is therefore included" (J. Jeremias, *Jesus' Promise to the Nations* [London: SCM Press, 1959], p. 70).

12

The Kingdom of God—Present and Future

Jesus proclaimed the coming of God's kingdom and the fulfillment of Israel's ancient hopes. Men and women were called to "repent and believe in the good news" (Mk 1:15). "The Kingdom of God" in the preaching and teaching of Jesus refers to God's act of reigning or ruling, rather than to God's realm, to God's dominion rather than to God's domain. It is the time when God's sovereignty and power are manifested. To enter the Kingdom of God primarily means to experience Christ's power, to be committed to him and finally to be united with him.

I

Jesus' teaching about the Kingdom of God distinguished him from John the Baptist, as well as from other religious groups or movements in ancient Judaism. John proclaimed that the Kingdom of God, the day of judgment, was about to come. To the ancient rabbis of Jesus' time, the expression "Kingdom of God" referred primarily to the future coming of God's power and God's rule. They did not envisage an overlapping of this age with the coming age. Jesus, by contrast, announced that the age to come had invaded this age with power: The Kingdom of God is already here,[1] although the

---

1 The Greek verb ἐγγίζω—which is used in Mk 1:15 in the past tense ἤγγικεν—and may mean "has come near" and "is here." Which of these two meanings is conveyed in Jesus' preaching? Analysis of the meaning of the Greek term alone is of little help. The only way to answer this question is to consider the interpretation of Mk 1:15 in the context of the entire teaching of Jesus. In Mt 11:4-5, for instance, the Kingdom is present in time; the Kingdom is intrinsically linked with the person of Jesus. Neither the verb ἐγγίζω nor the term "Kingdom of God" is used here, however. In another example, Luke reports a saying which has a parallel in Matthew: "But if it is by the finger of God that I cast out demons, then the Kingdom of God has come upon you" (Lk 11:20). Instead of using the "finger of God" to refer to God's power (as it does in Ex 8:19), Matthew substituted "the spirit of God" (12:28). Both Luke and Matthew used the verb φθάνω (ἔφθασεν), meaning "arrive" or "come." There is no ambiguity in the use of this verb. The Kingdom can no longer be considered solely a part of the future; it is present here and now. It should be added that there is no dispute among scholars regarding the authenticity of these two sayings of Jesus, given in Mt 11:4-5 and Lk 11:20 (Mt 12:28). They "are recognized as authentic" and "their meaning is clear"(see Xavier Léon-Dufour, *The Gospels and the Jesus of History* [London: W. Collins Sons, 1968], p. 230). In Matthew, John the Baptist preaches that the

end is still to come.[2]

With Christ's coming, "the time of preparation and expectation" was brought to an end, and the time of God's reign was inaugurated. The time of salvation had arrived. This was "without analogy" in the Judaism of Jesus' time. David Flusser writes that Jesus was the "only Jew known to us from ancient times" who brought the good news "that the new age of salvation had already begun."[3]

The Kingdom of God arrived with the coming of the Son of Man. He himself was the kingdom (αὐτοβασιλεία), in the words of Origen. When John the Baptist sent his disciples to ask Jesus, "Are you he who is to come, or shall we look for another?", Jesus answered them, "Go, and tell John what you hear and see: the blind receive their sight and the lame walk, lepers are cleansed and the deaf hear, and the dead are raised up, and the poor have good news preached to them" (Mt 11:3ff). The disciples of John asked, in essence, whether or not Jesus was the promised Messiah, and Jesus answered indirectly that the Kingdom of God was already the present reality. The same answer revealed the miracles as the fulfillment of God's promises and as signs that the Kingdom of God was present. The demons were cast out—"the Kingdom of God has come upon you" (Lk 11:20).

There are references in the gospels to the future kingdom as well. The most obvious is the petition in the Lord's Prayer: "Thy kingdom come" (Mt 6:10, Lk 11:2). Jesus taught his disciples to pray for the future manifestation of God's kingdom, which would be more clearly seen than

"kingdom of heaven is at hand" (3:2). Instead of using "God," Matthew used "heaven." The term "kingdom of heaven," therefore, has the same meaning as the Kingdom of God. In recounting the preaching of John the Baptist, the evangelist used the same verb form ἤγγικεν that occurs in the teaching of Jesus in Mt 4:17. The meaning of ἤγγικεν in these two passages, however, is not identical. It conveys a different meaning in each, derived from the gospel records of the teachings, attitudes and expectations. In John's message, it points to the future, whereas Jesus speaks primarily of the present.

2 See Oscar Cullmann, *Christ and Time*, 3rd ed. (London: SCM press, 1962). Cullmann writes that for the believing Christian the decisive point of time, which signifies salvation, no longer lies in the future. With the coming of Christ a new division of time was introduced. The end is not yet, but the power of the world to come is already operative in this world. The Christian hope for the future "can now be supported by faith in the past." The expectation concerning the future is not removed—the decisive battle has already been won, there is no doubt about its final outcome, but still "the armistice has not been signed." In these images, Cullmann presents the relation between "the Kingdom of God already realized" and "the Kingdom not yet fulfilled."

3 *Jesus*, 87, cited in Joachim Jeremias, *New Testament Theology* (*The Proclamation of Jesus*) (New York: Charles Scribner's, 1971), p. 108.

the present reign of God: While it now appears obscured, at the end, in the age of completion, it will appear in full glory and power. *Maranatha* ("Our Lord, come!"), a liturgical prayer of the primitive Church addressed to the Risen Christ, referred to both present and future aspects of the Kingdom (1 Cor 16:22, Rev 22:20). The Son of Man who has come is the same Son of Man who will come. The tension between the first and the second coming is not in thought but in the chronological present and future. With the second coming, Christ's work will be consummated. This tension is the basis of New Testament eschatology.

Several attempts have been made to adequately express or interpret the gospel teaching about the Kingdom of God. Two terms are widely known: "realized eschatology" and "futurist eschatology." For the proponents of the first view, the Kingdom of God was realized with Jesus and with his work, and nothing more can be expected in the future. The second theory lays all its stress on the new revelation that will be brought with the παρουσία, thus implying that almost nothing was accomplished with the ministry of Jesus. The proponents of these two eschatologies have one thing in common: they separate the present from the future, the fulfillment from the consummation, the "historic" from the "cosmic" Kingdom of glory. They remove the tension between the present and the future by neglecting one or another body of evidence from the gospels, in which both eschatologies are undeniably present.

A third view is that of New Testament scholars who define the gospel teaching about the Kingdom in terms of "inaugurated eschatology."[4] They take into account the complexity and diversity of the gospel evidence and the tension that exists between "already here" and "not yet." The two aspects of the Kingdom are kept distinct, but they are never separated from each other. The decisive battle has been won by Christ, yet the reign of God will appear in the fulness of its glory only at the end. Neither the present nor the future kingdom can be separated from the life and from the future coming of the Son of Man. This is the message of both the Gospel of John and of the Synoptic Gospels. While John stresses "realized eschatology," it also contains "future eschatology." Eternal life, a qualitatively new life, is possible now (Jn

4 The term "inaugurated eschatology" has been suggested by Georges Florovsky (see C.H. Dodd, *The Interpretation of the Fourth Gospel* [Cambridge: Cambridge University Press, 1953], p.447, fn.1).

3:36; 5:24; 6:47,54), but there are also references to a future resurrection (Jn 5:28-29), the last day (6:39), the final judgment (12:48), and the future coming of Jesus (14:3,18).

To prepare his own disciples for the final event, Jesus taught them "eschatological virtues," exhorting them to be ready and to watch, to have patience and confidence. While the apocalyptic authors were preoccupied with describing future events and with calculating "when" and "how" God would act, Jesus disclaimed any knowledge of "that day or that hour" (Mk 13:32). He was certain that it would come, however. While he used the title "Son of Man" from Daniel and I Enoch to claim messianic authority, he "was not one of the apocalyptists."[5] Neither his teaching nor his attitude was apocalyptic.

II

Jesus proclaimed the Kingdom of God in parables[6] which reveal that the day of salvation has arrived, that the new age has been inaugurated, that the "new wine" has been made available, and that the Messiah has come. The present and the future Kingdom are made known in the parables. The Kingdom of God is like a grain of mustard seed (Mt 13:31ff), and this small seed (the present Kingdom) becomes a large, nine-foot-high tree (the future Kingdom). The parables do not speak of the growth of the Kingdom as being a natural evolutionary process or an immanent

5 J. H. Charlesworth enumerates some of the main differences between Jesus and the apocalyptists. For example, the apocalyptists wrote down what they saw and heard from God; Jesus wrote nothing. The apocalyptists called upon God to destroy the enemies of Israel; Jesus exhorted his disciples to "love your enemies" (Mt 5:44). The apocalyptists moved God farther from the world of men; Jesus brought him nearer to them than ever before. Also, the apocalyptists "denigrated the earth;" Jesus expressed a deep appreciation of God's creation in his Sermon on the Mount (*Jesus Within Judaism*, pp. 38-39). Regarding this last difference between Jesus and the apocalyptists, it is worth quoting one of the rabbis: "He who walks along the road repeating the law and interrupts his repetition and says 'How lovely this tree is! How lovely this field is!' to him it will be reckoned as if he had misused his life." Hengel, recording and commenting on these words, writes that "by contrast, Jesus justifies his prophetic eschatological demand—which is conditioned by the nearness of God—by the radiant beauty of the spring flowers and the boundless freedom of the birds under heaven (Mt 6:25-34; 10:29ff) and not from apocalyptic calculations in the style of the Book of Daniel but rather from the fig tree (Mk 13:28f)" (*The Charismatic Leader and His Followers*, pp. 48f).

6 The art of parable was known and used before Jesus' time. The Old Testament records a few parables (2 Sam 12:104, 1 Kg 20:35-42, Is 5:1-7). Jesus, however, brought this art to perfection. Differing from previous storytellers in his subject matter, Jesus revealed his own character in these parables. His purpose was to lead the hearer to him and to compel a response to his challenge. Parables are never told to amuse people; they are not merely interesting or entertaining. They are of revelatory character.

development, nor as a magical change, but they emphasize its miraculous growth and transformation under God's power and guidance.

The parables about the Kingdom contain the same call to repentance that Jesus made when he started his public ministry (Mk 1:15). Many heard the parables, but few accepted their call. Jesus said to the Twelve: "To you has been given the secret of the Kingdom of God, but for those outside everything is in parables; so that they may indeed see but not perceive, and may indeed hear but not understand; lest they should turn again and be forgiven" (Mk 4:11-12). At a first reading, it might seem as if Jesus used the form of the parable to conceal his message and to keep outsiders in darkness. His teaching was not esoteric, however. With it, he gave his disciples "the secret of the Kingdom of God," that is, the knowledge that the end of the age was already upon them. This "secret" of the Kingdom of God was not to be kept by a few elect, but was to be revealed and proclaimed through the Twelve to the House of Israel. The mystery of the Kingdom is above all the mystery of Jesus himself.[7] For those who were "inside" with Jesus, that is, those who responded with repentance (*metanoia*) to his call, a parable was the revelation of the "secret of the Kingdom of God." For those "outside," however, the parables did not reveal that the Kingdom has arrived and were therefore heard as riddles. Both the Hebrew and the Aramaic words for parable may be translated as "riddle."[8]

7 For the meaning of Mk 4:11-12 in the context of the gospel, see Paul J. Achtemeier, *Mark*, 2nd ed. (Philadelphia: Fortress Press, 1986), pp. 72-73, 80-83.

8 The Hebrew and Aramaic words for parable, *mashal* and *mathla*, respectively, may also mean allegory, riddle, symbol, etc. Thus Jesus' statement that "for those outside everything is in parables" may be translated as "everything is in riddles" (Joachim Jeremias, *The Parables of Jesus* [New York: Charles Scribner's Sons, 1963], p. 20). A parable is not necessarily an allegory. While the former usually makes one point, the latter makes several, and this often gives an allegory an artificial character. In the gospels, however, we cannot always distinguish clearly between a parable and an allegory. Some of the stories of Jesus may be parables with allegorical features. Such is the case with the Parable of the Wicked Tenants of the vineyard (Mk 12:1-12), which gives the whole history of salvation, with Jesus as the central figure. This example of allegory in the gospels need not be considered a product of the early Church's elaboration upon a simple parable of Jesus. There is an allegorical song of the vineyard in the Old Testament (Is 5:1-7), and Jesus may have had this precedent in mind.

Modern scholarship has reacted against allegorical interpretation of the parables. There is much to be said against the exaggerated allegorism that is found in some of the early exegetes, such as Origen and Augustine. A good example of this type of exegesis is Augustine's interpretation of the Parable of the Good Samaritan. To Augustine, every sentence, every word even, meant something else (see C. H. Dodd, *The Parables of the Kingdom*, rev. ed. [New York: Charles Scribner's Sons, 1951], pp. 1-2). Adolf Jülicher, who published his book on the parables in 1898, severely

The quotation by Jesus of the prophet Isaiah (6:9), "Go, and say to this people: 'Hear and hear, but do not understand; see and see, but do not perceive'," does not mean that the parables were used to blind the people or to lead them to punishment, but to point out the responsibility of the people for their unwillingness to accept the message of the parables. Isaiah warned that the wicked will be punished on account of their way of

criticized this allegorical interpretation. Many have followed him on this point.

J. Jeremias, in his study *The Parables of Jesus*, considers their allegorical elements of secondary importance, as a matter of principle. To come to what is "authentic" in the parables, according to Jeremias, the exegete must first detect and isolate the allegorical elements in order to answer the question of what a parable meant for Jesus' audience.

Harald Riesenfeld has pointed out the limitations of Jeremias' view in his essay, "The Parable in the Synoptic and in the Johannine Traditions" (*The Gospel Tradition* [Philadelphia: Fortress Press, 1970], pp. 148ff.). He uses the Parable of the Lost Sheep (Lk 14:4-7, Mt 18:12-14) to demonstrate that the image of the Shepherd does not correspond to what we know about the role of the Shepherd from everyday experience. "It is scarcely possible to avoid seeing a conscious allusion in the parable itself "to the Shepherd of Ex 34:11ff ("Thus says the Lord God: I myself will search for my sheep, and will seek them out...I will seek the lost"). Jesus' parables are not free of "allegorical features," which are most probably their primary characteristic. Discovery of these allegorical elements is the product of critical investigation, which again makes us aware that the parables of Jesus are "simple and profound at the same time—simple in form and profound in substance" (Joseph Klausner, *Jesus of Nazareth*, p. 411).

The images that Jesus used in the parables of the Kingdom were not merely references to daily life in Palestine. "Sowing and harvesting" are also allusions to Old Testament passages. E. Hoskyns and N. Davey cite several passages from the Old Testament in which the metaphors of sowing and harvesting are employed. Among them the most telling are the following: Jer 31:27f, Hos 2:21-23, Is 55:10f, Jl 3:12f, and Ps 126:5f. "Other parables betray the same careful choice of simile and metaphor...The parables of wedding feasts and of the waiting of the virgins for the bridegroom are foreshadowed in the bethrothing of Israel to God and in the great feast of the coming age typified by the manna in the wilderness" (see *The Riddle of the New Testament*, pp. 130-133). See also Mary Ford, "Toward the Restoration of Allegory: Christology, Epistemology and Narrative Structure," *St. Vladimir's Theological Quarterly*, v.34, n.2-3 (1990), pp. 161-95. The author asserts that no method of interpretation is without its limitations, and that the modern rejection of allegory "is ultimately based on a secular world-view: a world-view which either does not understand, or does not accept, a traditional christology. Secularism fosters a distinct distaste for God as active in history and in individual human lives, as well as a distaste for the meaning influencing the picture part of a parable" (p. 194). The article is a valuable contribution to the ongoing discussion regarding the importance of allegorical interpretation.

Jesus told parables that were remembered, used, and adapted to the new situation after his death and resurrection. There is no doubt that certain changes occurred during their transmission and application due to a change of audience and of circumstances. Their universality only underlined their significance, which cannot be limited to the time of the public ministry of Jesus. Yet it is difficult to transform a good story. New elements may be added, but at the same time they can be detected. "A coherent image-story is resistant to change," writes Amos Wilder. "If a thing is well said there is only one way to say it, as in a poem" (*The Language of the Gospel: Early Christian Rhetoric* [New York: Harper & Row, 1964], p. 90).

life. While God did not will this turn of events, he saw that it would take place and warned the people through the prophet. This verse from Isaiah is characteristic of the Hebrew manner of expressing the predicted result of a prophet's mission rather than its purpose.[9] The mission of Isaiah was to open the eyes of the people of Israel, so that they might discern God's acts done on their behalf. The purpose of the parables was the same, and the result of their utterance similar, for when Jesus commanded, "Repent, and believe in the gospel," the people did not respond. To receive "the secret of the Kingdom of God," man must cease to belong to "those outside." Through repentance and faith he must come to perceive and understand that where Jesus is, the Kingdom is also.

The parables show what is meant by the Kingdom of God. They reveal how God acts to break through old customs and attitudes. Since they point to Jesus, to understand them is to recognize God's Messiah in Jesus of Nazareth.

III

The miracles of Jesus, as well as his parables, point to the present and future kingdom of God. Several types of miracles are recorded in the gospels. Jesus performed healings, exorcisms, resurrections (resuscitations), and miracles of the transformation of nature. In all these miracles the powers of the age to come were manifested. Each miracle was a sign of the Kingdom. The healing miracles were neither examples of faith-healing, nor the results of the victory of mind over body,[10] nor the products of a magic power. Rather, they were the manifestations of God's reign, the signs of God's presence in the world he created. They were also demonstrations of Jesus' messianic activity, the fulfillment of Isaiah's prophecies (Mt 8:17; 11:4-6).

9 See E. F. Sutcliffe, *The Monks of Qumran* (London: Burns and Oates, 1960), p. 73, and Vincent Taylor, *The Gospel According to St. Mark* (London: Macmillan Co., 1959), p. 256. See also *The New Jerome Biblical Commentary*, 41:27.

10 When mentioned in the context of a miracle, faith is not the "cause" but the "condition" of healing. The miracle is presented as the reward of faith. It is interesting to note that Jesus did not perform miracles before those who suffered from unbelief, and who therefore would not perceive their true meaning (Mk 6:1-6). Yet lack of faith could not stop his work of "alleviation of distress," to use a phrase of G. H. Boobyer in his commentary on Mark 6:5-6, for he was not practicing faith-healing. Still, "unbelief could obstruct the gospel of God." In his own country Jesus "could do no mighty work...except that he laid his hands upon a few sick people and healed them. And he marveled because of their unbelief" (Mk 6:5-6); see G. H. Boobyer and others, *The Miracles and the Resurrection* (London: SPCK, 1964), p. 56.

Jesus' exorcisms bore witness to the Kingdom of God that had "come upon us" (Mt 12:28, Lk 11:20). Confronted by Jesus, the demons admitted their defeat (Mk 5:1-20). In the miracles of exorcism there is a conflict between the powers of Satan and the power of the Kingdom; consequently, the exorcisms mirrored and were linked with the resurrection ("Behold, I cast out demons and perform cures today and tomorrow, and the third day I finish my course," Lk 13:31-32). Jesus' resurrection revealed what was already anticipated in his miracles of resuscitation: the victory of life over death. The nature miracles, like the feeding of the five thousand (Mk 6:30-44 and paral.) and Jesus' walking on the water (Mk 6:45-52, Jn 6:16-21), "[showed] not only that God can control nature and human life, but that he actually does so."[11]

The miracles, like the parables, were calls to repentance. "Woe to you, Chorazin, woe to you, Bethsaida!" Jesus reproached the cities where he did most of his miracles, "for if the mighty works done in you had been done in Tyre and Sidon, they would have repented long ago in sackcloth and ashes...And you, Capernaum, will you be exalted to heaven? You shall be brought down to Hades. For if the mighty works done in you had been done in Sodom, it would have remained until this day" (Mt 11:20-24). These mighty works (δύναμεις) were not wonders (τέρατα) but signs (σημεῖα) of the Kingdom and works (ἔργα) of Jesus. The miracles were not performed by Jesus to satisfy the curiosity of the people or to evoke their admiration, but to produce repentance as the response to his call—a call to an inward change of mind and heart, which would result in concrete changes in one's life: a call to follow Jesus and to accept his messianic authority.

The miracles of Jesus were manifestations of the saving power of God in the world and the revelation of Jesus as the bearer of the Kingdom of God. As Augustine wrote: "Let us ask of the miracles themselves what they will tell us about Christ; for if they be but understood, they have a tongue of their own...He was the Word of God; and all the acts of the Word were themselves words for us, they are not as pictures, merely to look at and admire, but as letters which we must seek to read and understand."[12]

Jesus ascribed ultimate significance to his miracles. "These very works

11 H. Van der Loos, *The Miracles of Jesus* (Leiden: E. J. Brill, 1965), p. 378.
12 Quoted in Alan Richardson, *The Miracle-Stories of the Gospels* (London: SCM, 1952), pp. 57f.

(ἔργα) which I am doing bear me witness that the Father has sent me" (Jn 5:36), Jesus declared. Those who do not accept this witness do not belong to his sheep (Jn 10:26). The miracles revealed both the arrival of the messianic age and the kind of Messiah Jesus was.

IV

Jesus proclaimed the Kingdom of God and created a new community, the nucleus of the restored Israel, which already lived in the last days. The restoration of Israel began with the call of the Twelve. His attitude toward women is without rabbinic parallel—he conversed with them (Jn 4), he healed them on the Sabbath day (Mk 1:29-31, Lk 13:10-17), they travelled with him (Lk 8:1-3), and he came to those who did not travel with him to teach them and to make them his disciples (Lk 10:38-47). This attitude towards women was again a sign of the new age inaugurated with Jesus' coming. His proclamation of the Kingdom and his creation of the messianic community took place in the period from his baptism up to his death and resurrection.

With Jesus' death and resurrection and the descent of the Holy Spirit, the Church came into existence, the community of those "upon whom the end of the ages has come" (1 Cor 10:11), of those who "have tasted the goodness of the word of God and the powers of the age to come" (Heb 6:5), as well as of those "in Christ," who already live in the last days and at the same time wait for the day of the Lord. The Church, as the Body of Christ and the Temple of the Holy Spirit, exists in the period between Jesus' resurrection and his parousia.

The Kingdom and the Church are related, but they are not identical. The *Didache*, a Syrian Christian document from the late first or early second century, expresses the relationship in a prayer:

> Remember, Lord, your Church, to save it from all evil and to make it perfect by your love. Make it holy "and gather" it "together from the four winds" (Mt 24:31) into your kingdom which you have made ready for it (10:5).[13]

The Church did not exist during Jesus' public ministry, but neither was the Church an unexpected development after his death and resurrection. It originated from Jesus and from his message. As soon as Jesus

13 Quotation and comment by Rudolf Schnackenburg, *God's Rule and Kingdom* (New York: Herder & Herder, 1967), pp. 230-32.

commenced his public ministry, he "appointed twelve" (Mk 3:14) whose mission was to proclaim the mysteries of the Kingdom. By choosing twelve, Jesus claimed that all twelve tribes of Israel belonged to him. The disciples gathered around Jesus did not represent a new sect within Israel, but symbolized the restored, eschatological Israel. The twelve were thus the foundation stones of the new messianic community.

The Twelve were "created" (ἐποίησεν, Mk 3:14) not simply to perpetuate their unique status, but also to "make disciples of all nations" (Mt 28:18). Jesus sent out the twelve as well as the larger circles of his disciples "into the harvest" (Mt 9:38, Lk 10:1ff). He also defined their conduct of living. He taught them the words of prayer (Lk 11:1ff), instructed them when to fast (Mk 2:18-20), and revealed to them that his mighty works were the call to repentance (Mt 11:21ff). They were exhorted to let their way of life shine before others (Mt 5:16). The ministry of Jesus, "the charismatic leader," therefore, "was characterized not only by charism but also by order"; the same can be said for the ministry of the Church in Jerusalem (Acts 1-6).[14] Jesus' followers, therefore, did not suddenly disappear from the world after the death and resurrection of their master and teacher, but became the leaders of the Apostolic Church. The members of the messianic community became the members of the Church of the Risen Christ.

The origin of the Church, nevertheless, should not be reduced to a single act of Jesus—the election of the twelve. The Church also "grew" out of Jesus' relation with his family, which in Mk 3:31-35 is shown to include all who follow God's will. The images that Jesus used to refer to this family, such as "little flock" (Lk 12:32), "the salt of the earth" (Mt 5:13), "the light of the world" (Mt 5:14) indicate a community that will extend and expand his work in history. Jesus' reply to Peter's confession of his messianic identity, "You are Peter, and on this rock I will build my church, and the powers of death shall not prevail against it" (Mt 16:18), contains the promise of a new people of God, the Israel of God (Ga 6:16), a new chosen race, a holy nation (1 Pet 2:9), a place of God's presence.[15] The words spoken at the Last Supper also point to a new

14 See E. Earle Ellis, *Pauline Theology, Ministry and Society* (Grand Rapids: Eerdmans, 1989), p. 92, n. 14.
15 See our article, "The Primacy of Peter in the New Testament and the Early Church," in *Primacy of Peter in the Orthodox Church* (Crestwood, NY: St. Vladimir's Press, 1992, forthcoming).

community. At the institution of the Eucharist, Jesus was present both physically and mystically—he was *with* his disciples as well as *in* them. The new Passover was to be celebrated in remembrance of him.[16] By instituting the Eucharist, Jesus showed that he desired to remain with his own disciples "to the close of the age" (Mt 28:20). Hence he reckoned with a period of history in which his Church would live and act. Finally, the title "Son of Man," from Dn 7:13 and 1 Enoch, which Jesus used for himself, embraces both the communal and the individual aspects of Jesus' work. The Son of Man did not come to live the life of an isolated individual, but to inaugurate the Kingdom of God and to lay the foundation to the eschatological community.

The choice of the Twelve, the confession of Peter, the institution of the Eucharist, and the title "Son of Man" all shed light on Jesus' self-understanding and his messianic mission. The meaning of his words and acts are revealed in two historical contexts: the period of his public ministry and the period of the post-resurrection Church. What he said and did leads to the birth of the Church. And in the final analysis "the question whether Jesus himself founded the church is really the question concerning his messiahship."[17] In many and various ways, Jesus revealed his messianic authority and the messianic mission. The rise of the Church is utterly incomprehensible without considering him to be its source and its origin.

---

16 According to Mark and Matthew, Christ pronounced these words over the chalice: "This is my blood of the covenant which is poured out for many" (ὑπὲρ πολλῶν, Mk 14:24, Mt 26:28). The expression "for many" is the Semitic way of saying "for all," for such a great number of people that they cannot be numbered. He died for all (ὑπὲρ πάντων, 2 Cor 5:15). Universal salvation is offered in the Eucharist. With the word "many" Jesus included both Jews and Gentiles. He had the Church in mind.

17 K. L. Schmidt, "The Church," in *TDNT*, III, pp. 521f.

Conclusion

The method of biblical criticism which prevails today is far from being perfect or free of subjectivity; but in spite of its limitations it is still the best method available. Through new literary and archaeological discoveries and increasing knowledge of the times and the culture in which Jesus lived, sensitive scholars have been improving and sharpening scientific methods to make them more reliable and less arbitrary. This particular scholarly effort will never end.

Neither in the past has there ever been a faultless method of biblical interpretation. The patristic approach, which looked for inner correspondences between some historical events or persons in the Hebrew Scripture and similar events in the New Testament, also had its shortcomings and led to certain excesses, such as the discovery of so many inner connections or patterns that they undermined the historical character of the two Testaments. Yet some results of typological interpretation, which was historically and theologically justifiable in the times of the Fathers, are still of enduring value. The Fathers of the Church defined the relation between the Old and the New Testaments, demonstrated the unity of the Bible in their exegesis, and expressed the theological significance of the life of Christ. They are still our teachers. They meditated upon the Scriptures, and their love for the Bible enabled them to reveal to their own age as well as to ours some of its mysteries and inner meaning. Their attitude toward Scripture is by no means incompatible with modern scholarship, although their method is not fully adequate to answer questions that are raised in modern times and that arise from our preoccupation with historical analysis.

Biblical criticism remains a crucial problem for the Orthodox Church today. The historical experience of the Church points to the organic link that has existed between biblical studies and creative theological development. A theological renaissance cannot take place without parallel advances in biblical studies. It belongs to the very mission of the Church to encourage its members in their pursuit of biblical research.

Like an icon, the gospel image of Christ emerges from the living tradition of the Church. Like the icons, the gospels are the product of a period of preparation, witnessing and meditation. Like the icons, they are the Church's expression of its faith. The gospels belong to the history of Christ and of his Church, and as such they are open to historical and critical research. Scholarly investigation of the basic sources of Christianity has proved to be rewarding both historically and theologically. The critical approach to the gospels has deepened and enlarged our historical knowledge of Jesus' contemporary Jewish environment and has given our age the possibility of answering in new terms the question of who Jesus is, an answer which will illuminate the living image of Christ in the Church.

Select Bibliography

Reference Works

The Encyclopedia of Religion, Mircea Eliade, ed. (New York: Macmillan, 1987).

Harper Bible Commentary, James L. Mays, ed. (San Francisco: Harper & Row, 1988).

Harper's Bible Dictionary, Paul J. Achtemeier, ed. (San Francisco: Harper & Row, 1985).

Jerome Biblical Commentary (1968) and *The New Jerome Biblical Commentary* (1990).

Léon-Dufour, Xavier, *Dictionary of the New Testament* (San Francisco: Harper & Row, 1980).

Theological Dictionary of the New Testament. R. Kittel, ed. (Grand Rapids: W. B. Eerdman's, 1964–1972).

Arndt, William F., and Gingrich, F. Wilbur, *A Greek-English Lexicon of New Testament and Other Early Christian Literature* (Chicago: University Press, 1957).

Books

Achtemeier, Paul J., *Mark* (second ed.) (Philadelphia: Fortress Press, 1986).

Alter, Robert, and Kermode, Frank, eds., *The Literary Guide to the Bible* (Cambridge: Harvard University Press, 1987).

Aulen, Gustav, *Jesus in Contemporary Historical Research* (Philadelphia: Fortress Press, 1976).

von Balthazar, Hans Urs, *Word and Revelation* (New York: Herder and Herder, 1964).

Bammel, Ernest, and Moule, C. F. D., eds., *Jesus and the Politics of His Day* (Cambridge: Cambridge University Press, 1984).

Barrett, C. K., *The New Testament Background: Selected Documents* (revised edition) (San Francisco: Harper & Row, 1989).

Brown, Raymond, *The Critical Meaning of the Bible* (New York: Paulist Press, 1981).

⸻, *The Gospel According to John* (New York: Doubleday, 1966).

Bruce, F. F., *Jesus and Christian Origins Outside the New Testament* (Grand Rapids: W. B. Eerdmans, 1974).

Charlesworth, James H., *Jesus Within Judaism—New Light From Exciting Archeological Discoveries* (New York: Doubleday, 1988).

Collins, Raymond F., *Introduction to the New Testament* (New York: Doubleday, 1987).

Cornfeld, Gaalyah, *The Historical Jesus: A Scholarly View of the Man and His World* (New York: Macmillan, 1982).

Cullman, Oscar, *Jesus and the Revolutionaries* (New York: Harper & Row, 1970).

Davies, W. D., *Christian Origins and Judaism* (Philadelphia: Westminster Press, 1962).

————, *The Sermon on the Mount* (Cambridge: Cambridge University Press, 1966).

Davies, W. D., and Daube, David, eds., *The Background of the New Testament and its Eschatology* (Cambridge: Cambridge University Press, 1956).

Dodd, C. H., *According to the Scripture* (New York: Charles Scribner's Sons, 1953).

————, *Historical Tradition in the Fourth Gospel* (Cambridge: Cambridge University Press, 1963).

Dunn, James D. G., *Christology in the Making* (Philadelphia: Westminster, 1980).

————, *The Evidence for Jesus* (Philadelphia: Westminster, 1985).

Ellis, E. Earle, *Pauline Theology, Ministry, and Society* (Grand Rapids: W. B. Eerdmans, 1989).

Fridrichsen, Anton, *et al, The Root of the Vine: Essays in Biblical Theology* (New York: Philosophical Library, 1953).

Gaster, Theodore H., *The Dead Sea Scriptures* (Garden City, NY: Doubleday, 1964).

Gerhardsson, Birger, *Memory and Manuscript: Oral Tradition and Written Transmission in Rabbinic Judaism and Early Christianity* (Uppsala: 1961).

Grant, Frederick C., *The Gospels: Their Origin and Their Growth* (New York: Harper & Brothers, 1957).

Grant, Robert M., *The Earliest Lives of Jesus* (New York: Harper & Row, 1961).

————, *Formation of the New Testament* (New York: Harper & Row, 1965).

Grant, Robert M., and Freedman, David Noel, eds., *The Secret Sayings of Jesus: The Gnostic Gospel of Thomas* (New York: Doubleday, 1960).

Hedrick, Charles W., and Hodgson, Robert, eds., *Nag Hammadi, Gnosticism, and Early Christianity* (Peabody, MA: Hendrickson, 1986).

Hengel, Martin, *Acts and the History of Earliest Christianity* (Philadelphia: Fortress Press, 1980).

————, *The Son of God* (Philadelphia: Fortress Press, 1976).

_____, *The Charismatic Leader and His Followers* (New York: Crossroad, 1981).

Hennecke, Edgar, *New Testament Apocrypha* (Philadelphia: Westminster Press, 1963).

Herford, R. T., *Christianity in Talmud and Midrash* (Clifton, NJ: Reference Book Publishers, 1966).

Horseley, Richard A., and Hanson, John S., *Bandits, Prophets, and Messiahs* (San Francisco: Harper & Row, 1985).

Hoskyns, Edwyn, and Davey, F. N., *The Riddle of the New Testament* (London: Faber and Faber, 1952).

Jaubert, A., *The Date of the Last Supper* (New York: Alba House, 1965).

Jeremias, Joachim, *The Eucharistic Words of Jesus* (London: SCM Press, 1966).

_____, *Jesus' Promise to the Nations* (London: SCM Press, 1959).

_____, *New Testament Theology (The Proclamation of Jesus)* (New York: Charles Scribners', 1971).

Jonas, Hans, *The Gnostic Religion* (second ed.) (Boston: Beacon Press, 1985).

Kee, Howard Clark, *Jesus in History: An Approach to the Study of the Gospels* (New York: Harcourt, Brace & World, 1970).

van der Loos, H., *The Miracles of Jesus* (Leiden: E. J. Brill, 1965).

Lossky, Vladimir, and Ouspensky, Leonid, *The Meaning of Icons* (Crestwood, NY: St. Vladimir's Seminary Press, 1983).

McKim, Donald H., ed., *A Guide to Contemporary Hermeneutics: Major Trends in Biblical Interpretation* (Grand Rapids: W. B. Eerdmans, 1986).

Meier, John P., *Christ, the Church, and Morality in the First Gospel* (New York: Paulist Press, 1979).

Mersh, Emile, *The Whole Christ: The Historical Development of the Doctrine of the Mystical Body in Scripture and Tradition* (Milwaukee: Bruce Publishing House, 1963).

Milik, J. T., *Ten Years of Discovery in the Wilderness* (London: SCM Press, 1959).

Moule, C. F. D., *The Phenomenon of the New Testament* (Naperville, IL: A. R. Allenson, Inc., 1967).

Murphy-O'Connor, Jerome, *Becoming Human Together: The Pastoral Anthropology of St. Paul* (Wilmington: Michael Glazier, 1982).

Neusner, Jacob, *Judaism in the Beginning of Christianity* (Philadelphia: Fortress Press, 1984).

Perrin, Norman, *Rediscovering the Teachings of Jesus* (London: SCM Press, 1967).

Price, James, *The New Testament, Its History and Theology* (New York: Macmillan, 1987).

Reicke, Bo, *The Roots of the Synoptic Gospels* (Philadelphia: Fortress Press, 1986).

Reisenfeld, Harold, *The Gospel Tradition* (Philadelphia: Fortress Press, 1970).

Robinson, James M., ed., *The Nag Hammadi Library* (revised edition) (San Francisco: Harper & Row, 1988).

Robinson, John A. T., *Redating the New Testament* (Philadelphia: Westminster Press, 1976).

Sanders, E. P., *Jesus and Judaism* (Philadelphia: Fortress Press, 1985).

Schnackenburg, Rudolf, *God's Rule and Kingdom* (New York: Herder and Herder, 1963).

Schweitzer, Albert, *The Quest of the Historical Jesus* (New York: McMillan, 1961).

Sherwin-White, A. N., *Roman Society and Roman Law in the New Testament* (Oxford: Clarendon Press, 1963).

Smalley, Stephen, *John—Evangelist and Interpreter* (Exeter: Paternoster Press, 1978).

Spicq, Ceslaus, *Agape in the New Testament* (St. Louis: B. Herder Book Co., 1963).

Sutcliffe, E. F., *The Monks of Qumran* (London: Burns and Oates, 1960).

Theissen, Gerd, *The Shadow of the Galilean: The Quest of the Historical Jesus in Narrative Form* (Philadelphia: Fortress Press, 1987).

Vawter, Bruce, *Biblical Inspiration* (Philadelphia: Westminster Press, 1972).

Wilder, Amos, *Early Christian Rhetoric: The Language of the Gospel* (Cambridge: Harvard University Press, 1971).

Articles

Breck, John, "Biblical Chiasmus: Exploring Structure for Meaning," *Biblical Theology Bulletin*, 17:2 (1987), pp. 70-74.

Dodd, C. H., "The Fall of Jerusalem and the 'Abomination of Desolation';" in his *More New Testament Studies* (Manchester: 1968), pp. 69-83.

Ellis, E. Earle, "Gospel Criticism—A Perspective on the State of the Art," in Peter Stulmacher, ed., *Das Evangelium und die Evangelien. Vortrage vom Tubingen Symposium 1982.* WUNT 28 (Tubingen: 1983).

Fitzmyer, Joseph A., "The Gospel in the Theology of Paul," *Interpretation*, 33:4 (1979), pp. 339-350.

Florovsky, Georges, "The Function of Tradition in the Ancient Church," *Greek Orthodox Theological Review*, 9:2 (1963), pp. 181-200.

_____, "The Predicament of the Christian Historian," in Leibrecht, W., ed., *Religion and Culture:Essays in Honor of Paul Tillich.* (New York: Harper & Brothers, 1959), pp. 140-66.

Flusser, David, "The Crucified One and the Jews," *Immanuel*, 7 (1977), pp. 25-37.

Hill, R. C., "St. John Chrysostom and the Incarnation of the Word in Scripture," *Compass Theology Review*, 14 (1980), pp. 34-38.

Hooker, M. D., "Christology and Methodology," in *New Testament Studies* 17 (1970), pp. 480-487.

Horbury, William, "The Passion Narratives and Historical Criticism," *Theology*, 75 (1972), pp. 58-71.

Kesich, Veselin, "Christ's Temptation in the Apocryphal Gospels and Acts," *St. Vladimir's Theological Quarterly*, 5:4 (1961), pp. 3-9.

_____, "Criticism, the Gospel, and the Church," *St. Vladimir's Theological Quarterly*, 10:3 (1966), pp. 134-162.

_____, "The Primacy of Peter in the New Testament and the Early Church," in *The Primacy of Peter in the Orthodox Church* (Crestwood, NY: St. Vladimir's Seminary Press, 1992 [forthcoming]).

Kingsbury, Jack Dean, "The Gospel in Four Editions," *Interpretation*, 33:4 (1979) pp. 363-375.

Lossky, Vladimir, "Tradition and Traditions," in L. Ouspensky and V. Lossky, *The Meaning of Icons* (Crestwood, NY: St. Vladimir's Seminary Press, 1983), pp. 13-24.

McKenzie, John L., "Problems of Hermeneutics in Roman Catholic Exegesis," *Journal of Biblical Literature*, 77:20 (1958), pp. 97-204.

Moule, C. F. D., "The Christ of Experience and Christ of History," *Theology*, 81 (May 1978), pp. 164-172.

Pearson, Birger A., "Early Christianity and Gnosticism: A Review Essay," in *Religious Studies Review*, v. 13, n. 1 (1987), pp. 2-5.

Schneemelcher, Wilhelm, "Gospel," in Hennecke, Edgar, and Scheemelcher, Wilhelm, eds., *New Testament Apocrypha*, R. M. Wilson, tr. (London: Lutterworth Press, 1963-1965), pp. 77-84.

Strousa, Gedaliahu G., "The Gnostic Temptation," *Numen* IIVII, 2 (1980), pp. 278-286.

Sweet, J. P. M., "The Zealots and Jesus," in E. Bammel and C. F. D. Moule, eds., *Jesus and the Politics of His Day* (Cambridge: Cambridge University Press, 1984), pp. 1-9.

Index

Index of Biblical References

John